G000108297

**Based on the collection of the
English Place-Name Society**

RICHARD COATES

Ensign
PUBLICATIONS

First paperback edition published in 1993 by
Ensign Publications
a division of Hampshire Books Ltd.,
2 Redcar Street,
Southampton SO1 5LL.

Originally published as *The Place-Names of Hampshire* by
B. T. Batsford Ltd., 4 Fitzhardinge Street, London W1H OAH

Publisher David Graves.
Cover design by The Design Laboratory.
Cover photo. by Terry Heathcote.
Printed by Short Run Press, Exeter.

ISBN 185455 090 X
[Original ISBN 0 7134 5625 6]

CONTENTS

ACKNOWLEDGEMENTS

My thanks are due to the following people, whose assistance during the preparation of this book has been most valuable in a variety of different ways: Mark Bateson and John McNeal Dodgson of the English Place-Name Society and University College London; Gerald Gazdar and Amanda Davey of the University of Sussex; John Pile of Bedhampton; Ken Richardson of Basingstoke Library; Alex Rumble of the University of Manchester; and Karl-Inge Sandred of the University of Uppsala. Andy Clews of the University of Sussex solved for me the very complex problem of alphabetizing by computer the entries which I had compiled in more or less random order, and I owe him a large debt of thanks. The largest single debt is to Kenneth Cameron, Honorary Director of the English Place-Name Survey, for permission to use the Survey archives, the circumstances of which are explained in the introduction. I am of course solely responsible for any use made of their views and their work on my behalf.

The book is dedicated to my parents Aylmer and Kathleen Coates in gratitude for their constant support.

RICHARD COATES

Falmer, Sussex

INTRODUCTION

Definition of Hampshire

Hampshire occupies some forty miles of the central southern coastline of England and about forty miles of country northwards from the Solent. Its boundaries have changed a little from time to time, and an inclusive policy has been followed in this book. Places that used to be in Hampshire but are now, since various local government reviews in the late nineteenth century and later, in Berkshire, Dorset and Sussex, are treated; as are Berkshire, Wiltshire and Dorset places that have become part of Hampshire in the same period. The Isle of Wight is systematically excepted. Its place-names are covered in a book published in Sweden in 1940 by Helge Kökeritz (see Bibliography, pp. 188–93). The present book follows the English Place-Name Society in ignoring changes to the boundaries of other counties that took place in 1974. Places mentioned are allocated to their pre-1974 counties.

The scope of this book

A book of this size cannot possibly include the name of every minor feature: field, stream, wood, cottage. Such an enterprise will need the attention afforded by the English Place-Name Survey, which has published volumes for many counties of England under the auspices of the English Place-Name Society (EPNS). Unfortunately no such book exists for Hampshire, and the EPNS will certainly not publish one this century. No editor for the county has yet been appointed. Until such a survey appears in print, the present book is intended to provide interested readers with information on the major names of the county (towns, suburbs, villages, civil parishes, manors, some tithings and hamlets, rivers, forests). In addition, I like to think of it as a pilot study of these major names, allowing the more problematic ones to be fully discussed in advance of any future EPNS work. There exists in some libraries in Hampshire a typescript volume prepared for the EPNS by the late J.E.B. Gover, which never found its way into the publication schedule. By the kindness of Professor Kenneth Cameron, Honorary Director of the Survey, I have been able to draw on Mr Gover's collection of spellings, put together in the late 1950s. This has been an invaluable aid, and has saved incalculable amounts of time which would otherwise have been lost in duplicating work already done, and which will have to be redone to a certain extent anyway when the EPNS eventually treats Hampshire. On the other hand, this is not merely a rehash of Mr Gover's book-that-never-was. Firstly, it covers only a subset of the names covered in the typescript, as will become apparent below. Secondly, the field of place-name studies has changed radically since 1960 or so when Mr Gover was finalizing his work, and the recent discoveries and analyses by such scholars as Dr Margaret Gelling, Professor John McNeal Dodgson, Professor Kenneth Jackson, Dr Alexander Rumble and other Council members of the EPNS have had to be taken into account. There are new views on the meaning of particular place-name elements, some of which are set out below in this introduction, and there are new views on the chronology of name-types; in fact this topic occupies much less space in this book than it would have done in an antique EPNS volume, and there is rather less emphasis on the detailed characteristics of naming-practices in the earliest period of Anglo-Saxon settlement than is customary in books of this kind. For instance, I have simply assumed that -ingas names, like *Worting*, *Eling* and *Wymering*, represent an early type, without embarking on a fine-grained chronology of the relation of these names to the -hām and -ingahām types. Thirdly, I have views of my own, and have differed with Mr Gover over matters of detail in many cases, and not infrequently in major matters too.

My choice of what to cover has been guided by a feel for what is a major name. All the manors of Domesday Book (1086) appear, and the bulk of the places mentioned in the fourteenth-century *Nomina villarum*, in the Lay Subsidy of 1586, on Moule's county map of c. 185 (excluding, usually, individual houses), and printed in type over a certain size on the second-series 1:50000 sheets of the Ordnance Survey (OS) dating from around 1984. No doubt this scheme will not satisfy all readers, and they will find numerous of the most tantalizing ones missing; but I hope the 850 or more covered will be found tolerably representative. I have also put in some names which are likely to attract attention merely by virtue of their form, like *Criddlestyle*, *Smannell*, *Tiptoe* and *King's Garn Gutter*.

Previous work on Hampshire place-names

Mr Gover's work has already been mentioned. In addition to this, Dr G.B. Grundy published in the *Archaeological Journal*, in the 1920s, a large collection of Hampshire documents from the Anglo-

Saxon (AS) period containing place-names in their main text and in their boundary-clauses. Hampshire is exceedingly fortunate in the number of its early charters which are still in existence. This is due, in large measure, to the fact that Winchester was the capital of Wessex, and indeed of England, for significant parts of the AS period, and that the royal court and its scribes were often there. Again, land-grants by the king were often of estates in the vicinity of Winchester. Religious houses favoured by successive kings were also established in Hampshire: for instance Hyde Abbey and St Swithin's in Winchester; Romsey; Wherwell; Southwick. Many documents from their archives have also survived, either as originals or in medieval copies. Such documents contain the primary evidence for the names of the county before the Norman conquest. Dr Grundy's work has proved useful in preparing this book, especially his topographical interpretations, but his linguistic speculations need to be treated with scepticism in many cases. It is not an adequate alternative account of Hampshire place-names. Professor Ekwall's *Dictionary of English place-names* covers the names of Hampshire as it does of all other English counties, but it was last revised in 1960 and there is much recent scholarship which it does not take into account. It was an admirable work in its time, but now needs to be used with care. The work of these three writers – Gover, Grundy and Ekwall – is drawn upon a great deal in this book, and a bare mention of one of their names is a direction, unless otherwise stated, to the books or articles just referred to. Other writings on Hampshire tend to be rather dependent on one of these authorities. A select bibliography – including precise details of these three works – can be found at the end of this book. My own fuller bibliography of Hampshire names has been published separately (1988) by Younsmere Press (Brighton).

The organization of this book

The book consists largely of an alphabetical dictionary giving the origin and meaning of the names in the range just discussed. A few names are treated out of sequence during the discussion of others, and these are indexed on p. 200. For each name treated, some spellings representative of the range found (over at least nine centuries in many cases) are listed. The more doubtful the name, and the more susceptible to different interpretations, the more spelling evidence is given. I have not been dogmatic where doubt seems reasonable. All major spelling traditions are mentioned, i.e.

all those which point to different possible origins or different later understandings of the name in question. Spelling-variety due to well-understood aspects of Old and Middle English phonology, which does not cast doubt on the origin of a name, is treated less, or not at all, except insofar as it is used as evidence to decide on a particular origin in the first place. For places with something less than parish status, an indication of their location is given after the heading to the entry. (Mr Gover's parish assignments are usually followed; but the New Forest parishes alluded to are those in existence in 1966.) Obviously the status of some places will have changed through time, and no attempt is made to trace the entire history of a place from ancient parish to vill to deserted medieval village (DMV) to modern suburb, for instance, although some interesting changes are noted. The information given is intended merely to be something more user-friendly than an OS grid reference, though the latter might have been preferable, and has been used in some cases in the text where special precision about the locality is necessary. If no information is given with the heading, it can be taken that the place was a parish at some point in the Middle Ages and probably persisted as such till at least the last century.

The dictionary entries

The place-name to be treated is sometimes given in more than one spelling in the heading to the entry, for example **Kilmeston**, **Kilmiston**. This is intended as a statement that the spelling has vacillated in recent times (defined as since 1800). No judgement is implied about which is the 'correct' form in cases like these, nor even about which is preferable. Places which are 'lost', i.e. whose names do not appear on modern maps, are given in bold italics, thus: ***Achelie***.

After the heading to the entry, which may be followed by an indication of where (or sometimes what) the place is, comes the evidence on which the interpretation is based. This consists of spellings, with dates at which they are recorded. For spellings from the Anglo-Saxon period, the date of the manuscript in which they occur is also given, in parentheses. These dates have been checked against the scholarship represented by the most recent standard handbook, P.H. Sawyer's *Anglo-Saxon Charters: An Annotated List and Bibliography* (1968). Thus '901 (*c*.14)' means that the spelling ostensibly dates from 901, but appears in a fourteenth-century copy only. Judgements about the reliability of medieval transcriptions is a matter for expert opinion. Opinions on offer before 1968 may be found summarized in Sawyer's *Charters*. Where no parenthetical date is given, the spelling is taken to be contemporary with its apparent date, i.e. the manuscript in which it appears is original. I have also treated some forms from the *Old English (Anglo-Saxon) Chronicle* from the tenth century onwards in this way. I have not, in general, stated from which document the spelling is taken. This may well be a defect of the book, but this information – usually presented in place-name books in a highly condensed and abbreviated style – has been omitted to stop it becoming too formidable for the general reader. The indulgence of specialists is requested; I have to ask them to believe that I have followed the best modern scholarship when proffering dates. Gover and Ekwall (see above) standardly give mentions of the documents involved, even if they (especially the former) make occasional errors of attribution or dating.

For post-Conquest documents, a single date is given: the ostensible date. If any form is in a late copy, that fact has rarely been found to influence the etymology that I would have arrived at had the document been original. By the simple expedient of omitting manuscript dates, therefore, space has been saved and legibility improved at the cost of a lot of apparatus of no great value to my main purpose – to explore the original meanings of the place-names. If my main purpose had been to date precisely the variant spelling traditions for the names, a different decision would have been made. But this is a matter touched upon only where it seems to be of specially great interest. As with Anglo-Saxon documents, only a date is given and not an indication of the nature of the manuscript involved.

After the evidence of the spellings, an etymology is suggested. Language-names are given in abbreviated form: see List of Abbreviations (pp. 17–18).

A large number of names treated are of OE origin, i.e. they originated in the Anglo-Saxon period. Since Hampshire was the heartland of Wessex, Old English (OE) words are quoted in their West Saxon dialect form. Where it is unclear whether the name originated before or after the Norman conquest, I write 'OE/ME', but arbitrarily quote the suggested original form as if it were OE. After the language-name comes a brief translation. Some of the elements involved are discussed in greater detail below in this introduction; otherwise there is some amplification in the dictionary entry itself. Here is a sample entry:

Slackstead, two hamlets in Farley Chamberlayne
903 (c16) *slastede*; 1269 *Slacstede*; 1350 *Slaghstede*
OE *★Slāhstede* 'sloe-place/site'. The [k]-sound for earlier [x] (OE
h) is paralleled in e.g. **Heckfield**, and in *Hickstead* (Sx). For
stede, see Sandred (1963). The chalk downs are góod blackthorn
country. Distinguished now as *Upper* and *Lower S.*

Slackstead is located in the parish of Farley Chamberlayne. It is first
recorded as *slastede*, ostensibly in 903, though this is only in a
sixteenth-century transcript. Two medieval spellings are mentioned.
An origin in OE is suggested, and an original form for the name
proposed (in the OE nominative case), preceded by ★ to show that
it is conjectural and not actually attested in the spelling record. A
minor problem in the history of its pronunciation is shown to have
its parallel in places not too far remote. Bold type indicates that the
place with which their comparison is being made has its own entry
in the dictionary. The form is translated literally on the assumption
that all the spellings are compatible with it. (If they are not, some
fuller discussion of the discrepancies is offered.) For discussion of a
difficult element, a reference to specialist literature is given; the book
mentioned is in the bibliography at the end of this one. A brief note
follows suggesting that the proposed name is ecologically plausible.
Finally it is observed that historically the name has attached, and
still does attach, to two adjacent places.

The convention has been adopted of spelling OE forms with a
lower-case initial letter, unlike later forms. AS-period scribes made
no systematic use of capital letters for names, and moreover it is
not always easy to tell the difference between names and descriptive
expressions in the charter boundaries that are a principal source of
material for our investigation. When the scribe writes *on broccæs
hlæw*, does he mean 'to [the] badger's barrow' or 'to Badgersbarrow';
and when he writes *on cyneburgan hyrstæ*, is this 'to Cyneburh's
wood' or 'to Cyneburh's Wood'? The difference is not simply to
do with whether the definite article is expressed; in one and the
same charter, the scribe writes in almost adjacent lines *þonne on
þone weg* 'thence to the way ...', and *þonne andlang weges*, which
we can hardly avoid translating as 'thence along THE way ...'
rather than as 'thence along Way ...'. Twelve clauses later he writes
þonne andlang þæs wæges ... explicitly 'thence along the way ...'. I
have therefore chosen not to symbolize typographically whether a
given attested expression is a name or a definite description, even
where there is little or no doubt. As an incidental benefit, this
decision enables readers to see at a glance whether a given recorded
spelling is ostensibly OE or not.

Linguistic aspects of interpretation

We need to discuss in more detail the languages we will draw on in interpreting the place-names of Hampshire. It is not possible to say what the inhabitants spoke in the Bronze Age, nor in the earlier part of the Iron Age, though there is the odd tantalizing glimpse of this remote past (see for example *Solent, Winchester*). By the later Iron Age, and certainly during the Iron Age C, the period just before the Roman conquest, the language of the bulk of Britain was British, technically a Brittonic or P-Celtic language, the ancestor of modern Welsh, Cornish and Breton. It is customary to call British after approximately the middle of the sixth century by the names of the languages into which it developed. From this time to the final extinction of Celtic in Hampshire we will say that Primitive Welsh was spoken, following the system of periods established by Professor Kenneth Jackson. This language has left place-name traces (see for example *Andover, Cams Hall, Candover*, the *Cleres, Crow, Micheldever*, and *Silchester*). The study of Celtic names needs delicate handling. In the past, various names have been claimed to be Celtic where all that can reliably be said is that they predate English. No totally convincing Celtic etymology can be given, for example, for the crucial elements in *Everton, Itchen, Meon, Test*, and *Wallop*, even though there is a fair presumption that they are pre-English.

The bulk of the names of our area have been formulated in English, and most of those which appear in this book can be traced to the Old English period, to be equated roughly with the period of Anglo-Saxon cultural dominance (c.400-1100). There has been much scholarship devoted to discovering the precise application of Old English words in place-names, and it is not always possible to do justice to it in a work of this kind. Some elements have been systematically translated by a bare modern English equivalent, where a lengthy historical or cultural note would have been preferable. An attempt is made here to compensate for this brevity in the dictionary by listing and discussing some of the most frequent elements and contrasting those which are liable to be confused with each other.

hām, hamm

OE *hām* is a habitative term, i.e. one which actually *means* an inhabited place, translated 'estate'. It is now accepted that many *hām* names belong to the earliest layer of English place-names; as in, for example *Cosham, Enham*, and *Popham*. The use of *hām*,

7

except in the expression *nīwan hām* '(the) new estate', *Newnnam*, is largely confined to the eastern, earlier-settled, part of England, suggesting that its usage petered out as anglicization proceeded westwards. A further piece of evidence suggesting that it belongs to the early period is its frequent use with *-ing-* derivatives of personal names, inflected in the genitive plural (like *Ellingham*, the only example from Hampshire). *Hām* was very often applied to large, important, and diverse agricultural centres that are in many ways analogous to what were called *manors* in the Middle Ages. Probably a large majority of places named *hām* are still manors in Domesday Book. Some *hām* names may denote estates which were taken over as functioning entities from their Romano-British occupants, though continuity is hard to prove. The element enters into some significant compounds which underline its high importance. OE *wīchām* is now known to have meant 'small Roman town, villa', as in *Wickham; wealdhām* was '(royal) forest estate', as in *Bishop's* and *North Waltham*. *Hām* of course denoted a farm in some sense, but in this book 'farm' is used as a standard translation for OE *tūn* (see below), which carries no specific connotations of antiquity, size or importance.

Hām may easily be confused with the element *hamm*; in the absence of Anglo-Saxon period spellings it may be impossible to decide which of these elements is contained in some names. If such spellings exist, and if they include forms in *hom(m)*, this reliably indicates that *hamm* is involved, for technical reasons having to do with well-established facts of OE pronunciation. Otherwise certainty is impossible. *Hamm* is a topographical term crudely translated 'hemmed-in land' in this book. This is intended to convey the etymological relationship between *hamm* and the word *hemmed,* and to provide a translation which is neutral between the several different applications of the word which have now been established. The fundamental meaning seems to have been 'land surrounded on all sides but one by some impassable or clearly defined feature'. Thus *hamm* sites include land within a river-bend, promontories into water or marshes, and projecting hillspurs. There is good evidence that in later times it was used less specifically in such applications as riverside meadows, dry land ('islands') in marshes, land taken in for cultivation in more marginal sites, and artificially-delimited plots or enclosures. But the earliest use is of good agricultural land delimited by well-marked topographical features. *Hamm* names in this book, for example *Elvetham*, *Northam*, and *Rownhams*, are often accompanied by a 'Dodgson number', which relates to John McNeal Dodgson's classification of the relevant sites:

8

1 'land in a river-bend'
2a 'promontory into water or marsh'
2b 'hillspur' or the like
3 'riverside meadow'
4 'dry land in marsh'
5a 'intake in marginal land'
5b 'enclosed plot'
6 'valley bottom with higher land on several sides'

A major obstacle to discovering whether a particular name contains *hām* or *hamm* is that there is no reason why a *hām* should not occupy a *hamm* site. One term is habitative and the other topographical. At first glance, one might assume *Southampton* was a *hāmtūn* 'home farm, major estate' name, but the spread of spellings make it clear that whilst it may have *been a hāmtūn*, it was *called* *Hammtūn*, from its Dodgson-2a position on land between the estuaries of the Itchen and Test.

hām, tūn, stoc, wīc

The first two of these OE words are translated in this book as 'estate' and 'farm'. As explained above, *hām* is an early term, applied to places of major importance and size, becoming obsolete relatively early. No such specific connotations attach to *tūn*. This is not to claim that a *hām* can always be distinguished from a *tūn*; the frequency of the compound *Kingston* shows that places of significance could be called *tūn*. However it also occurs in words for dependent farms like *dēortūn* 'deer-farm', and *beretūn*, literally 'barley-farm', i.e. '*Barton*', along with *stoc*, 'secondary settlement', especially 'grange farm, farm devoted to the upkeep of a religious establishment' and *wīc*, originally 'specialized farm', 'dairy-farm; salterns'. The use of *tūn* continued till after the Norman conquest, possibly as late as the fourteenth century; see for example *Monxton*, *Sarson*, and *Thruxton*. The original sense of *tūn* may have been 'deliberately-enclosed place', for the relatives of the word in other Germanic languages have senses like 'fence', 'hedge', 'garden'; and of course the word continues in modern English in the guise *town* – the earliest towns so called were walled, fortified, places.

wyrð

This element is translated 'curtilage', a legal term meaning the plot of land on which a house stands. This sense is covered approximately by the word *toft* in Danish-influenced areas of Britain. Names including this element appear therefore to have been names for inhabited sites without consideration of their legal or physical place in larger estates and with no consideration of their appurtenances. The difficulties in interpreting the single Hampshire *Worthy* name are discussed under that name in the dictionary. A late development of the word *hamm* makes its sense hard to distinguish from that of *wyrð*, and it is *hamm* whose use continues into ME times in occasional field-names like *The Ham* (1301 *le Hamme*) in Crawley. Other words which may be glossed as 'enclosure', for example OE *gehæg, hege*, ME *howe*, are discussed where necessary in the dictionary.

lēah

Some general books give apparently incompatible meanings for this term, including 'wood', 'clearing', and 'meadow'. The last sense is unlikely in genuinely early place-names in Hampshire, for the change of application was a dialect development which filtered down from the north during the Middle English period (c.1100–1450). It may have been affected by the sense of the slightly similar word *læs* (dative case form *læswe*) pasture, meadow', which may survive as *leas(e), leasow* in minor local names. The meanings 'wood' and 'clearing' are not really incompatible. It appears that 'wood' is the earliest sense in English; the great Wealden forest was called *Andreslēah* from the time records began, for instance. Margaret Gelling argues (1984: pp. 198–207) that names of administratively important places containing *lēah* as their final element are likely to stem from patches of woodland, and in particular patches of the primeval woodland which agriculture in England has now all but cleared. (*Cold*) *Henley*, for instance, may have meant 'high wood' in a sense not dissimilar from that of the modern expression. Other types of wood, i.e. those which were managed to provide woodland products (spars, poles, wattle, etc.) or which gained significance by being dominated by a single species (perhaps even plantations in some cases), were often, but by no means always, referred to by different words like *grāf* and *holt*. (Compare *Sparsholt* with *Pilley*, for instance.) *Lēah*, on the other hand, may typically have been used for the exercise of common rights like pannage (the right to allow pigs to forage) and fire- and hedgebote (the rights to collect firewood and fencing materials). Into these vestigates of ancient woodland, incursions were made in times of rising population to set up new settlements. Where these settlements (assarts) flourished, we may find *lēah* names. So a name like *Baddesley* 'Bæddi's wood' or *Durley* 'deer wood' may be simultaneoulsy thought of as a name for a (part of a) wood or as a name for the settlement in a clearing within it. I have usually glossed *lēah* as 'wood/clearing', intending that the distinction in sense between these terms in modern English should not be thought of as applying in the case of the Old English term — it is not really one word-form with two meanings but a single lexical notion. However I have sometimes chosen one word rather than the other where it seems appropriate; the various *Farley/Farleigh* names are glossed 'bracken clearing' because bracken will not grow as undergrowth in the wildwood itself but only in openings within it. This is just an accommodation with common sense as applied to the botanical facts of life and not a departure from the principle I have just expressed; the woods in question will still have had the bracken place within them and I might just as well have written 'bracken wood/clearing'. The same goes for *Headley* 'heath clearing' and *Bentley* 'bent-grass clearing'. On the other hand, I have rendered *Oakley* as 'oak wood' for obvious reasons.

Gelling suggests that in at least one part of England, the West Midlands, a cluster of *lēah* names indicates settlements in a stretch of wildwood existing at the time the Anglo-Saxons gave the place-names, whilst an isolated *lēah* may indicate an isolated patch of ancient woodland in open country. To be sure of this we would have to show that the settlers automatically gave *lēah* names when the occasion to do so arose. It appears that in later times the sense of 'glade' became dominant over the sense of 'wood'; the cases of *Farley*, *Headley*, and *Bentley*, may properly be instances of this later development. The relative chronology, within this outline, of names including words for domesticated animals, like *Hursley*, is not clear. *Lee/Leigh/Lea* as a simplex name is not likely to mean 'wood', as it seems to be a relatively late type. Few indeed are recorded before 1086, although there are many places with this name. By this date, an isolated wood seems likely to have been called *wudu*, judging by the fact that, over England as a whole, places called *Wootton* 'wood farm' tend not to occur in forest or thickly-wooded areas (Gelling 1984: p. 227).

There is scope for a further exhaustive study of this difficult element and its meaning-developments in contrast with terms like *wudu*, *grāf* and *holt*, although Johansson (1975) and Gelling have made a valuable beginning. It is probably the most frequent of all place-name elements occurring in major (parish, manor, and hamlet) names.

-ing

Names containing final *-ing* fall into several distinct groups, though for present purposes they can be treated as if of two broad types.

There are singular -*ing* names, where the suffix is taken to be just an element by means of which a place-name can be formed (*Nursling, Sholing*). This sometimes appears in a fossilized oblique case-form (*Hampage Wood*). The second type of -*ing* names are those in a plural form. These are usually referred to as -*ingas* names, and are held to contain the names of peoples, in some loose sense – whether of tribes or of smaller associations around a single person whose name may form the stem to which the suffix is attached (*Basing, Wymering, Eling*). It used to be thought that these -*ingas* names were the oldest English place-names in England, though work done in the late 1960s by John McNeal Dodgson suggests that this cannot be literally true. For instance, their distribution does not precisely coincide with the earliest Anglo-Saxon remains discovered by archaeologists. Nevertheless such names are probably relatively early (say before c.600). Their value has been diminished only as indicators of where the invaders first put down their roots. (See further below.)

Name-changes

A matter which is rarely discussed, for lack of evidence, but which needs to be borne in mind, is that of name-changes. It is usually assumed that the Old English names whose traces we find on our present-day maps are the first and original names given to the places by the Anglo-Saxons. This may very well be true in a large number of cases, but we know of sufficient changes taking place in Anglo-Saxon times to make us wary of assuming automatically that locations, once named, bore that name for ever and ever. It may well have been that names were more fluid in the earliest times before a centralized administration and bureaucracy were established, for example that a farm typically bore the name of a current tenant rather than of his/her remote forebear. This is why it may not make a great deal of sense to describe some particular name-type as characteristic of the earliest ('original') period of settlement, since we cannot know what changes took place between the incursions of the fifth century and the period from which a great number of documents survive, say from the later eighth century onwards. (This problem is even more acute in counties for which virtually no pre-Conquest documentation survives; Hampshire is well served by comparison.) We should also bear in mind the period of settlement disruption which archaeologists call the Middle Saxon Shuffle. We do not really know whether this period was characterized by the transfer of old names to new settlements (or to what extent settlement was redistributed within existing administrative boundaries) or by the creation of a whole battery of new names reflecting some new tenurial pattern. There are also persistent indications – though not always clear ones – that names were being created up to the Conquest, and perhaps even beyond it, for places which had existed for centuries already. It is in the light of these problems that all questions of the chronology of place-name elements, and their utility as indicators of the chronology of settlement, should be seen, and treated with great caution.

Geological, topographical and ecological aspects of interpretation

Hampshire consists geologically of a central mass of gentle chalk hills dissected by rivers and dry valleys with a certain amount of Coombe Rock on their floor. The highest hills of this area are sometimes capped with clay-with-flints, with decreasing intensity as one proceeds eastwards. On the north side of the chalk is a zone of post-Cretaceous rocks including Reading beds, London clay and Bagshot sands. On the east is the western extremity of the Weald with its greensands, gault and Weald clay. On the south side is the so-called Hampshire Basin, the southern counterpart of the Thames Valley geology on the north flank, consisting (especially in the New Forest) of highly complicated patterns of recent sands and clays. Naturally this structure has had profound implications for patterns of settlement and land use, aspects of which are preserved in the place-name record. Thus, for instance, the soils least hospitable to agriculture are in areas showing none of the ancient name-types alluded to above; the New Forest itself has no certain -hām or -ingas names. On the other hand, the area north of Portsmouth has an extremely attractive pattern of water supply, due to the junction of the chalk with later overlying Eocene deposits, and it is here that the largest concentration of place-names with allusions to Roman activity is to be found (see for example *Havant*, *Boarhunt*, and *Wickham* in the dictionary). Other examples of significant relations between water supply and place-naming may be found at *Alton*, *Thedden*, and *Dummer*.

In a good few cases, the linguistic interpretation of the forms available is inconclusive, and in these cases we need to appeal to non-linguistic (geological/topographical or ecological) evidence to help us select the most likely etymology. This is illustrated by the discussion in the dictionary of what sort of *hamm* is likely to be denoted by *Elvetham*. Non-linguistic evidence can, of course, also

13

reinforce our linguistic deductions, even if there is no ambiguity in the name. *Popham*, apparently 'flint estate', is on the chalk downs, but consulting the OS geological map of the area reveals that it stands on a patch of clay-with-flints. The etymology proposed for *Calmoor* is strongly backed by the known geographical distribution of seakale and the history of market gardening in Hampshire. The plausibility of any given interpretation is always subject to scrutiny in the light of such criteria. The origin proposed for *Slackstead* above would have had to be ditched at once, no matter how plausible from the purely linguistic viewpoint, if blackthorn could never have grown at the site in question. This is why the apparently most plausible interpretation of *Hatherden* – from *heather* – is rejected. It is easy with hindsight to raise a wry smile at the efforts of early place-name scholars who produced 'hill' names in pancake-flat sites, and names said to testify to boats being pulled up a bank by windlass where there is only a tiny stream, but we need to be vigilant: one of the greatest of all place-name scholars produced a reference to the capercaillie in Hampshire where the right ecological conditions for ths bird can never have existed (see *Worldham*).

Historical and cultural aspects of interpretation

We need to ensure that our interpretations are drawn from languages known to have been spoken at the relevant period in the area. There have been no particular problems on this score in Hampshire. The difficulty of a Scandinavian personal name appearing with an English element far outside the Danelaw in *Thruxton* is only apparent, for it is clear that the name in question must have become a fashionable *English* name when borne by the man who gave his name to Thruxton, just as, for example, modern *Sean* or *Siobhan* (spelt with or without accents) applied to their children by English parents are clearly not Irish names in any unqualified sense, i.e. they could be given irrespective of whether the namers knew they were of Irish origin.

It is possible to discern changing fashions in naming. A little has been said about the chronology of different name-types within the Anglo-Saxon period. This matter especially excites the attention of historians because of the light it may throw on the question of whether Bede's account of the settlement of the area, involving West Saxons and Jutes, is accurate. Accepting for the purposes of argument that there is some truth in the account, the place-name evidence turns out to be rather disappointing. If the Saxons entered the future Hampshire from the north and the Jutes from the south, they seem to have left rather similar place-name types behind them. We find *-ingas* names in the north (*Worting, Basing*) and the south (*Wymering, Eling*). (The only *-ingahām* name is on the margin of the New Forest.) We find *-hām* names in the north (*Enham, Popham*) and more in the south (*Cosham, Upham, Waltham*). There is not much help here with chronology among the elements usually considered to be diagnostic. The Jutes appear to have left their 'tribal' name in an old name for the New Forest, *Ytene*; see also *Itchen Stoke*. Other peoples appear to be commemorated in *Canterton* and *Exton*, and much less probably in *Marchwood*. For recent work on these questions, the reader should consult, for example, Biddle (1976), Hills (1979), Evison (1981), Sims-Williams (1983), and Copley (1986).

The overwhelming bulk of the more significant places bore the ancestors of their present names by 1066, but amongst those known to have arisen (or to have been altered) after then we see first a French stratum dating from the period before c.1350–1400 when the aristocracy were on the whole French-speaking. There are purely French names like *Beaurepaire, Beaulieu* and *Freemantle*, some coined in England and others possibly transferred from northern France. Others add a French family name as a token of feudal overlordship to an English name, as in *Shipton Bellinger, Weston Corbet* and *Stratfield Turgis*. Such names are sometimes French place-names by origin, for example *Sutton Scotney, Penton Grafton* and *Stratfieldsaye*. When English had come to be the culturally dominant vernacular language again, a later fashion was to rename aristocratic houses in a somewhat whimsical way (in Hampshire *The Vyne* for *Sherfield Coudray* is the only notable early case); and later, but over a lengthy period, after the landowner's family, either by attribution – *Temple Farm* (Selborne) for *Temple Soddington*, or *St Clairs* for *Benstead St Clairs* – or by complete replacement (*Lisle Court* for *Sharprix*).

By the eighteenth century we find, as a consequence of the taking-in of land not previously used for settlement or agriculture, a glut of 'remoteness' names (*Canada, World's End*). The occasional ultra-modern place-names in the landscape show again a kind of whimsicality, in that, like *The Vyne* of earlier times, and like recent house-names, they do not necessarily contain toponymic elements (*Buckskin, Solent Breezes, Salt Grass* near Keyhaven). Antiquarianism, the passion for ancient things which led people to reinterpret present states of affairs in the light of the real or supposed past, active mainly (but not exclusively) in the eighteenth century, has had a hand in *Norsebury Ring, Oliver's Battery* and *East Anton*, and has also been responsible for the reintroduction of earlier spellings into the landscape or the introduction of specious ones (*Easeborne Manor* in Hurstbourne Tarrant and *Ormersfield* in Dogmersfield; *Anna Valley* in Upper Clatford).

Commemorative names of any other kind are a relatively recent phenomenon. Events in distant places are enshrined by such names as *Waterlooville* and the occasional *Bunker's Hill*. The tide of high society fashion is followed by *Lansdowne Hill* (with its associations with the Marquis of that title who helped to make Southampton, briefly, a fashionable resort), and by *New Brighton* in Emsworth, named after the rise of its big rival along the coast.

Tailpiece

The remarks above are not a study, but a foretaste of the dictionary. They give an idea of the principles and techniques used in place-name study, as well as of which issues are considered important by present-day researchers. The relation of place-name study to other disciplines is also emphasized. Scholars in this area cannot work in a geographical, biological, historical or cultural vacuum.

Note on some other elements

Some recurrent PN elements not treated in this introduction may be conveniently looked up as follows: *cumb* under Faccombe; *denu* under **Priors Dean**; *healh* under **Hale**, **Hawley**; *scēat*, *Scīete* under **Kempshott**, **Sheet**. *Hat*, *Inclosure* and *Plain* have separate entries in the dictionary.

LIST OF ABBREVIATIONS

County names

Bd	Bedfordshire‡	Mx	Middlesex‡
Bk	Buckinghamshire‡	Nb	Northumberland
Brk	Berkshire‡	Nf	Norfolk
C	Cambridgeshire‡	Np	Northamptonshire‡
Chs	Cheshire‡	Nt	Nottinghamshire‡
Co	Cornwall	O	Oxfordshire‡
Cu	Cumberland‡	Ru	Rutland
D	Devon‡	Sa	Shropshire
Db	Derbyshire‡	Sf	Suffolk
Do	Dorset‡	So	Somerset
Du	Durham	Sr	Surrey‡
Ess	Essex‡	St	Staffordshire‡
Gl	Gloucestershire‡	Sx	Sussex‡
Ha	Hampshire	W	Wiltshire‡
He	Herefordshire	Wa	Warwickshire‡
Hrt	Hertfordshire‡	We	Westmorland‡
Hu	Huntingdonshire‡	Wo	Worcestershire‡
K	Kent	Wt	Isle of Wight
L	Lincolnshire‡	YER	Yorkshire, East Riding‡
La	Lancashire	YNR	Yorkshire, North Riding‡
Lei	Leicestershire	YWR	Yorkshire, West Riding‡

English Place-Name Society county surveys exist in whole or in part for the counties marked ‡.

Language names

Lat.	Latin
RB	Romano-British (Latinized British, British forms in a Latin guise)
Brit.	British (pre-Roman or Roman-period British Celtic)
PrW	Primitive Welsh (c.400–800)
OE	Old English (c.400–1100)
WSax	West Saxon dialect of OE
ME	Middle English (1100–1450)
eModE	Early Modern English (1450–1600)
ModE	Modern English (1600–date)
PrE	Present-day English (contemporary)
NF	Norman French
AN	Anglo-Norman

Gmc.	Germanic, the ancestor language of English, German, Danish, etc.
OHG	Old High German
MHG	Middle High German
ON	Old Norse

Other abbreviations

AS	Anglo-Saxon
c	(before a numeral) century
c.	(before a numeral) circa, approximately
Cy	Country (as in WCy, NCy, SCy)
DB	Domesday Book
DEPN	Dictionary of English Place-Names, by E. Ekwall (see Bibliography)
DMV	deserted medieval village
e.	early
EPNE	English Place-Name Elements, by A.H. Smith (see Bibliography)
EPNS	English Place-Name Society
FN	field-name
IA	Iron Age
l.	late
m.	mid
OS	Ordnance Survey
PN	place-name
s.-e.	self-explanatory
t.	in the time (reign) of, followed by the abbreviation of a monarch's name (Hy II, John, Ed III, Eliz I, etc.)
TA	Tithe Award
VCH	Victoria County History (see Bibliography)
x	(between 2 numerals) between the two dates indicated
★	(before a spelling) a hypothetical reconstructed form whose former existence can reasonably be inferred
?	possible, possibly

The compass points are abbreviated by their first letter, upper case.

A

Abbot's Ann, Amport, Little Ann Three manors, two parishes
901 (c14) (*at*) *annæ*, (*to*) *anne*; 1086 *Anna*.
Usually taken to be a Celtic river-name based on ?Brit. **onno-*
'ash'. The OE forms would be good spellings for this. But words
for trees are not found unadorned as Celtic river-names; they are
suffixed or compounded. Rivet and Smith (1979) experiment with
various pre-Celtic etymologies for the possibly related RB name
Onnum, but the name still remains obscure. There is actually no
clear evidence that this really is an old river-name, because the
earliest mention of Pillhill Brook, to which it would have to refer,
is 1228 *aqua de Anne*, which could just as easily contain *Anne* as a
district name. It is true that the manors are strung out along Pillhill
Brook. But I suggest that the name is a village or estate name
deriving from the PrW plural form **onn* 'ash-trees' as a simplex
name, like **Ashe** and *Ash* (Sr). Whether the stream had a distinct
early name is uncertain. The modern name is not found before
1826. Scholarship has left its mark, for the appearance of the name
in DB in the form *Anna* has motivated the recent naming of *Anna
Valley*, beside the stream in Upper Clatford, in effect a suburb of
Andover. The immediate motivation may be the chapter-title *The
Vale of Anna* in D.H. Moutray Read's *Highways and Byways in
Hampshire* (1908).

The villages are distinguished as Abbot's Ann, Little Ann and
Amport. Abbot's Ann belonged to Hyde Abbey (the grant is in the
document of 901 cited) and is c.1270 *Anne Abbatis*. Little Ann is
1540 *Anne Parva*. Amport was held by the important Hampshire
landholder Hugh *de Port* at the time of DB, and appears as 1248
Anne de Port, 1379 *Portesanne*. See also **Monxton**, **Sarson** and
Thruxton. **Ann** is sometimes spelt **Anne**.

Abbot's Worthy
See **Worthy**.

Abbotstone DB manor and shrunken village in Itchen Stoke
c.970 (c12) *abbodestun*; 1086 *Abedestune*.
OE 'abbot's farm'. Itchen Stoke was held by Romsey Abbey,
though by DB this manor was held by Hugh de Port, not the
Abbey. The medieval spellings show the replacement of the OE
abbod by the borrowing from French *abbat* (1203 *Abboteston*).
Predictable later developments include 1579 *Aberston* and the
transmutation of the last syllable into *stone*.

Abbott's Barton

t. Hy I *Abbotesberton*; 1250 *Bertone*.

OE *beretūn* (literally) 'barley farm'; (later) 'grange farm'. The word *barton* is recorded as a Hampshire dialect word by Cope (1883: 5). The farm belonged to Hyde Abbey, hence the full name, and also the alternative 1606 *Hyde Barton*.

Abshott Hamlet in Hook

t. Ed I *Abbeshute*; t. Ric II *Abbechute*.

OE **Abbansciete* 'Abba's *sciete* or angle of land', formerly at the eastern end of Hook parish abutting Titchfield Common, hence *sciete* in its typical administrative sense.

Achelie Two lost DB manors in the New Forest.

These names are clearly OE **Āclēah* 'oak wood'; maybe represented by the two modern *Oakley Inclosures*, NE of Burley. Cf. also **Oakley**.

Aldershot

1171 *Halreshet*; 1248 *Alreshete*; 1287 *Alresshate*.

OE **Alorscēat* 'alder corner', or more pedantically **Alrescēat*, 'corner at the place called *Alre*' (i.e. 'at the alder tree'). The infant river Blackwater forms the county boundary with Surrey here, and describes a broad arc leaving part of Hampshire projecting a little between Weybourne and Ash in Surrey. This is probably the *scēat* 'corner' in question (cf. **Grayshott**). Alders beside the stream are probable enough. There was another 'alder shot' in Droxford recorded in 826.

In view of the later military associations of Aldershot, it is interesting to note that alder-charcoal was preferred for the making of gunpowder (Rackham 1980: 306).

Alice Holt Forest

1167 *Alsiholt*; 1168 *Alfsiholt*; 1190 *Alsiesholt*.

OE/ME **Ælfsigeshoit* 'managed woodland of Ælfsige'. Gelling (1984: 196) suggests that a typical *holt* was a wood of a single species, and it may be that the central settlement name of *Bucks Horn Oak* is indicative. But the modern forest is quite large and there is room for more than one *holt*.

Allenford In Damerham, former submember of parish of Toyd Farm, once in Dorset

c14 *Elyngford*; 1518 *Alyngforde*, *Elyngford*.

Forms are too late for certainty. Uncertain whether it has anything to do with **Ellingham** (and hence with **Eling**). Stands on the river

Allen, a name-type which is often pre-English, but no early spellings for the river-name have come down to us and it may be a back-formation from the farm-name.

Allington Manor in South Stoneham

1086 *Ellatune*; 1154×1158 *Aldintona*; 1186 *Aldintone*; 1229 *Aldung-tona*.

OE 'Ealda's farm', either in a genitive formation (*Ealdan*) or an -*ingtūn* formation. Forms without *d* are found from the early c15.

Allum Green In Brockenhurst

1086 *Alwinetune*; 1331 (*boscus qui vocatur*) *Alwenne*; 1589 *Allem greene*; 1606 *Allen Green*.

The modern name preserves, rather than continues, the DB name, which was either OE ⋆*Ælf-*/*Æðelwynnetūn* 'Ælfwynn's farm' or 'Æðelwynn's farm', in either case the owner being a woman; or the second element of the personal name might have been the male -*wine*, in which case the formation without -*s* is unusual in this region (but cf. **Awbridge, Wolverton**). The identification with modern Allum Green rules out Gover's suggestion that *Allum* represents a Brit. river-name of a familiar type, as in *Aln* (Nb). Cf. *Alum Chine* in Bournemouth (1759 *Allam Chine*), which may be appropriately compared with *Alum Bay* (Wt). Cornelius de Vos had been extracting alum in the Isle of Wight under monopoly licence in the mid c16. James Blount, sixth Baron Mountjoy, took over de Vos' patent in 1576 to exploit the deposits of shale and iron pyrites under Bourne Heath to produce alum and copperas. The attempt ruined him (Young 1957: 15–16).

Alre River

A back-formation from *Alresford*, first recorded in 1724, but known earlier as *Alresford river*. The OE charter boundaries make it clear that this river was considered to be the headwater of the Itchen, whilst what is now known as the upper reaches of the Itchen was called *Ticceburna* (see **Tichborne**).

Alresford, New and **Old**

701 (c12) (*to*) *alresforda*; 947×955 (c14) (*to*) *alresforda*; 1167 *Alresford*.

OE 'alder ford', with the possible but not certain implication 'at the alder tree' because of the genitive singular form of the first element. The tradition showing no -*s* is later and only sporadic. Most forms from 701 all through the Middle Ages are of the type *Alresford*. The modern pronuncication may be first hinted at in 1408 (*Allesford*). *New Alresford*, founded by bishop Godfrey de

Lucy in 1200, is first distinguished in the mid c13 (*Nova Villa de Alresford*), later 1332 *Chepyng Alresford*, i.e. 'Alresford Market (-town)'. Alresford does not take its name from the river **Alre**, but vice versa.

Alton

1080×1087 *Auueltona*; 1086 *Aultone*; t. Hy I *Auelton*; c.1124 *Awelton*.

OE *★Æwielltūn* 'spring farm'. The river Wey rises at several points around Alton, and one source (or all of them) gives its name to the place. It may be the one which rises at *Will Hall*, whose medieval spellings, in the dominant tradition, suggest derivation from *wielle* 'spring'. (The *Wildehel* of 1086 is out on a limb. The c14 scribal tradition with *Wyne-* is an aberration.) Alton stands on the chalk just where it meets the Upper Greensand, and the combination of a steep hydraulic gradient and the Stockbridge anticline in the chalk makes for strong springs (Cole 1985: 7).

The two manors of Alton were known as *Westbrook* and *Eastbrook*, 'west and east of the brook', being divided by a headwater of the Wey. Both names survive as house-names.

It is possible formally that the first element is OE *awel* 'hook, etc.' in some topographical sense (cf. *Awliscombe* (D)), but that hardly seems worth considering in the light of the above.

Alverstoke

948 (c12) (*æt*) *stoce*; 1086 *Alwarestoch*; c.1127 *Alwarestoke*; c.1170 *Alwarstok*; 1174 *Stokes juxta mare*.

The place was originally just *Stoc* 'dependent farm, place'. Tradition relates that a Saxon lady called *Alwara* (i.e. *Ælfwaru* or *Æðelwaru*) bestowed the manor on St Swithin's, Winchester (cf. *VCH* III: 203). The forms cited do not contradict this. (She may also be commemorated in 1279 *Aylwarstrete*, the north part of what is now *Jewry Street*, Winchester. If this is the same person, then she was *Æðelwaru* not *Ælfwaru*.) Some forms of the c13 and later show that the first element was taken to be the common man's name *Æðelweard*.

Ambersham Detached part of Steep, now parish in Sx

963 (c12) *æmbresham, embresham*; 1166 *Ambersham*.

OE 'estate of Æmbre', the name apparently being from a side-form of *Ambre* 'the Ambrones', though not necessarily in any tribal sense when used as a personal name. Absorbed into Sx by the Act of 1844.

Ampfield Modern parish carved out of Hursley
1208 *Anfelda*; 1292 *Amfelde*; 1307 *Aumfelde*.
A very difficult name; apparently containing OE *ān* 'one, single'
and *feld* 'open land'. If there were forms like **Anefeld* in the Middle
Ages, we could confidently translate 'lonely open land'; but there
are none. Perhaps it is a three-element compound with the middle
one lost (a so-called *Klammerform*), e.g. **Ānsetlfeld* 'hermitage
open land'. But there is no certainty.

Amport
See **Abbot's Ann**.

Andover
955 (c14) *andeferas*; 962 (*æt*) *andeferan*; 994 (*to*) *andeferan, ande-*
f(e)ron.
The name appears to be a plural form in OE, representing a form
like Brit. **Onnodubrī* or PrW **Ondiβr* 'ash waters (streams)' (cf.
Jackson 1943: 285). Translation at the grammatical level is implied,
suggesting bilingual contact. The streams would be the **Anton** and
the right tributary joining it above the town. If this is an old area
name, Pillhill Brook may also be referred to (see **Abbot's Ann** for
some relevant discussion).

Andwell Extraparochial area adjacent to Mapledurwell
t. Hy I *Enedewella*; *1199 Anedewelle*; 1351 *Andewell*.
OE **Enedwiell(e)* 'duck stream' (or better, it appears, **Eneda-*
'ducks'). The river Lyde broadens out here to form a pond. A very
common type of name. There was in AS times another **Ænedawiell(e)*
in Tadley.

Andyke Ancient earthwork in Barton Stacey
c13 *Auntediche*.
This must have been already here when the Anglo-Saxons arrived,
for they called it **Entadīc* 'giants' dyke', a typical name for
prehistoric earthworks before the name of the Devil became
associated with them in Christian times (cf. the *Devil's Ditch* at St
Mary Bourne). A further earthwork in King's Worthy was referred
to in 1026 as *ænta dic*, the same expression. An OE poem ('The
Ruin') describes Roman remains as *enta geweorc* 'work of giants'.
Other ancient earthworks in the county were attributed to *Grīm*,
supposedly a by-name for Woden; the end of one of the Grims
Dykes in Breamore is called 1297 *Grymesdichesende* and Grims
Ditch in Linkenholt was 1272 *Grimesdich*.

Anstey Manor in Alton

1086 *Hanstige*; 1157 *Anestiga.*

Following Gelling (1984: 63–4), this is OE *ānstiga, ānstig* 'amalgamation of two (or more) rising paths in a col', though Gelling admits it is difficult to justify in this particular case. It depends how one views the medieval importance of the roads that fan out from Alton and from Cuckoo's Corner, east of Anstey. The older view was that the element meant 'single-file path'.

Anton, East Hamlet, now suburb, of Andover

1582 *Eston towne*; 1611 *Estentowne.*

OE *★ēastan tūne* 'east of the town' (i.e. Andover or possibly Charlton); or, since it is recorded late, its ME derivative. Cf. *Easton Town* (W). It has been misunderstood as *east* followed by a PN, in a glaring example of misapplied antiquarianism. The MS of Tacitus' *Agricola* in which a PN *Antona* appears was well known in the c18. This is a corruption of *Trisantona*, the river-name *Trent* or *Tarrant*. Someone has clearly associated this ghost-name with that of Andover, discovered *Estentowne* in the parish, and jumped to a hasty conclusion. By pure coincidence, East Anton is really the site of a Roman settlement where the Roman roads (numbered following Margary (1973)) 4b (Port Way) and 43 cross.

Anton River

1756 *water of And.*

A modern name back-formed from **East Anton** and/or **Andover**. It is earlier called by the less elliptical name c.1540 *Andever water.*

Aplestede Lost DB manor in Portsdown hundred

OE 'Apple place'.

Appleshaw

1200 *Appelsag'*; c.1250 *Appelschage*; 1273 *Appelshawe.*

OE/ME *★Æppelsceaga* 'apple wood or strip of woodland'. Probably with reference to crab-apples, for *sceaga/schawe* does not mean an orchard or any managed wood. The element is not common in the SCy.

Arford In Headley

1256 *Areford.*

Of uncertain meaning, perhaps OE *★Ēarford* 'gravel ford'; or maybe the first element is *ærne* 'fit for riding', as in *Arnford* (YWR).

Arnewood Manor and hamlet in Hordle, now in Sway
1086 *Ernemude*; 1488 *Arnewode, Ernewode.*
Probably OE **Earnawudu* 'eagles' wood'. The DB spelling with
-*m*- is an error.

Ashe
1086 *Esse*; 1167 *Aisse*; 1258 *Esshe.*
OE **Æsc(e)* '(at the) ash-tree'. Recorded in 1354 as *Ashe Maners*,
from being held by the family of John *de Maners.*

Ashley Near King's Somborne
1275 *Asselegh.*
Not in DB as Gover claims; that is Ashley near New Milton. OE
*Æscléah 'ash wood'. There are two other **Ashley**s having the same
origin: one near New Milton (1086 *Esselie, Esselei*), occasionally
East Ashley (1285 *Est Assely*); and one near Ringwood (1236 *Essileg*,
1390 *North Ascheley*). The last two are named directionally in
relation to a common point of importance, perhaps Christchurch.

Ashley Walk Part of Fordingbridge within the New Forest,
extraparochial
1280 (*boscus de*) *Assle.*
OE/ME **Æscléah* 'ash wood'. The *walk* is one of the forest walks
(1670 *Ashley Walk*).

Ashmansworth
909 (c12) *æscmæreswierðe*; 934 (c12) *æscmæres wyrðe, æscmeres
weorþ*; 1171 *Esmeresworde.*
Since no personal name *Æscmǣr* is known, the first element is likely
to be a PN **Æscmere* 'ash pool'. Grundy (1921: p. 90; 1927: pp. 281–
3) drew attention to the lost *escmeræ* mentioned in an AS-period
charter alongside Buttermere (W), about five miles away just over
the county boundary. He showed that *Æscmere* comprised the modern
Vernham's Dean and **Linkenholt**. The present name is therefore
'curtilage (perhaps here "secondary settlement") of Æscmere'. Ancient
PNs compounded with *wyrð* are, however, rare (Smith, *EPNE* II:
274).
  The spelling *wierð, wyrð, weorð* are a feature of West-Saxon
documents. For a little discussion see Smith (*loc. cit.*), Kitson
(forthcoming).
  The resemblance of the first element to OE *æscmann* 'pirate' is pure
coincidence. Forms in *n* are not found till 1398 (*Asshmansworthe*).

Ashton Tithing of Bishop's Waltham hundred in Bishop's Waltham
1248 *Esseton*; 1307 *Assheton.*

OE *Æsctūn 'farm of the ash tree(s)'.

Ashurst Former hamlet in Colbury, now estate in Eling by Forest bounds, and Forest walk
1331 *Assh(e)hurst.*
OE/ME*Æschyrst 'ashwoodedhill'.

Aston
See **East Aston**.

Avington
961 (c12) (*to*) *afintune*; 1181 *Avinton.*
OE *Afingtūn 'farm associated with Afa'.

Avon River
688 (*c.* 1300) *abon*; 672 (c12) *afen*; 961 (*on*) *afene*; 1234 *Avene.*
The common PrW word for 'river', *aβon, cf. W *afon*. The name is frequent elsewhere, cf. the Warwickshire and Bristol Avons.

Awbridge DB manor, scattered settlement in Michelmersh
1086 *Abedric*; 1207 *Abberugge*; 1218 *Abbederugge*; 1238 *Abbede-rigge.*
OE *Abbodhrycg 'ridge of the abbot'; the lack of the genitive -*es* is noteworthy (cf. **Wolverton**). The manor belonged to St Peter's Abbey, Winchester. Later c13 forms begin to show the substitution of the French derivative of the Latin *abbas* (1256 *Abboterigge*). There is no support for Smith (EPNE I: p. 1) in his belief that it contains *brycg* not *hrycg*. There is no ancient bridge nearer than **Kimbridge** in Mottisfont or Greatbridge and Stanbridge in Romsey; Awbridge is on a hilltop as viewed from Michelmersh.

Axford Hamlet in Nutley
1272 *Ashore*; 1280 *Axore.*
OE 'ash-tree slope'. Gelling's translation of *ōra*, 'foot of a slope' (1984: 179), is highly suitable for Axford. The first element is either a metathesized form of OE *æsc* (*æx*) or its genitive plural form *acsa. The spelling of 1272 might, but need not, suggest the alternative *Æscōra.

B

Baddesley, **North** and **South** Parish, and hamlet in Boldre
1086 *Bedeslei* (both); 1135×1154 *Betheslega* (N); 1167 *Badeslea* (both); 1212 *Badeslie* (S); 1235 *Baddeslegh* (N).
OE ★*Bæddeslēah* 'Bæddi's wood/clearing', presumably a settlement in a stretch of ancient woodland. On this man's name, cf. Coates (1988b). The two names are presumably quite separate in origin, even if linguistically the same, since the places are on opposite sides of Southampton.

Badley DB manor, now **Clare Park**, in Crondall
1086 *Baddeleie*; 1248 *Badelegh*.
OE 'Badda's or Bada's clearing/wood'.

Badminston Part-tithing of New Forest hundred (1586) in Fawley
1296 *Brightmaneston*; 1334 *Brygmanneston*; 1525 *Barkemaston*; 1586 *Barkmeston*; 1681 *Brickmanston*; 1759 *Badminston*.
OE ★*Brihtmannestūn* 'Brihtmann's farm', though the name has undergone all manner of irregular developments including the stopping of [x] to [k] and the completely unaccountable modern transformation. The form of 1681 is out of line and seems to depend on the earlier tradition.

Baffins In Portsmouth
From the surname of the Tudor explorer of western Greenland, William *Baffin*?

Bagmore In Herriard
c.1245 *Baggemere*; 1273 *Baghemeresfeld*.
The word ★*bagga* is now generally assumed to have existed and to have meant 'badger' (cf. **Baughurst**). This name is OE ★*Bagganmere* 'badger pool'.

Banister's Park In Southampton
Perpetuates the memory of the *Banastre* family (of Tidworth) who owned the land in the c14, and in particular of Thomas Banaster, alive in 1502, who gave his name to *Banaster* (or *Banisters*) *Court*.

Bank In Lyndhurst
Bank is on a low sandstone ridge, between streams, and between the lower Barton Clay and Headon Beds areas.

Bar End Suburb of Winchester
1541 *Barende*.

The *bar* of Winchester is recorded t. Hy III ((*extra*) *barram Wynton'*) presumably denoting a barrier erected in the East Gate, beyond which Bar End lies. For the general sense, cf. the street-name *Above Bar* in Southampton.

Bartley Heath In Odiham
1086 *Berchelei*; 1236 *Berkeleg'*.

OE **Beorc(a)lēah* 'birch wood' (it is c.1350 *Barkele boscus*). The heath, on valley gravel/sand, is first documented in 1586. The form with *-t-* is purely modern, and is paralleled in the surname *Burtenshaw*, a variant of *Birkinshaw*. Thus also *Bartley* (Grange and village) in Copythorne (1236 *Berkele*, 1586 *Bartlie Regis*).

Barton Peveral In South Stoneham, later in Eastleigh
1223 *Barton'*.

OE *beretūn* 'barley farm, grange farm', as in **Abbott's Barton**. In 1223 the manor was held by Robert *Peverel* (NF 'pepper-corn'), the family name being commemorated also in 1391 *Peverelleswey*.

Barton Stacey
c.1000 (c14) (*æt*) *bertune*.

For *Barton* see **Abbott's Barton**. *Stacey* is a c14 corruption of the family name of the tenant in 1199, Roger de *Saci*, whose surname is from the PN *Sacy* (presumably the one in Marne *département*). The same change is found in the name of *Newton Stacey* (903 *Niuuetone*, c14 *Nyweton Sacy*) in the same parish.

Barton-on-Sea Seaside resort in Milton
1086 *Bermintune, Burmintune*; 1262 *Bereminton*; 1327 *Bermeton*. Probably OE **Beormantūn* or **Beormingtūn* 'Beorma's farm'. *Beorma* would be a regular short-form for a name like *Beornmund*. The forms quoted refer to the ancient manor; the modern resort has grown as a natural eastward extension of the Bournemouth conurbation convenient for the New Forest. The name has been assimilated to the common *Barton*.

Bashley
1053 (c14) (*æt*) *bageslucesleia*; 1086 *Bailocheslei*; 1152 *Bailukesleia*.

OE **Bægloceslēah* 'wood/clearing of Bægloc'. (The first *-s-* in the 1053 form is a mistake.) This uncommon name was borne by an c8 abbot. The transformation to *Bashley* can be understood by looking at the intermediate form 1606 *Balloxley*; it is a euphemism, and in 1664 we find, among others, the present spelling.

Basing or **Old Basing**

871 (*c*.890, *c*.1120) (*æt*) *basingum, basengum*; *c*.894 *basengas*; 945 (c14) (*ad*) *Basyngum* (Latin form); 1086 *Basinges*.

OE *Basingas, an OE folk-name based on the personal name *Basa, not in evidence in OE records but which has a secure parallel in continental Germanic. Its existence must be assumed to handle PNs like *Basford* (Nt) and probably *Bassingbourn* (C); and according to Copley (1954: 125) also the old name of Ankerwyke (Bk).

Basing Park In Froxfield

1453 *virgat' terr' vocat' Basynge in decenn' de Langenhurst*, 'a yardland called Basynge in Langhurst tithing'. The last word in this expression is the original name for the place (1307 *Langehurst*), OE *langan hyrste* 'long wooded hill (oblique case form)'. It takes its later name from the family *de Basyng*, who held it in the c14. They took their surname from **Basing**, q.v.

Basingstoke

990 (c12) (*on*) *embasinga stoc*; 1086 *Basingestoches*; 1167 *Basingstoke*.

OE *Basinga stoc 'dependent settlement of **Basing**' or 'of the Basingas'. The peculiar first form may, according to Tengstrand, include OE *ef(e)n* 'near', here appearing as *em*. The form of 1086 (and others like it) shows the common AN apparent plural form (cf. Smith, *EPNE* II: 155).

Bassett In North Stoneham

This place grew in the late c18 as a retreat for rich people outside (and away from civic responsibilities in) the borough of Southampton. A family of *Basset* is known in South Stoneham in the early c15, and the PN may be from their name.

Batchley DB manor in Milford-on-Sea

1086 *Beceslei*; c13 *Bachesle*; 1397 *Bacchesle*.

OE * *Bæcceslēah* 'wood/clearing of Bæcci'.

Battle Down Farm In Wootton St Lawrence
See **Herriard**.

Battramsley Manor in Boldre, New Forest bailiwick

1086 *Betramelei*; 1212 *Batrameslie*; 1236 *Baterhameslie*; 1272 *Beterhemeleg'*.

A most difficult name. A secondary PN, the *lēah* 'wood/clearing' of a place apparently called **Betraham(m)* 'better estate/hemmed-in land', for whose name there are no parallels and whose site is not known. Perhaps rather of **Bēateraham(m)* 'beaters'/boxers' estate/hemmed-in land', with a 'professional' first element as in *Bemerton* (W) 'trumpeters' farm', and cf. **Kempshott**.

Baughurst

909 (c12) (*on*) *beaggan hyrste*; 1175 *Baggeherst*; 1189 *Baggehurst*. Ekwall and Gover translate 'Beagga's wood', claiming *Beagga* to be a short-form of a man's name like *Bēagmund, -nōð*. This is possible. But the OE form may be in error. All the medieval development is compatible with an OE name *Bagganhyrst* 'badger wooded-hill'. *Bagga* is not recorded, but PN scholars have long accepted its existence (Smith, *EPNE* I: 17–18). The name would be parallel to the numerous *Bagleys* and *Bagshaws*. (Note that there is a *Brock's Green* (probably 1245 *Brochurst*) about 4 miles away in Ecchinswell.) Moreover *hyrst* rarely appears with a personal name as first element. Unusually, therefore, I prefer to take an attested OE form as misleading. (The document (in B.L. Add MS. 15350) is spurious, in fact.)

The modern (irregular) pronunciation is first shown by 1558 *Bogorste*, 1741 *Baugust*. The parish name has also influenced and/or been influenced by the name *Haughurst*, in Baughurst parish, which was 1256 *Hauekehurst* 'hawk wooded-hill'.

Beaulieu

1205 (*de*) *Bello Loco* (*Regis*); 1208 (*usque*) *Bellum Locum*; c.1300 *Beulu*; 1341 *Beuleu*; 1381 *Bewley*.
AN 'lovely place', a name created for the abbey established in 1205. Often appearing in a Latin form, as in the first two examples. Anglicized over the years and still pronounced in the English way. 'The king's' (*regis*) because in the forest and therefore in the king's gift (John's, in this case).

Beaulieu River

The river takes its name from the village. But it was known c.1200 (c17) as (*aque que vocat'*) *Otere*, 1236 *Otere*, perhaps *Otorēa* 'otter stream', cf. *Otterwood*, the DB manor of *Otreorde* (1236 *Oterwud'*) 'otter wood'. Three streams descend from the vicinity of this hamlet to the river.

Beaurepaire Mansion in Sherborne St John

1272 *Beaureper*; 1298 *Byaureper*.
AN *beau repaire* 'fine retreat', but the form of 1298 and another of 1300 appear to be in a northern French dialect. This PN recurs elsewhere, e.g. *Belper* (Db), *Beaper* (Wt) and *Berrepper* (Co).

Beauworth
938 (c12) *beowyrð*; 963x975 (c12) (*æt*) *beowyrðe*; 1208 *Beworda*; 1280 *Buworthe*.
OE **Bēowyrð* 'bee curtilage', i.e. presumably a farmstead where the inhabitant kept bees rather than one which specialized in honey.

Beckley DB manor in Christchurch
1086 *Bichelei*; 1294 *Beckele*.
These are the only medieval spellings known. OE 'Beocca's clearing/- wood', or perhaps 'Bicca's'. Cf. *Beckton* in Hordle, less than 5 miles away, which Gover believes to contain the same name.

Bedhampton
1086 *Betametone*; 1167, 1242 *Bethameton*(a); 1236, 1248 *Bedham*(p)*ton*.
Far from obvious. Apparently OE **Betehǣmatūn* 'farm of the inhabitants of **Betehām*, an unknown place called 'beet-estate'.

Beech Hamlet (now village) in Alton
1239 *la Beche*; 1334 (*atte*) *Beyche*.
ME 'beech tree'.

Beenham Manor in Kingsclere
1428 *Edmundesthrop Bienham*; 1586 *Edmonstrop Beanam*.
The present name is the manorial specifier (from the family *de Bynam* (i.e. Beenham (Brk), c.7 miles away) who held the manor in 1327) of the earlier village name *Edmondsthorpe* (1167 *Ædmundestorp*, 1236 *Eadmundestrop*) 'secondary settlement (OE *þrop* (*þorp*)) of Ēadmund'. Now mapped as *Cheam School*; the prep school was moved here in 1935 (Gover).

Belmont Reputed manor in Bedhampton
Not recorded till Tudor times (t. Eliz. *Beamonds*), but enshrining the family name of Geoffrey *de Bello Monte*, a Latin version of the common French PN *Beaumont* 'lovely hill'.

Belvidere In Southampton
Italian architects of the c16 invented the *belvedere*, literally 'nice view'; it had two related senses, 'lookout tower or gallery (on a house)', 'gazebo (on a hillock) with all-round views'. The Southampton *Belvidere*, with its latinized spelling, is now in a heavily industrial area, but a good view up and down the Itchen might be obtained from it by peering between the wharves and other buildings. A typical l. c18/e. c19 name in an expanding town. It directly parallels the earlier *Bellevue House*, equally having views over the Itchen, built for Nathaniel St André in the early 1700s.

An interesting parallel is *Buonavista Farm* in Milford-on-Sea (Napoleonized 1797, 1800 as *Boneyvest(ae)*).

Bentley Liberty
963×975 (c12) (*æt*) *beonetleh*; 973×974 (c12) (*to*) *beonetlegæ* (*gemære*); 1167 *Benetlea*; 1208 *Benetlega*; 1272 *Bunetleye*; 1341 *Bientelegh*. OE **Bēonetlēah* 'bent-grass clearing' or less likely 'meadow'. *Bennets* is recorded as a Hampshire dialect word by Cope (1883: 7). Bent-grass is especially well adapted to grow in acid soil. Bentley is established on or adjacent to Denchworth association soils, which are said to be especially good for grass. The northern boundary of Bentley liberty shadows that of the Upper Greensand outcrop.

Bentworth
t. Hy I *Bintewrde*; 1130 *Binteworda*.
OE **Bintanwyrð* 'Binta's curtilage'. No such OE man's name is on record, but there is a precise continental German parallel *Binizo*, and the name may recur in *Benton* (Sr).

Bere Forest Two forests
1168, 1185 *la Bera*; 1237 *foresta de Ber'*.
From OE *bær* 'swinepasture', i.e. one where rights of pannage were exercised. There is a significant name in Soberton, in the eastern forest, viz. *Mislingford*, which appears to contain a lost PN **Mastlēah* '(beech-)mast wood/clearing', the favourite food of the foraging pigs being beechmast. The two forests are distinguished as *East* and *West*, or the smaller western one as 'near Winchester' (1280 *la Bere de Asshele juxta Wynton'*). Its name survives in *Forest of Bere Farm* in Ashley.

Bessete DB manor in Neatham hundred
Unidentified. Possibly OE **Bēosscēat* 'bentgrass corner' or **Bēoset(t)* 'bentgrass bed'.

Bevois Mount; Bevois Town; and Bevois Valley In Southampton
In the 1720s the Earl of Peterborough developed for himself a mansion called *Bevis Mount*, commemorating the medieval legendary hero Sir *Bevis* (AN, usually understood as if *beau vis* 'handsome face') of Hampton. The lower part of the estate towards the river Itchen came to be called *Bevis Valley* (sometimes with the eccentric spelling *Bevois*, which has now prevailed). This area was developed for housing in 1852–67 when the former Peterborough estate was broken up; it is now called *Bevois Town*, and contains the commemorative *Peterborough Road*.

Bickton Manor in Fordingbridge
1086 *Bichetone*; 1227 *Biketon*.
OE *Bīcantūn* 'beehive farm'; or possibly an OE man's name *Bīca*
is involved. Names of this type are discussed by Dietz (1985).

Bighton
959 (c14) *bicincgtun*; 1086 *Bighetone*; 1158 *Bicentona*; 1229, 1253
Byketon; 1255 *Bikinton*.
The earliest spelling (from a MS. judged authentic by the best
authorities) suggests an *-ingtūn* derivative of the man's name *Bīca*;
if so, 'Bīca's farm'; but see previous entry. The medieval spellings
indicate the possible coexistence of synonymous names descending
from *Bīcingtūn* and *Bīcantūn*. The first clear indication of the
change from [k] to [x] (spelt *gh*) comes in the c16.

Bile DB manor in Boldre hundred
Unidentified. Possibly **Pilley** in the same hundred, but that would
leave the DB manor of *Pisteslei* unidentified instead. As it stands,
it appears to be OE *Bīlēage* 'by the wood/clearing'. Lloyd (1964:
184) identifies it with **Burley**, otherwise nameless in DB.

Binley Hamlet in St Mary Bourne
1184 *Benelega*; 1269 *Bynleghe*; 1334 *Bienlygh*.
Maybe OE *Bēona lēah* 'bees' clearing/wood' (except that *bēo* 'bee'
never seems to occur in the plural in PNs) or *Bynnan lēah* 'Bynna's
clearing/wood'. However, given the universal importance of beans
in the medieval peasant's diet, we should consider *Bēanlēah* 'bean
clearing'. The medial syllable only appears in two recorded medieval
forms. Ekwall relates several other PNs (e.g. *Bincknoll* (W)) with
-ie- in spellings of the first syllable to OE *bēan*.

Binstead
1086, 1201, 1240 *Benestede*.
OE 'place where beans grow' (but the medial *e* raises questions).
In the c14 its manors had the feudal names *Bynstedepopham*,
Bynstedekyng; the Pophams were from **Popham**, and there was
royal interest in this estate before the time of DB. In 1375 the other
manor was adjudged to have reverted to the king by the death of
John de Bensted senior and his son's minority (*VCH* II: 483).
Bēanstede was also the older name of **St Clairs** in Corhampton
and of *Binstead* (Wt).

Bishop's Sutton

982 (c14) *sudtunam*; 1086 *Sudton(e)*.

OE **Sūðtūn* 'south farm'. It is south-east of Old Alresford and south of Bighton. It was held by the bishop of Winchester in 1086, as was Alresford; Bighton was not; so direction from Alresford is the likely source of the name.

Bishopstoke

959 (c14) (*apud*) *itinstokan*; 960 (c12) (*æt*) *yting stoce*; 1086 *Stoches*; c.1270 *Stoke Episcopi*.

OE *stoc* 'grange farm'. Despite appearances the OE forms belong here and not to **Itchen Stoke**. Their import is obscure, but they may contain a reference, of very great antiquity, to Jutes (WSax OE *Ȳte*, cf. Ekwall 1953: 132); however the form *Yting* appears to be a singular *-ing* name here. Bede (*HE* I, xv) refers to the Jutes of Hampshire (*Iutarum natio*). *Ytene* persisted as a name for the **New Forest** (q.v.), according to the post-Conquest chronicler Florence of Worcester. The estate is associated by name with the bishops of Winchester from the c13, though it is held by the see as early as Domesday Book.

Bisterne Manor in Ringwood

1086 *Betestre*; 1187 *Bettestorn'*; 1190 *Budestorn'*; 1219 *Butestorna*; 1300 *Budesthorne*.

Spellings in *-t-* are more frequent than *-d-*. OE **Byttesþorn* 'Bytti's (haw)thorn'. The man's name is related to a form *Buttinga graf* found in a boundary clause of Worcestershire (see Ekwall under *Butley*). Ekwall suggests **Biedenes-* for the Ha PN, but that is based on a single untypical form (1190 *Bedenestorn*).

Bitterne

c.1090 *Biterne, Byterne* and thus pretty well throughout the Middle Ages.

Ekwall derives this from OE **byhtærn* 'building by a bend' with reference to a 'horseshoe-shaped ridge' close by. Gover accepts this formal origin but sees a reference, in *byht*, to the prominent bend in the river Itchen here; this is more likely. But old Bitterne is a good mile from the bend. An alternative possibility might be **bit(e)ærn* 'building for bits', i.e. in one of the senses associated with tools or horse-tackle. The word *ærn* in OE often formed compounds with words denoting what it contained.

It is generally thought that Bitterne riverside was the site of the RB town of *Clausentum*, and it is regularly marked on local maps. This name is interpreted by Rivet and Smith (1979) as if from

British words meaning 'nail' and 'path', and they speculate that there was a causeway or pontoon or suchlike here to give rise to the name. However, this does not precisely suit the Antonine Itinerary distances to Winchester and Chichester, for which Wickham gives a better match (Rivet and Smith 1979: 166–7). The origin just proposed for the RB name is less obviously suitable for Wickham.

Bittles Farm in Hambledon
1448 *Botevyleyns*; 1597 *Butvillens*.
A 'manorial' name containing the surname *Buttevileyn* (thus in Hambledon in the c13), a morally ambiguous name meaning either 'bash/kick-villein' or 'provide-boots-for-villein' (probably the former). It replaces an earlier *Burwell* (1236 *Burewelle*) 'spring by the fortification'. The *burh* '"fortification"' is in all likelihood the Roman building at SU 645144, which also gives its name to the adjacent *Bury Lodge* (OS 1:50 000; 1263 *la Burgh*). Burwell tithing was an anomalous detached part of Meonstoke hundred within Hambledon hundred.

Black Dam District of Basingstoke
The dam controls a right tributary of the Loddon; pools are visible by the Southern Ringway bypass road. They are said locally to be the remains of cress-beds. Some reasons for *black* PNs are given by Field (1972: 22).

Blackbushe Airport In Elvetham
t. Hy III *Blakebushe*.
Self-explanatory, a dark thicket.

Blackfield Estate in Fawley
S.-e. Presumably from the soil colour. In this area occur soils of the Bolderwood association, some of which are described as black, and which tend to be marshy. There is a *Blacklands Farm* in Exbury (1609 *Blakelande*), and *Blackwell Common* is adjacent to Blackfield.

Blackmoor In Selborne
1168 *Blachemere*; 1200 *Blakemere*.
Probably OE *Blacan mere* '(at the) black pool', but it cannot entirely be discounted that the first element is OE *blāc* 'pale, white'.

Blackwater River, and hamlet of Yateley
1298 *Blakwatere* (river); 1588 *Blakwater* (village).
S.-e. Gover attributes such names to the appearance of the river-bed in sandstone areas. The river was originally called 1272 *aqua de Swalewe*; the name duplicates that of the *Swale* in YNR. Ekwall

says that the river-name is related to that of the bird, citing 'move, plash' as the rather weak link connecting the meanings, but giving interesting continental cognates like MHG *swalm* 'whirlpool' (better perhaps *swall* 'surge (of dammed water)'). The old river-name survives in *Swallowfield* (Brk), through which the Blackwater flows. Another *Blackwater* is a right tributary of the Test.

Blashford Hamlet in Ellingham
c.1170 *Blachford*; 1248 *Blecheford*; 1429 *Blaschforde*.
OE **Blæcceanford* 'Blæccea's ford'; but the personal name is unattested. It is a derivative of *blæc* 'black'.

Blendworth
c.1170 *Blednewrthie*; 1207 *Blendeword'*; 1256 *Bledenewrth*; 1280 *Blenteworth*.
An OE man's name *Blǣdla* is on record, and this name may contain a dissimilated form of it. 'Blædna's curtilage', containing the word *wyrð*, also earlier perhaps *worðig*, cf. **Worthy**.

Boarhunt, East and West Parish and two manors, North Boarhunt
1086 *Bor(e)hunte*; 1170, 1184 *Burhunt(e)*.
OE **Burhfunta* 'spring of (or at) the fortification or town'. The spring is that at *Offwell Farm*, whose name also contains a reference to it. *Funta* is taken to testify to signs of Roman activity (see **Havant**). The modern pronunciation is shown by forms like *Burrant(e)* to date from at least the c16.

Boldre and East Boldre Two modern parishes
t. Ste *Bolra*; 1152 *Bolre*.
Usually said to be the old name of the **Lymington** river. In a document of t. John we find *usque fossatum quod descendit in Bolre* (etc.) 'up to the ditch which goes down to the Boldre', and the river is clearly alluded to in the name of *Bolderford Bridge* (1331 *pontem de Bolre*), above Brockenhurst, and possibly in *Bolderwood Walk*, further still up-country. Origin quite uncertain. Ekwall's final suggestion involves the source of the dialect word *boulder* 'bulrush', therefore '(river marked by) stands of rushes'? The village name would then be from the river. However, some of the forms (e.g. 1236 *Balre*) suggests rather **bī alre/alrum* 'by the alder(s)', i.e. a primary PN, with phonology as in **Bure Homage**. (The definite article is normally absent in PNs of this structure.) If Ekwall's earlier suggestion of **bolærn* 'bole or plank house' is the right one, then again it is a primary PN and not a river-name.

East Boldre is at the extreme eastern margin of the former

undivided parish.

In the midst of all this uncertainty, the DB forms *Bovre(ford)* do not fit in at all, unless they are for *★bī ofre* 'by the (flat-topped) ridge', in which case all the later medieval forms would have to be explained as containing hypercorrect *l* for *v*, interpreted as *u*; scarcely likely. The manor of before 1066 was depopulated by the Conqueror, and the site repopulated only later. The name *Boldre* may therefore be a new one for the site. *Bovre* may duplicate **Bure Homage**. It should not be confused with 1300 *la Boverie* where Beaulieu Abbey had a grange chapel (Hockey 1974: lxv), which was AN *bouverie* 'ox-stall'.

Bordon Hamlet and army camp in Headley
c.1230 *Burdunesdene*.
The medieval form means 'Burdun's valley', where the *de Burdon* family lived t. Ed. III. This surname appears to be from a genuine local place-name, but since there are no other early spellings, it is hard to speculate on what the name might have meant. The final element was probably *dūn* 'hill'; the first may have been *būr* 'cottage, bower', *burh* 'fort, manor', *gebūr* 'peasant', *★burg* 'burrow', or maybe even *bord* 'board', perhaps in a sense 'flat-topped hill', suitable for the site of Bordon camp, at least. On the other hand, if *de* is an error for *le*, then the family name was AN *burdun* 'honeybee'.

Boscombe Suburb of Bournemouth, now in Do
1273 *Boscumbe, Boscumbas*.
Apparently OE 'Bōsa's valley(s)', cf. **Bossington**. But the scarcity of early spellings makes this doubtful. Smith (*EPNE* I: 43) postulates the existence of an OE *bors*, meaning some spiky plant, to account for various modern PNs, not including *Boscombe*. In each case the modern name has lost its *r*: *Boasley* (D), *Boscombe* (W) and *Boseleys* also in W. (Cf. common dialectal *hoss* for *horse*.) This may account better for the Hampshire *Boscombe*.

Bosley Heath and farm in Hurn
t. Hy I *Borstel*; 1152 *Borstele*.
Gover suggests OE *burgsteall* 'steep path up an escarpment' (especially common in Sx). But since there is no significant scarp here, the *burh* referred to may be Christchurch Castle or the *borough* itself, for they are nearby, or it may be 'site of an earthwork'. The later medieval forms may suggest *Burgsteall-lēah* 'clearing at *Burgsteall*'. In DB we find *Bortel*, and this has been identified with Bosley. The present spelling is modern.

Bossington

1086 *Bosintone*; 1167 *Bosinton*; 1200 *Bossinton*.

OE ⋆*Bōsingtūn* 'Bōsa's farm'. The name *Bōsa* is found in that of *Bosmere* hundred in the far SE of the county, and in *Bosham* just over the border from it in Sx.

Botley

1086 *Botelie*; 1184 *Botlai*; c13 *Bottel(e)(y)e*; 1349 *Botlegh*.

OE 'wood or clearing of Botta', a man's name, perhaps a diminutive of a name like *Bōt(w)ulf.*

Bourne Rivulet

Thus on the 1:50 000 OS map. This is a modern name for the stream referred to in the name of **Hurstbourne**, a right tributary of the Test.

Bournemouth Now in Do

1407 *la Bournemowþe*; t. Hy VIII *Bowurnemothe*; 1574 *Borne mouthe*; 1575 *Burnemouthe*.

ME 'mouth of the stream', formerly a locality in Holdenhurst parish. The first record commemorates the stranding of a whale. *Bourne*, i.e. the name of the stream which enters the sea near the pier, is all that appears on some maps in this area as late as 1817. Some of the oldest plans of the area, and some early references by inhabitants, also show just *Bourne* as the name of the place.

Boyatt Wood Suburb of Chandler's Ford

Enshrines the name of *Boyatt*, a DB manor in Otterbourne and later tithing of Mansbridge hundred.

1086 *Boviete*; 1207 *Bovegat*; 1211 *Buviet*.

OE ⋆*būfan geate* 'above (the) gate'. The 'gate' must be the point where the Itchen Navigation canal meets the main course of the river Itchen; the valley narrows noticeably at this point, though not as significantly as at e.g. *Symonds Yat* (He), also containing *geat*.

Bradley

1086 *Bradelie*.

OE ⋆*Brādan lēage* '(at the) broad clearing/wood'. A very frequent name-type.

Braishfield Hamlet in Michelmersh, later parish

c.1235 *Braisfelde*; 1287 *Brayesfeld*.

Possibly OE 'undergrowth-covered open (relatively treeless) land'. The first element is probably the ancestor of the dialect word *brash*, and may be found in *Bracebridge* (L). The reference may be to woodland regenerating on open land, suitable for coppicing for small poles, etc. But Cope (1883: 11) gives as a Hampshire dialect word *brashy* 'full of small stones', which may suggest an alternative origin.

Bramdean

824 (c12) (*ofer*) *bromdene*; 932 (c12) (*to*) *brom dene*; 1045 (c12) (*andlang*) *bromdene*.
OE *Brōmdenu 'broom valley'. In a fairly broad-bottomed valley, in Chalk country where broom is not usually endemic. Cf. **Breamore**. The modern *a* vowel is found from the c15.

Bramley

1086 *Brumelai*; 1167 *Bromelega*; 1241 *Bromleye*.
OE *Brōmlēah 'broom clearing', like *Bromley* (K, Mx etc.). We find late *a* for *o* as in the same element in **Bramdean**, **Bramshott** and the etymologically identical *Bramley* (Sr); cf. **Breamore**.

Bramshaw Formerly partly in Wiltshire

1086 *Brammesage*; 1158 *Bremscaue*; 1186 *Brumesaghe*; 1272 *Brambelshagh*.
The c13 form suggests OE *Brēmelsceaga 'bramble-bush wood' or 'bramble strip of wood', and is typical also of the c14. The earlier ones are a medley. That of 1158 is of a type that used to be attributed to a ME *brame* 'bramble', whose existence is now disputed. That of 1186 suggests, perhaps, OE *brōm* 'broom', as could that in DB, but there is much to cause doubt. If that of 1158 had a medial syllable, we might consider OE *bremen 'broom-covered'. We can say for sure only that the first element is a plant-name, and that it probably denoted one of the stiff-branched or prickly kind. It is particularly provoking that the forms *Bremeshawe*, *Brumschawe*, *Brambles(h)awe* and *Bremelshawe* all occur in a Forest document of 1280. The other *brōm/brēmel* names **Breamore**, **Bramley**, **Bramdean**, **Bramshill**, **Bramshott**, whilst presenting minor philological problems, are by no means as variable as this one.

Note *Bramble Hill Walk* (cf. 1595 *Brambelhill*) in this parish. *Sceaga* usually denotes a small wood, copse or woodland strip (Gelling 1984). As it becomes phonetically reduced, it appears confused with *shire* (1670 *Bramshire/-sheere*).

Bramshill Modern parish carved out of Eversley

1086 *Bromeselle*; 1167 *Bromeshelle*.
An unusual genitival compound, OE *Brōmeshyll 'broom hill'. (Bramshill stands on sandy heathland.) We find the same unrounding of *o* to *a* from the c15 that we find in **Breamore**, etc.

Bramshott

1207 *Brembelsete*; 1230 *Brembelchete*; 1280 *Bremlessate*; 1316 *Brembelshute*.

OE *★Brēmelscēat* 'bramble corner', the second element alternating between *scēat* and its derivative *scīete*.

Bransbury Manor in Barton Stacey

1046 (c17) *brandesburi*; 1086 *Brandesberee*.

OE 'Brand's manor' (not 'fort'; there is only the earthwork **Andyke** here, which is not what is usually called a *burh*). *Brand*, like *Osmund* in **Ossemsley**, is a name of Scandinavian origin. If *byrig* (dative case of *burh*) is here 'manor', the PN may be a precise parallel for *Brondesbury* (Mx), where the person named is actually known to history.

Bransgore Hamlet, then village, in Christchurch

1759 *Bransgoer Common*; 1817 *Bransgrove* [*sic*].

The name is recorded too late for certain interpretation. The second element is probably ME *gore* 'triangular piece of land'.

Bratley Inclosure; **Bratley Plain**; **Bratley Wood**; and **Bushy Bratley** In Minstead and Broomy Walk

1365 *Brottele*; c.1490 *Bratteley*.

OE/ME 'brittle clearing/wood'. The ME word *brotel* is used of a tree (c.1325) and (figuratively) of ground (c.1395). See also **Inclosure**.

Breamore Liberty

1086 *Brumore*; c.1130 *Brommore*.

OE *★Brōmmōr* 'broom(-covered) marsh or moor'. The village is beside the Avon and surrounded by ponds. Forms representing the modern pronunciation, whose origin has not been accounted for, are seen from 1245 *Bremmora*, 1544 *Bremmer*. There may have been a ME adjective *★brēmen* 'broom-grown' whose form could have influenced the PN (and cf. **Bramshaw**). The element *brōm* shows an oddly frequent, and early, tendency to unround the vowel to *a* when shortened (cf. **Bramley** and ctrst. **Totton**).

Every parish in Hampshire whose name includes *brōm* or a relative has unenclosed common surviving today (Tavener 1957). This is testimony to the durability of soil conditions. Common is in general rather rare in Hampshire away from the SW and extreme NE of the county. The survival of a pocket of it in **Bramdean**, a chalkland parish in the centre of the county, is striking.

Bridgemary In Alverstoke liberty, suburb of Gosport
1759 *Bridge Mary*.
A John *atte Brigge* lived in Alverstoke in 1327; the church of
Alverstoke is dedicated to St Mary. This may be enough to account
for the PN.

Brighton Hill District of Basingstoke
Directly from a no longer existent local farm, and indirectly from
the name of the hill above Kempshott. The origin of this is uncertain.
The district consists largely of streets named after composers, from
Handel to Borodin to Grainger to Dankworth to McCartney.

Broad Halfpenny Down Hill in Hambledon
1647 *Broad Halfpenny*.
Famous as the birthplace of cricket. *Broad* is s.-e. for this wide open
space. *Halfpenny* remains obscure. Coin names in place-names
usually have to do with geld or rent payable, or are value-judgments
on land quality.

Broad Laying In East Woodhay
This appears as *Broad Lane* in 1859, and the relation between these
forms is unclear.

Broadlands Mansion in Romsey
1541 *Brodeland*; 1547 *Brodelandes*.
A s.-e. early ModE name. It is on the wide left bank of the Test
below Romsey. There is a lake at Nursling bearing the same name.

Brockenhurst
t. Hy I *Brokenhurst*; t. Ste *Brokeherst*; 1181 *Brochenherst*.
Traditionally supposed to be 'badger wood'; beginning in the mid
c16 we find *Broknest* (a perfectly possible phonetic development of
the original name), which has been reanalysed by later commentators
as having to do with *brock*. The persistent may also point to the
DB form *Broceste*. The name is no doubt really OE *Brocenhyrst*
'broken wooded hill', in the sense of being marked by broken-up
or dissected terrain. There are numerous small streams in little
valleys here.

Brockhampton In Havant
1086 *Brochematune*; 1236 *Brockhampton*.
'Farm of the Brōchǣme', i.e. 'brook-dwellers'. The brook is the
Brockhampton Stream of the OS first series map, unless the element
brōc is to be understood in the sense of 'wet meadows, marshes'
met with in Sx.

Brockhurst In Gosport

1200 *Brochurst.*

Perhaps '(wooded) eminence (*hyrst*) by a brook'. OE *brōc* in Sx and K may mean 'marshland adjacent to water', and this seems more suitable for the topography of Brockhurst, close to the western shore of Portsmouth Harbour.

Brook Tithing of King's Somborne

1362 *le Broke*; 1586 *Brooke.*

OE/ME *brōc* either 'stream', or, as typically in Sx, 'streamside watermeadow'. The place lies low by the river Test.

Brookley Manor in Brockenhurst

OE/ME 'brook wood/clearing'. There are several streams flowing to the Boldre river near the site of this DB manor.

Broomy Walk Part of Ellingham within the Forest, extraparochial Recorded from 1787, in association with *Broomy Lodge.* The chain of spellings is ambiguous between two older PNs meaning 'broom hill' and 'broom clearing', and an adjective *broomy* qualifying *Walk* and *Lodge*; it is never found alone. The third seems preferable; i.e. the PN means what it appears to. There was a PN *Broomy Close* in Christchurch (1878 (TA)) and another in Exbury (1609 (NF)); and no doubt many more. Broom is a typical plant of the sandy heaths, though a reference to gorse is not out of the question since that is far commoner in the New Forest.

Broughton

1173 *Burchton*; 1176 *Berchton*; 1212 *Bergeton*; 1219 *Bereweton*; 1235 *Borgheton.*

On balance, this seems to be OE **Beorg(a)tūn* 'hill, barrow farm'. There are at least five barrows on the crest of Broughton Down and Broughton Hill overlooking the village in the valley of the Wallop Brook. The persistent *u*–spellings, which are also implicated in the modern name, must be put down either to dialect phonology or to confusion with the common name-type *Burton* from *burhtūn*. Discounting the 1086 form *Breston*, forms with *Br-* are first found from 1485. The modern spelling may also have been influenced by the adjacent **Houghton**.

Brown Candover

See **Candover**.

Brownwich Manor in Hook with Warsash

962 (c12/c13) *brunwic* (*were*); 1086 *Burnewic*; 1199 *Brunwich'.*

OE 'brown specialized farm', probably 'dairy farm', not 'salterns', even though the place is on the coast. The sense of the compound is unclear. *Brown* is not very common in PNs, and I know of no other case of its occurrence with a habitative term. The reference of 962 is to an associated 'weir' (fishtrap), on the adjacent stream.

Broxhead Manor in Headley
1086 *Brocheseve*; 1236 *Brokesheved*; 1280 *Brockesheved*.
OE **Broccesheafod* 'badger's head' or 'hill'. The *head* names were discussed by Dickins in PNSr, where the theory was advanced that at such places animal (or occasionally human) heads were put on display for some religious, ritual or totemic reason. Modern scholars prefer to interpret *heafod* as 'hill' and the qualifier as descriptive of the shape of the hill (e.g. Gelling 1984). Gover notes that the spelling *Brocashead* in 1639 is due to the *Brocas* family holding the manor.

Buckholt Parish west of Broughton
1086 *Bocolt*; 1231 *Bocholte*.
These forms actually relate to an extinguished manor in the New Forest, in Redbridge hundred, but there can be little doubt that the parish west of Broughton (modern spelling 1817) has a name of identical origin. OE **Bocholt* 'beech wood'. *Holt* usually means a grove or managed woodland, very often of a single species (cf. Gelling 1984: 196); hence this name.

Buckholt Forest
1086 *Bocolt*; 1254 *la Bokolt*.
OE **Bocholt* 'managed beech wood'. See previous entry.

Buckland Manor in Portsmouth
1086 *Bocheland*; 1280 *Boclaunde*.
OE *bocland* 'land whose ownership or tenure is confirmed in writing' (or better, 'by royal charter'), cf. Kennedy (1985), Rumble (1987). A further Buckland is in Lymington (1262 *Bocland*); though the earliest spelling of this, 1236 *Buckeland*, distinctly suggests the OE genitive plural of *bucc* '(fallow) buck', the others do not.

Bucklers Hard Village in Beaulieu
1759 *Montague Town vulgar Bucklesbury*; 1789 *Bucklers Hard*.
Hard, as along much of the coat of Ha and Sx, means 'firm landing-place'; here probably originally of current-deposited pebbles. The Montagues have been lords of Beaulieu since the c18, but the village gained its permanent name from the less illustrious *Buckler* family established there since at least 1664. The first example is interesting, because it suggests that *bury* was still thought of as a living PN element in the mid c18; cf. **Colbury, Exbury.**

Bucks Horn Oak
See **Alice Holt**.

Buckskin District of Basingstoke
From *Buckskin Farm* (reason for name unknown), now submerged by suburban Basingstoke.

Bullington Parish and hamlet
1002 (c14) *bulandun*; 1218 *Bulindon*; 1236 *Bulendun*; 1280 *Bolyngton*.
OE *Bulandūn* or **Bulingdūn* 'hilltop dwelling-site of a bull' or 'of a man called Bula'. It is not clear whether the original reference is to the slopes S of the river Dever or the hill to the N of it on which is **Tidbury Ring**. The former is possible since the church is on that side of the river. The village and hamlet are *Lower* and *Upper* Bullington (OS 1:50 000), earlier 1228 *West-* and *Est-*. The *-ington* forms may be by analogy with the common type seen in e.g nearby *Avington, Hannington, Ovington*, and the earliest forms of *Tufton*.

Bure Homage In Highcliffe
t. Hy II *Beura*; c.1170 *Beora*; 1248 *Bures*; 1256 *Bure*; 1272 *Bur*.
Probably OE *bī ōran* or 'by the bank/shore' (cf. Gelling 1984: 173–82), less likely *bī ofre*. Bure is close to the present seashore. *Homage* commemorates the place's relationship with Christchurch Priory, and is the only survivor of several such medieval PNs in Ha.

Burgate, **Upper** and **Lower** Manor, tenement in Fordingbridge of Beaulieu Abbey
1086 *Borgate*; c.1250 *Burgate*.
OE/ME 'gate of/at the fortification or town'. The reference appears to be to the 'camp' across the river Avon at Godshill, called *Godmanes Ca[m?]p* on early OS maps. But perhaps, since Upper Burgate is on the northern limit of Fordingbridge parish, it is 'gate of the town or borough', if Fordingbridge was ever called this. The two tenements are distinguished from the c14 as *Op-/Over-* and *Nethere-*. A grant of c.1249 mentions a moor and a meadow called *la Burmore, la Burmede*. Often associated in Beaulieu documents with *Gorley* (c.1210 *Garleia, Gorlega*, OE **Gārlēah*) 'triangular wood/clearing'.

Burghclere
See **Clere**.

Buriton
1227 *Buriton*.
OE **Burh-* or **Byrigtūn* (*byrig* dative case of *burh*) 'farm by the

fortification'. The reference is to the IA earthworks on Butser Hill, which may also feature in *War Down* (OS 1:50000), perhaps containing OE *(ge)weorc* '(earth)works'. The older name of the parish was **Mapledurham**, which survives only in the name of a farm. This was OE **Mapuldorhām* (1086 *Mapeldresham*, 1214 *Mapeldurham*) 'maple-tree estate'.

Burley Parish, that part of Ringwood within the Forest, Forest walk
1178 *Burgelea*; 1212 *Borlegh*; 1301 *Borghley*.
OE **Burhlēah* 'fort wood/clearing', perhaps with reference to the earthwork called *Castle Hill* (modern, OS 1:63 360). But if Morris is right that the DB entry for Ringwood mentioning four hides in the Forest refers to Burley, then we may be justified in taking *burh* in its later sense of 'borough, town', and the name would mean 'clearing/wood of the town' (i.e. Ringwood). cf. **Bile**

Bursledon
c.1170 *Brixendona*; 1208 *Bursedona*; 1218 *Burxedun'*; 1228 *Brexheldene*; 1245 *Bercildon*; 1248 *Bursindene*; 1263 *Bursuldon*; 1288 *Bursyngdon*; 1343 *Bruseldon*.
Several traditions are represented in the records of this name. It originally contained *dūn* 'hill' rather than *denu* 'valley'; its situation is not that of a typical *denu* (see Gelling 1984: 97–9). The *dūn* is the low hill between the river Hamble and its last tributary. As to the first element, **Beorsa*, a hypothetical pet-form of the frequent man's name *Beorhtsige*, first the bill, though some of the earliest forms suggest that the full-name may have been involved. Either, therefore, OE **Beorhtsigingdūn* or **Beorsandūn* (or both), 'Beorhtsige's hill', with *l* for *n* by dissimilation. A medieval tradition associates the name with ME *bristle*, *berstle* (e.g. 1404 *Brisseldon*).

A quasi-medieval spelling of the parish name has been used to name *Brixendone* farm (SU 495102), and Gover says there is also a house called *Brixedon*. The spelling *Brixendona* appears c.1170.

Burton Village in Christchurch East
c.1100 *Buretone*; 1236 *Buriton*; 1248 *Burton*.
Possibly OE *Burhtūn*, *Byrhtūn* 'fortified settlement', or, more likely, 'farm of the borough', i.e. Christchurch, cf. Gelling (1978: 145). For the form of the earliest mentions, cf. **Buriton**.

Bury Farm in Eling
Found in 1518–29 as *Bery*, ME 'manor', abbreviating the earlier 1331 *Newton Bury*. The older name is OE/ME 'new farm'; its position on the boundary of Marchwood and Eling testifies to this.

Bushy Bratley
Cf. **Bratley Inclosure**.

Butser Hill In Buriton
956 (c13) (*on*) *bryttes oran*; 959x963 (c13) *byrthes oran*.
OE 'Briht's slope'. *Ōra* is often used inland for quite prominent hills.

Buttsash In Fawley, district of Hythe
1212 *Bottesesse*; 1269 *Bottesasshe*; 1280 *Butesasse*.
ME 'ash-tree of *But*'. There was a William le But in Fawley in 1327. The family also gave its name to the local *Butts Bridge*.

C

Cadnam Hamlet in Copythorne
1272, 1280 *Cadenham*.
OE/ME 'Cada's estate or hemmed-in land'; the topography gives
no real clues. Gover notes that a ford in the parish is 1279
Kademannesford, and suggests that *Cada* may have been a short-
form for this name. The man's name looks remarkably as though
it could be for PrW *Cadṃãn* (the source of OE *Cædmon*), i.e. the
PN could date back to the earliest contacts between Welsh and
English; but the forms are far too late for certainty. At any rate,
the frequent *Cada* is likely to derive as a name from the Brit.
element *Catu-* (PrW *Cad*) 'battle'.

Calmoor or **Calmore** In Netley Marsh/Eling
c13 *Cauwelmor*; 1276 *Caulemore, Kaulemor*.
OE *Cawelmōr* 'cabbage marshland'. The reference is almost
certainly to seakale (*Crambe maritima*) since the place is adjacent
to the once-tidal marshes of the Test. Its seeds disperse through tidal
action on sandy and pebbly beaches. The seakale of Southampton
Water was famous as a wild food, and an c18 Hampshire man,
William Curtis, popularized it among London gourmet palates. It
was especially common locally on the sands near Calshot Castle.
(Cf. Grigson 1959: 63.)

Calshot Castle Spit of land and fort in Fawley
980 (c12) (*æt*) *celcesoran*; c11 (c14) *celces(h)ord*; c.1300 *Calchesores*;
1347 *Calchesorde*.
The bulk of forms for this name suggest OE *Cælcesord* 'spit of land
(*ord*) of the chalice'. The difficulties involving this were discussed
by Gover *et al.* (1942: 85–6) in relation to *Chelsea* (Mx); Cole
(1987) takes *Chelsea* to include OE *cealc* 'chalk', to which there are
objections, and *cealc* cannot be directly responsible for modern
Calshot. The earliest form has *ōra* 'shore, bank'. It is not clear
whether the change of name reflects a change in topography due to
local geological and tidal conditions. As often, the element *ord* in the
Middle Ages is sometimes taken for *ford* (1344 *Kelcheforde*). Come
the c16, the modern form with *shot* is found, as if for the common *scēat*
of N Hampshire, but the reason for the change is unclear. The Tudor
fort is first *Calshot castel* on Saxton's map of 1579.

Camdentown In Gosport
Possibly taken direct from the name in London, which dates from

c.1800, commemorating the first Earl Camden, who took his title from *Camden Place*, Chislehurst (K). This name derives ultimately from that of the great c16 antiquary William *Camden*.

Cams Hall Two manors in Fareham
1242 *Kamays*; 1248 *Kamuse*; 1259 *Kamus*; 1268 *Cameys*; 1280 *Cames*.
A highly unusual name derived from PrW **cambes'*, the ancestor of W *cemaes* 'shallow bend in a river, shallow bay'. Gover derives it ultimately from Brit. **cambo-* 'crooked', with reference to Wallington River. There is a marked bend here, not just a slight one; there is a most noticeable bag-shaped bay downstream. Credibility attaches to this explanation because the place is adjacent to **Wallington**, whose name attests the presence of Welsh speakers into the AS period.

Canada Settlement in West Wellow
A modern name denoting a remote part of a parish, in this case a neck projecting into the New Forest. PNs of this kind typically date from the later c18 or the early c19. (Canada was especially in the news in the 1750s.) They often represent intakes of previously marginal land; Canada is on the Bagshot Sands.

Candover Three parishes, **Brown**, **Chilton** and **Preston Candover**
701 (c12) *cendefer* (stream); 880×885 (c.1000) *cendefer* (at least Brown Candover); 901 (e. c11) *kendefer* (stream); 903 (c16) *candeverre* (at least Brown Candover); 1086 *Candevre, Candovre* (all three, Preston Candover); 1204 *Candevra* (Brown Candover).
The parishes take their name from the stream whose name (following Ekwall) may have been from Brit. **Caniodubrī* 'beautiful waters', PrW **Cen'diβr*.
   The three specifiers come into use for the separate parishes/manors in the c13. The family *Brune* held land in *Brown C.* in the c15/16, but it is not known what, if any, connection they had with the place before that. In the c13/14 the place was alternatively *Abbot's Candover* (1279 *Candever Abbatis*) from being held by Hyde Abbey since 901.
   Chilton Candover may be an amalgamation of two PNs. Around 1300–1400 the parish is alternatively recorded as just *Chilton*. But a slightly earlier tradition has e. c13 *Chiltecandevere* and the like. The place may therefore have been called either OE **Ciltantūn* (or maybe that was the name for what is now called *Chilton Manor* (OS)) or ME **Chilte Candever* 'the Candover at *Chilte*'. Either

way the first element appears to be the *cilta̅ discussed under
Chilcomb. The east bank of the stream is overlooked by a fairly
steep slope, on which the manor farm is situated. However one c13
document shows a form *Childe Candever*, suggesting that the first
element is really OE *cild* 'young retainer' (or the like), as in other
Chiltons (e.g. Brk, So). Despite being backed by only one recorded
spelling, this solution may be the better one. This view is reinforced
by the discussion below.

Preston Candover is 1262 *Prestecandevere*, clearly OE *Prēostacan-
defer* 'priests' Candover'. Gover speculates that the black monks of
Southwick Priory are referred to. DB states merely (29,2) that
'*clerici*' hold it and (69,8) that Edwin the priest holds a virgate from
the king there. From 1255 forms like *Preston Candovere* are found,
suggesting an alternative name deriving from *Prēostatūn* 'priests'
farm', therefore perhaps parallel with the *Cildatūn* mooted above.
The late form 1442 *Preston in Candeveresdene* 'Preston in the valley
of the Candover' seems to be unique.

Either the *tūn*- forms are 'rationalizations' of earlier forms in the
genitive plural -*a*, or they represent alternative OE PNs which are
not recorded till ME times. This matter is still to be resolved.

A person hailing from Candover gave his name to *Candover's
Farm* (1369 *Hertele Candevere*) in Hartley Maudit.

Canterton Manor in Minstead
1086 *Cantortun*; 1212 *Kantarton*; 1227 *Canterton*.
Often said to be from OE *Cantwaratūn* 'farm of the Kentish men'
(thus Ekwall 1953). Hampshire is pockmarked with places whose
names denote, or appear to denote, settlements of people who were
not West Saxons; cf. **Exton, Marchwood, New Forest**.

Castle Malwood Hamlet and Forest walk in Minstead
1272 *Malewode*; 1280 *Mallewode*; 1565 *The Castle of Malwood*.
Originally perhaps OE 'Mealla's wood', in view of the persistent
double *l* in medieval times. Otherwise it would be tempting to
suppose OE *Maluwudu* or *Malwewudu* 'wood by a gravelly
ridge' (topographically suitable) or *Mealuwewudu* 'mallow wood'.

Catherington
1015 *Cateringatun*; 1176 *Cateringeton*.
One of a notoriously difficult group of names, cf. e.g. *Caterham*
(Sr), *Chadderton* (La). It used to be thought (1) that *cater* represented
the Brit. *cater-*, PrW *cader*, the equivalent of Irish *cathir* 'fortified
town', or (2) that *cater-* was borrowed from VL *cat(h)edra* 'chair',
and that it was a topographical word. However this word gives

PrW *cadeir*, and all names derived from it in English should show *d*. This appears only once in the record for Catherington, and clearly another story is needed for at least some of these difficult names (see Jackson 1953: 555). Some of the OE forms have been explained as containing an OE personal name *Cat(t)or*, of PrW origin (seen in Malory's Sir *Cador* of Cornwall). The present name means 'farm of the Cateringas', a folk-name perhaps meaning 'dwellers at (the) *Cater*' (of whatever origin such a (?) hill-name may be) or 'people associated with Cat(t)or'.

The present spelling has influenced the church-dedication to St Catherine – the medieval church was All Saints (ex inf. Mr J. Pile).

Catisfield In Fareham

1233, 1245 *Cartesfeld*; 1245 *Kardesfeld*.

The association with cats is late. The name is very difficult, but, if of OE origin, may contain an early borrowing of Lat. *carta* 'document, charter', the whole meaning 'open land of the charter', perhaps analogously to *bōcland* (on which see Kennedy 1985, Rumble 1987). Even so there would be much still to explain, e.g. the gender of the borrowed element *cart*. If the name is of the highest antiquity, it may contain a Brit./PrW personal name allied to the first element of the name of the British queen *Cartimandua* (unless her name contains a reduced form of Brit. *carat-* 'dear'). (*Cart* in the sense of 'wagon' is a borrowing from Danish and cannot be relevant here.)

Chalton

1015 *cealctun*, *cealhtun*; 1167 *Chaulton*; c13 *Chalcton(e)*.

OE 'chalk farm'. The place is on the Chalk downs. Its name seems to make sense only if taken to mean that the site was in some way unusual: Cole (1987: 47) reports that the downs here are nearly denuded of topsoil and appear white. The loss of the stop consonant can be observed in a string of medieval spellings showing the fricative [x], spelt *gh*, e.g. 1282 *Chalghton*. Contrast **Chawton**. The settlement has moved from the adjacent hilltop site of Church Down.

Chandler's Ford Modern parish carved out of North Stoneham

909 (?c11) *searnægles ford*; 1280 *Sarnayllesford*; 1759 *Chandlers Ford*.

The ancient name appears to mean 'ford of Sēarnægel', which would have to be a nickname since it means 'withered or dry nail' in OE. The modern form may assimilate the old form to the common word *chandler* or may be an entirely new name. The *le Chaundler* family is known in nearby South Stoneham from the c14. The ford carried a Roman road (Margary 422) over Monks Brook.

Chapel In Southampton

So called from the chapel variously referred to in the c13 as *capella s(an)c(t)e Trinitatis de Suhamt'* and the chapel of St Mary's church (*ecclesia s(an)c(t)e Marie cum capella*). St Mary's was the mother-church of old Southampton, and Patterson (1966: 7) reports that this area beyond the medieval town walls was long referred to as *Old Hampton.*

Charford Two parishes, later one, now manor and farm in Breamore

1086 *Cerdeford*; c.1200 *Sherdiford*; 1236 *Chardeford*; 1240 *Cherdeford.*

Nothing can be made of this name unless it is linked with the *Cerdices/Certices ford* of annal 519 of the *Old English Chronicle*, recurring in a recension of c.1000 with the qualification *in fluvio Avene* 'on the river Avon'. It is 'Cerdic's ford', the site of the battle at which Cerdic and Cynric routed the Welsh in the Wessex heartland once and for all. If we can take the *Chronicle* at face value, then this might be the battle at which the present boundary of Hampshire was established here. There is no earlier mention of Cerdic or his dynasty any further west or north. They do not fight in the present Wiltshire till the mid c6.

The *Chronicle* also says that battles against the Welsh took place in 495 at *Cerdicesora* and in 527 at *Cerdicesleag*, his 'bank' and 'wood/clearing', both unidentified places.

Chark In Crofton

1256, 1262 *Cherk*; 1256 and from then on *Chark.*

(A fancy spelling is preserved in *Cherque Farm.*) Gover compares the English name for a Welsh town *Chirk*, from W *ceiriog* 'rocky'. The Ha name appears, by that theory, to be for W *carreg* 'rock'. It is not known what rock is alluded to. Perhaps rather an inexplicable alteration of OE *cert/cært* 'rough common', found in simplex names in Sr and K. Chark 'Common' is on an outlier of the Barton/Bracklesham Tertiary sequence of rocks, said to be 'poor in texture, ill-drained, acid and highly podsolized' (Tavener 1957: 33).

Charlcot Farm in Whitchurch

c.1230 *Chorlecote*; c.1235 *Cherlecote.*

OE *Ceorlacote 'cottages of the semifree villeins', see **Charlton**.

Charlton Hamlet, now suburb, of Andover

t. Hy II *Cherletone*; 1192 *Cherleton.*

OE *Ceorlatūn 'farm of the churls', i.e. free peasants of the lowest rank (cf. Finberg 1964b). The plural first element suggests a communal enterprise. Places called *Charlton* are often found on the fringes of important estates; Andover was a royal manor in the king's own hands before and after 1066. They may represent special foundations whose inhabitants could be called upon to perform boonwork on such estates; i.e. they were less free than the use of the term *churl* implies.

Charminster Suburb of Bournemouth, now in Do
The name of a road in 1805; an 'obvious importation' (Young 1957: 187) (from *Charminster* (W)).

Chawton
1086 *Celtone*; 1167 *Cautona*; c.1195 *Chalton*; 1242 *Chauton*.
Ekwall takes a form c.1230 *Chalvedone* to refer to Chawton; if so the place is OE 'calves hill'. For Chawton such a spelling is unique in two ways, and Gover believes it is not for Chawton anyway. More likely this is OE either *Cealftūn 'calf farm' or *Cealctūn 'chalk farm'; Chawton is on the Chalk downs. Compare **Chalton**; but the sequence of spellings is different for the two places.

Cheriton
1162 *Chiriton*; 1208 *Cheritona*; 1218 *Cheriton(a)*.
The analogy of names in Devon and Kent makes it likely that this is OE *Ciricetūn 'church farm', i.e. farm by a church or one whose produce was devoted to the upkeep of one. However, there is a conspicuous long barrow on the hillspur just east of the village (in addition to the gravemounds of the victims of the battle of 1644), and we may wonder whether *cirice* is not here an anglicization of PrW *crüg 'barrow' as it is in the similar name *Churchill* (O). The fact that the tumulus is in Hinton Ampner parish is not necessarily a bar to this, as it is only 0.75 miles from Cheriton church, and the hamlet of *Hinton Marsh* is actually in Cheriton.

Chewton Bunny In Highcliffe-on-Sea
Cope (1883: 12–13) notes that *bunny* is a specialized term of the New Forest area, of unknown origin, for a narrow rift or valley, what is called on Wt or in Bournemouth a *chine* (OE *cinu*). This *bunny* is at *Chewton* (c.1170 *Chiventon*, 1247 *Chuuton*, 1280 *Chyveton*) 'Ceofa's farm', or perhaps, as Ekwall suggests, 'Cifa's'. There is also a *Beckton Bunny* in Hordle, and records of one in Exbury (1609 *Bunn(e)y meade, coppice, Bonnye*), and a *Bunny Copse* in Mottisfont, where the bunny is recorded as early as 1466 (*le Bony*). Cf. also Young (1957: 191).

Chidden In Hambledon

956 (c12) (*æt*) *cittandene*; 1218 *Chitedene.*

Apparently OE **Cittandenu* 'Citta's valley'; but there is a group of spellings from the AS period like 958x975 (c12), 1042 (*on*) *citwara mearce* 'to the boundary of the people of Chid(den)', and it is unusual for this type of abbreviated expression to be based on a personal name rather than on a PN element proper.

Chilbolton

909 (c11) *ceolboldingtun*; 934 (c12) (*æt, in*) *ceolboldinc*(*g*)*tun*(*e*). OE **Cēolbealdingtūn* 'Cēolbeald's farm'.

Chilcomb or **Chilcombe**

t. Æthelwulf (c12) *ciltacumb*; 909 (?c11/c12) *ciltancumb*; 963x975 (c12) (*of*) *ciltancumbe*; 1171 *Chiltecumbe.*

OE 'valley below the steep slope', or 'valley below **Cilta*' where this is a word in a pre-English language meaning 'slope', surviving to English times as a name. This element is fully discussed in Coates (1984a). The slope is the abrupt scarp of Deacon Hill, or of Magdalen Hill Down, or both.

Chilling Farm in Hook

t. Ed I *Chullyng*; 1440 *Chyllyng.*

The reference dating from 982 in the *Hyde Chartulary*, (*on*) *ceolling* (*burnan*), is to a place in the Isle of Wight (Finberg 1964a: 58), and not to Chilling, as is sometimes said. The present PN seems to be a singular -*ing* derivative of *cēole* 'throat, gullet', its application here being unclear. If we could assume some changes in local coastal topography, we might be able to derive it instead from *cēol* 'ship', but this is speculative. Hook Lake, a mile or so to the W, can never have admitted ships of much consequence.

Chiltlee Manor in Bramshott

1086 *Ciltelei*; 1194 *Chiltelega*; 1338 *Cheltele.*

OE 'wood/clearing at **Cilta*' or 'at the slope'. This element is discussed by Coates (1984a); see **Chilcomb**.

Chilton Candover

See **Candover**.

Chilworth

1086 *Celeorde*; 1230 *Cheleuuorth*; 1334 *Chuleworthe.*

OE **Cēolanwyrð* 'Cēola's curtilage'.

Chineham Hamlet in Monk Sherborne

1086 *Chineham*; 1206 *Chinham.*

The Basingstoke-Reading railway line passes between two low hills here, and the feature may have been designated OE *cinu* 'ravine, rift' (cf. **Chewton Bunny**), though this seems like poetic licence here. If so, OE 'rift estate'.

Chingescamp Lost DB manor in Broughton hundred
The name means 'king's *camp*' where *camp* is 'uncultivated land on the edge of a villa estate' (Gelling 1978: 74–8). In this hundred (called *Thorngate* in the Middle Ages) we find the Roman road from Old Sarum to Winchester (Margary 45a). Roman buildings have been found at East and West Dean, and the name **Mottisfont** also testifies to Roman activity.

Cholderton, East
1086 *Cerewaretone*; 1174 *Chelewartona*; 1200 *Chel(e)warton*.
OE *Cēolwaratūn 'farm of Cēolwaru', a woman's name of regular formation but not attested. The form of 1174 *Chelewardtun* is exceptional, and probably not evidence for the man's name *Cēolweard*, the most telling point against which is the complete absence of medial -*s*- in the records. Forms with *Chol-* appear in the c15. The *East* is a purely modern feature distinguishing it from the 5 miles distant *Cholderton* just over the border of W, which has a different origin, probably OE *Cēolrǣdingtūn 'Cēolrǣd's farm'.

Christchurch Town, hundred
t. Will. II *Christi ecclesia de Twinham*; c.1125 *Christecerce*; 1176 *Cristescherche*.
S.-e. The document copied from one of William Rufus' time gives the older name for the place, *Twinham*, which is 901 (c11) (*æt*) *tweoxneam*, 934 (copy) (*at*) *twynham*, and persists as an alias into the c15. This name derives from OE *betwēonan ēam* 'between the rivers', i.e. the Avon and Stour. The older form may be seen in annal 901 of the *OE Chronicle*, *betwēoxn ēam*, where it is treated as an obscured PN: 'at Betweenwaters'. A much reduced form of the PN is seen in the c16: 1528 *Crichurche*, 1536 *Crechurche*.

Church Crookham
See **Crookham Village**.

Chute Forest
1222 *foresta de Cet*; 1245 *Schet(e)*; 1298 *Chut*.
A PrW word for 'woodland', *cēd, is the basis of this PN and **Melchet Park**, as well as numerous names in other counties, though precisely which ones is debatable. The modern form appears to descend from the West-Saxonized form *Cīet. Sometimes in the c13 taken to be *scēat*, *scīete* 'angle, nook', an element often associated

with words for trees (cf. **Aldershot**) and other plants (**Bramshott**).

Cildeest A lost DB manor in Egeiete hundred
Gover identifies this with 1339 *Childenhurst* in Brockenhurst; thus
'wooded hill of the young nobles', though ★*Child(er)hurst* might
have been expected.

Clanfield
1207 *Clanefeld*; c13 *Clenefeld*.
OE ★*Clǣnefeld* 'clear or cleared open land', i.e. free or cleared of
scrub.

Clanville Manor in Weyhill
1086 *Clavesfelle*; 1259 *Clanefeud*; 1263 *Clanefelde*.
OE ★*Clǣnefeld* 'clear or cleared open land', cf. **Clanfield** and further
places of the same name in O and in Bishops Waltham (alleged by
Ekwall). The name now attaches to *Clanville Lodge*, the former
Blissmore Hall (1198 *Besemerishale*, c13 *Busemerehale*, 1648 *Blismer-
hall*, OE 'nook at ★*Bēosmere/Bēosmersc* 'bentgrass pool or marsh').
The 'nook' was presumably the northern end of Weyhill parish
(now Penton Grafton).

Clare Park In Crondall
See **Clere**.

Clarken Green In Oakley
Found 1859 as *Clerkengreen*. Looks as though it contains the plural
of ME *clerke* 'cleric', though the form is too late for certainty.

Clatford, Upper
1086 *Cladford*; 1156 *Clatford*; 1306 *Upclatford*.
OE ★*Clāt(e)ford* 'burdock ford'. In some parts of the SCy, *clote*
(the descendant of OE *clāte*) means 'water-lily', but surely the
Pillhill Brook flows too fast for these to grow. *Up(per)* because
further up the Anton valley than **Goodworth Clatford**, part of
which was formed out of *South Clatford*.

Clatinges Lost DB manor in (Charford in) Fordingbridge hundred
961 *claetinc* (charter of Coombe Bissett, W, cited in DB Hants);
1086 *Clatinges*; 1330 *Clattyng*.
Apparently OE ★*Clǣting* 'burdock place', cf. **Goodworth Clatford**
and **Clatford, Upper**.

Clere Three parishes **Burghclere, Highclere, Kingsclere**
749 (c12) *cleran* (Highclere/Burghclere); 873 x 888 (c11) (æt) *clearan*
(Kingsclere); 931 (c12) (æt) *clere* (Ecchinswell); 953 (c12) (æt) *west
clearan* (Highclere); 955 (c14) *clearas* (Burghclere); 959 (c14) (æt)

clearan (Highclere/Burghclere); 1086 *Clere* (Kingsclere); 1167 *Clara* (Kingsclere, Highclere).

The existence of AS-period forms rules out ME *clere* 'clearing', from the French. No OE lexical word is known which could fill the bill. The OE name appears to be in the plural in at least one of its occurrences (955). Ekwall compares two Hampshire charter boundaries containing a reference to one and the same place: 901 (e. c11) (*to*) *cleara flode*, 909 (c12) (*æt*) *clearan flode*, where Micheldever meets North Waltham. *Flōde* is 'channel, ditch, watercourse'. There is no stress at this point, but Grundy (1927: 285) mentions that there was a *Cocksford* in Popham which must have been over the same water; perhaps therefore there was once a winterbourne there, which no longer flows because of changes in the water table. If *cleara(n)* is a lexical word, its sense is unknown (the origin of the PN *Clearbury Ring* (W), not recorded before 1632, is unknown). If it is a name, it perhaps derives from PrW *clijár, the source of Welsh *claer* 'bright' (*claear* 'lukewarm' hardly makes sense for a bourne-flow, though this word seems to have the same etymological source as *claer*). What such a name could refer to in the case of Kingsclere, Highclere and Burghclere is unknown; they share no single stream, and we cannot assume that the various streams of the area all bore the same name.

Kingsclere was a royal demesne manor before and after 1066, though part of it was given to St Peter's, Winchester, by William I, and the rest to St Mary, Rouen, by Henry I, though it was again in royal hands t. Ed II. It appears as t. Hy I *Kyngesclere*, c.1270 *Clara regis*. The name of *Highclere* (1208 *alta Clera* but previously 'West Clere' (see above)) ought to be s.-e., but only the ridgetop site of Highclere Castle is notably high. The village is slightly higher than the other two. This was the Bishop of Winchester's holding at the time of DB, and the site of a palace of his; but 1241 *Clere le Evesk*, 1320 *Bisshopes Clere* are names for *Burghclere*, once a single episcopal manor with Highclere, though having a separate reeve from earliest times (*VCH* IV, 256f.). The name of Burghclere (1171 *Burclere*) at first sight appears to allude to the *burh* or ancient earthwork on Beacon Hill, mentioned in 943 (c12) as (*to*) *weard setle* '(at the) watchhouse'. Indeed, Old Burghclere (see below) is close to the foot of the hill on which it stands. But it is possible that we have late OE/ME *burh* in the sense of 'manor, great house', from the bishop's palace. The absence of this element in OE forms may suggest the latter interpretation, though there is no firm way of deciding the issue at present. The bishop had a market here, and the mention 1218 *novus burgus de Clere* (analogous to *Newbury*

(Brk), see **Newtown**) makes it superficially possible that the name is to be taken as 'borough (market-town) Clere'. But the market was established in the second decade of the c13, whilst Burghclere's name is on record from the late c12. *Burghclere* may, then, be 'fort Clere' or 'manor Clere'.

The most populous part of modern Burghclere, and the part named as such on the OS 1:50000 map, is a relatively modern development; hence *Old Burghclere* for the ancient settlement.

Morris, in the *Hampshire Domesday*, identifies the holding of William son of Baderon in Kingsclere hundred with *Earlstone* (1167 *Erlestona*, 1233 *Erlestune* 'earl's farm'). It was held of the king by Saxi before 1066, who held three other parcels of land in Ha from the king and was clearly a man of substance.

John *de Clere*, who took his name from here, lived in Crondall in the early c13 and his name eventually became attached to *Clare Park* in that parish, previously **Badley** 'Bad(d)a's wood/clearing'.

Under **Sherfield-on-Loddon**, the thorny question is examined of whether the *Sher-* forms descend from OE words for 'bright' or 'shire'. It is curious to see along the Ha/Brk boundary a group of parish names in *Clere* in the west and a group in the east, almost abutting, in *Sher-*. It gives the impression that the RB/PrW name of the region involved the British word for 'bright', which the Saxons adopted and incorporated, in translation, in their own PNs. More investigation is required; there is a case for assuming that *Sher-* in these names means 'shire(s)'.

Cliddesden

1194 *Cledesdene*; 1219 *Cludesdene*; 1240 *Clydesdene*.
Ekwall postulates an OE form *clȳde* deriving from *clūd* 'lump, mass'. Rather than multiplying new lexical elements it might be better to suggest that *Clȳde* is from the dative/locative case-form of an old PN *Clūd*, viz. *Clūdi*, which is now lost. The present name would be 'valley of (a place with the fossilized PN) *Clȳde*'. This might have been a name for the adjacent Farleigh Hill (see **Farleigh Wallop**).

Colbury Modern parish carved out of Eling, now split between Dibden Purlieu and Eling
c.1250 *Colebir'*; 1280 *Colebur'*.
Probably ME 'Cola's manor'. I know of no ancient earthwork here. One *Cola uenator* 'Cola the hunter' held the DB manor of **Ellingham**; see this name for its relation to **Eling** and therefore its relevance to the interpretation of *Colbury*. He also held land in Langley (1086 *Langelie*), adjacent to Colbury. In 1441 there was a

Coltrowlane in Eling, so perhaps the *trow* 'tree' commemorated him too.

Cold Henley Manor in Whitchurch
909 (c12) (*on*) *hean lea*; 1167 *Hanlea*; 1272 *Henley*.
OE '(at the) high wood'. *Cold* presumably from being dominated by E and NE facing slopes of the chalk downs.

Colden Common Common in Twyford, modern parish
1208, 1245 *Colvedene*.
A difficult name. The second element is OE *denu* 'valley', presumably that to the NW of Owslebury, taken later as *-down* (1540) and *-end* (1759). The first may be a metathesized form of OE *clofa* 'cleft', i.e. *★colfa*. The valley in question is steep-sided and narrow.

Coldharbour A common house/farm name
Some *Coldharbours* are known from the Middle Ages, though the name really became popular from c.1600 onwards, in commemoration of a property of the Earl of Shrewsbury in London which had descended in the world from a palace to a rack-rent slum. There are over 300 places with this name in England, most dating from after 1600. In Ha we find them in Kingsley and Wickham, at Lee near Nursling, and in St Mary Bourne, for instance.

Coldrey House and extraparochial area adjacent to Froyle
973×974 (c12) (*to*) *colriðe*; 1253 *Colrethe*.
Seems to be unmistakably OE '(char)coal stream(s)', though for exactly what reason is not known. It may be significant that a mile or so away is *Isnage Farm* (973×974 (c12) (*of*) *isen hyrste* (*gate*), 1205 *Isonhirst*), whose name means 'iron wooded hill'. If so, the charcoal would have been used in smelting. There is a dammed stream here, a left tributary of the Wey.

Colemore or **Colmore**
1086 onwards *Colemere*; 1196 *Culemere*.
OE *Cōla mere* '(the) cool pond'. I can detect no pond on the map. Perhaps the reference is to be a dewpond, whose waters are traditionally said to be cold.

Combe Now in Berkshire
See **Faccombe**.

Compton
1086 *Cuntone*; c.1195 *Cumton*; 1202 *Cumpton*.
OE *★Cumbtūn* 'valley farm'. The valley is that in which *Compton End* (OS 1:50 000) now stands.

Conford In Bramshott

An unknown quantity. If it is the same as 1429 *Tonford* in the Selborne Chartulary, one form or the other is due to the confusability of *c* and *t* in gothic script.

Connigers Copse In Brockenhurst

One of the numerous Ha instances of ME *coni(n)gre* 'rabbit-warren'. Rabbits were introduced in the late c12, and warrens multiplied rapidly from c.1240–60, largely on marginal land, waste or forest.

Coombe Tithing of East Meon
As **Combe**.

Copnor In Portsmouth

1086 *Copenore*; 1248 *Copponore*; 1272 *Coupenore*.
OE **Coppanōra* 'Coppa's shore/bank'. The man's name *Coppa* is inferred from other PNs. One of the numerous names between Southampton and Bognor Regis that show *ōra*. This fact leads Gelling (1984: 179) to speculate that the whole district was called *Ōra* 'the shore'.

Copythorne Modern parish carved out of Eling

t. Ed III *Coppethorne*; 1754 *Copped Thorne* (*Common*).
ME 'pollarded (haw)thorn', a PN also in evidence in Hrt and Sr as *Copthorne*. (Cf. also the **Cut Thorn** in Southampton.) ME *copped* could apparently also mean 'having the upper part removed', of a house, or conversely 'having a high top', and there is a recurring house-name type *Copthall* (e.g. Mx). There is, coincidentally, a *Copied Hall* in this parish. Which meaning is intended, only local knowledge can decide. There is also a *Pollard Moor* (sometimes appearing on modern maps as *Pollards Moor*), which may involve a surname.

Corhampton

1201 *Cornhamton*; c.1225 *Cornhampton*; 1232 *Corhamtune*.
OE **Cornhāmtūn* 'corn estate'. OE *hāmtūn* denotes a place of considerable significance.

Cosham Modern parish formed of Widley and Wymering

The majority of early spellings, including one in the Laud text of the *OE Chronicle* (e. c12) (*s.a.* 1015), are of the type *Cosham*, without a trace of the medial *e* which would license the interpretation 'estate or hemmed-in land of a man called Cossa', though DB and some c13 spellings point in that direction. If it is not that, then what it might be is anybody's guess. It might contain OE *cost* (1) 'excellent', or (2) 'tansy', but the lack of *t* in any recorded form offers difficulties worse than derivation from *Cossa*. On balance, the first interpretation is more likely. There are odd spellings of the type *Corsham* in the c13 which are hard to account for. *Corsham* (W) shows the same development, and seems to be of the same origin as Cosham.

County Gates Between Bournemouth and Poole (Do)
This place is at the old (pre-1974) county boundary with Do. In fact the gates referred to were those of the drive to a private house, *Branksome Tower*, erected in 1855 (Young 1957: 86).

Cove Modern parish carved out of Yateley
1086 *Cove*.
OE *cofa* means at first 'enclosed chamber' and may denote a building of some kind. It develops topographical senses like 'rock hollow, cave, den', etc., later. The application is unclear in the present name; Cove is in what was once open level countryside north-west of Farnborough.

Cowplain
1859 *Cow-plain*.
This is the only one of the spots called *plain* in the Forest of Bere which has achieved distinction as a biggish inhabited place. These will have been forest plains in the technical sense (cf. Rackham 1976).

Cranbourne District of Basingstoke
Cf. the mention of 1443 *Camburnecroftys*. The present name may be a false association with the common name-type *Cranbourne* 'crane (heron) stream', of which the nearest to Basingstoke is the one in Wonston.

Cranbourne Grange In Wonston
901 (e. c11) (*to*) *cramburnan*; 1174 *Craneburna*.
OE *★Cranburna* 'crane stream', i.e. presumably referring to herons. The stream is a right tributary of the Dever. Other *Cranbournes* in the county have the same origin.

Crawley
909 (c12), c.965 (c12) *crawanlea*.
OE *★Crāwanlēah* 'crow wood'.

Criddlestyle Hamlet in Fordingbridge
c.1220 *Cridelistruhe*; 1341 *Cridelestrowe*.
The last element in the name is highly variable (1248 *-ton*', 1377 *-stowe*, modern *-style*), but it seems originally to have been OE

Crideles trēow 'Cridel's tree'. The form of c.1220 also allows the possibility of *trog* 'trough', *þruh*, 'water-conduit', and the more so since Criddlestyle is at a place where the river Avon runs in more than one channel and there are leats, to judge by the OS 1:50 000 map. *Cridel*, though unattested, would be a regularly constructed pet-form of the name *Creoda/Crida*; this name was borne by a son of Cerdic, one of the first kings of the West Saxons.

Crofton New parish carved out of Titchfield
Recorded at all times since 1086 as *Crofton* or *Croftone*, this is 'croft farm', i.e. a farm with a smallholding attached to it, or consisting of one.

Crondall Parish and hundred
873 x 888 (c11) (*æt*) *crundellan*; 955 x 958 (c14) (*æt*) *crundelan*; 968 x 971 (c12) (*æt*) *crundelom*; 1086 *Crundele*.
OE 'at the (chalk-)pits'. The chalk outcrops here over a platform of the Upper Greensand. The word *crundel* was discussed especially in relation to minor place-names of this area by Grundy (1922 – and ctrst Baring 1907). It appears to have meant literally 'crooked diggings', and to have been applied to more irregulary shaped diggings than *dell* was. Other instances of the same word are found, e.g. in *The Crundle* (Buriton) and in numerous OE boundary marks (Smith, *EPNE* I: 116–17).

Crookham Village Modern parish carved out of Crondall, and **Church Crookham**, suburb of Fleet
1200 *Crocham*.
Apparently 'crook estate' or 'crook hemmed-in land', but it is not clear in what sense of 'crook' (OE *crōc*) and it cannot be decided whether OE *hām* or *hamm* is involved. It is possible that the first element is OE *crōh* 'nook', as in *Crookham* (Brk), in which case the nook would be the notch in the 76m contour line south of Crookham Village, cut across by the Basingstoke Canal.

Crookhorn Farm In Farlington
1256 *Crevequor*; 1302 *Crevequeor*; 1312 *Creuker*.
A primary French PN, NF *Crevecuer* 'break-heart', also known in surnames, though there is no indication that this is 'manorial', i.e. from a surname. The modern name is folk-etymological. Possibly gave its name to *Crookhorn Copse* (1840 *Crookhorns*) in Exton.

Crow Manor in Ringwood
1086 *Croue*; 1300 *Crowe*.
Appears, from its situation, to contain PrW *crïw* 'ford, weir, (in

the plural) stepping-stones', like *Crewe* (Chs). Gover suggests a relation with W *craw* (actually *crau*) 'hovel', which may suit the forms better, though Padel (1985: 73) notes that the two elements are readily confusable in English PNs of Cornish origin. Both words are discussed by Wakelin (1969).

Crowdhill In Owslebury
May take its name from the family of *Croude* ('fiddle') mentioned in Owslebury in 1350. The place is on record since 1307 (*Croudehull*).

Crux Easton
801 (c13) *eastun*; 961 (c13) (*æt*) *eastune*.
OE 'east farm'. It is SE of Ashmansworth and NE of Hurstbourne Tarrant. The reference-point is probably the hundred-head manor of Hurstbourne. Crux Easton is in a detached part of Hurstbourne hundred (later called *Pastrow*), east of the main block.

The manor was held in 1086 by *Croch venator* 'Crōc the huntsman', and his descendants continued to hold it into the c13. It is thus 'Crōc's Easton', *Crux* appearing in 1607 (Smith, EPNE I: 117 is wrong; it is not Latin *crux* 'cross').

Cupernham Hamlet, now suburb, of Romsey
1248 *Cuperham*; 1272 *Kiperneham*; 1316 *Cupernam*; 1586 *Kippernam*.
OE/ME *Cyp(e)ærnahamm* 'hemmed-in land with (fish-)basket buildings'. The first element may alternatively be the OE *cupe*, same meaning, not attested till ME and the ancestor of ModE *cup*. The *hamm* is a typical site for such a name between two rivers (a version of Dodgson's *hamm*-2a classification (1973)), namely a branch of the Test and its left tributary which rises at Ampfield.

Curbridge
1236 *Kernebrugge, Curbrugge, Kerebrigge*; 1272 *Cornebrigge*; 1286 *Kernebregge*.
OE *Cweorn(a)brycg* 'quern bridge'. It can hardly be 'bridge by a quern', as Gover suggests. The association of the two words is very difficult. OE *cweorn* appears to exist as a simplex name in *Quorn* (Lei), but this is actually a reduction of OE *Cweorndūn* 'hill where quernstones were got'. The forms of our name suggest 'bridge of quernstones', for the first element seems to show traces of the genitive plural ending -*a*. Whether it is credible that a bridge over the widening river Hamble could be made of stones suitable for or recycled from handmills is a question I prefer to leave open.

Curdridge Modern parish carved out of Bishop's Waltham
901 (e. c11) (*to*) *cuðredes hricgæ*; 1208 *Curderigge*.

OE *Cūðrǣdeshrycg 'ridge of Cūðrǣd', a man's name. It stands on a low eminence between the river Hamble and a left-bank tributary.

Cut or **Cutted Thorn** Location in Southampton
This spot on Southampton Common was the site of the Southampton courts leet. Gover says it served as a borough boundary mark. It is recorded e.g. as 1254 *Cuttethorne*, 1488x1490 *Cutted thorne* (*crosse*) (*VCH* III: 492). A pollard hawthorn is the most likely source of the name, but a reference to ritual tree mutilation (usually however confined to ashes) is not out of the question. Cf. also *Cutbush Lane* in Bitterne and **Copythorne**.

D

Damerham Formerly in Wiltshire
873×888 (c11) (æt) *domra hamme*; 944×946 (c14) (æt) *domerhame*; 975×991 (c11) *domarham*; 1186 *Domerham*.
OE *dōmera hamm 'hemmed-in land of the judges'. Apparently a riverside *hamm* site of Dodgson's type 3. Damerham was a royal manor, and its proximity to Salisbury might account for the name: a residence provided for travelling justices, or, more likely, one whose revenues were dedicated to their support. The form with -a- is first found 1231 (*Damerham alias Domerham*).

Danebury Hill Earthwork in Nether Wallop
The earliest records, 1491 *Duwnebury Hill*, 1637 *Dunbury*, make it quite clear that it has nothing to do with Danes. It is rather 'hill fort'. The tendency to invent history may also be seen in *Norsebury* in Micheldever, another hillfort (902 (*to*) *næsan byrig*, t. Ed. I *Nosebury*), which is really 'fort at the ness' (later 'nose'), i.e. the western end of the little ridge between the valleys of the Dever and Cranbourne, on which the fort is placed west of its highest point; and in *John of Gaunt's Deer Park* in King's Somborne (John held the manor only through his wife, and the authentic name was *How Park* (cf. 1200 *Howude* 'hillspur wood')).

Daneshill District of Basingstoke
A modern name commemorating the battle of Basing, fought unsuccessfully by the West Saxons against the Danes in 871. It is close to **Lickpit/Lychpit** farm, a site which tradition associates with the burial of corpses from the battle.

Darby Green Hamlet in, now suburb of, Yateley
1759 *Darby Green*.
To be associated with the descendants of William de *Derby* mentioned in an Assize Roll of 1277.

Dean, East
1086 *Dene*; 1167 *Estdena*.
Partner of *West Dean*, straddling the border with W but administratively in W. Both originate in OE *denu*, plain 'valley', i.e. the valley of the river Dun, and are distinguished as *West* and *East* from the c12. Ths twin village may continue the estate of the Roman villa around which West Dean has grown. Cf. also **Dunbridge**.

Deane

1086, 1212 *Dene*.

OE *denu* 'valley'. Deane is in the dry upper reach of the valley of the river Test, which rises at Ashe, the next village westwards. The village contributes its name to the post-1974 district of *Basingstoke and Deane*.

Denmead In Hambledon

1205 *Denemede*.

OE **Denumǣd* 'meadowland in the valley'. The valley is that of a headwater of the Wallington river.

Denny Civil parish, that part of Beaulieu within the Forest, a forest walk

c.1300 *Dunie*; 1331 *la Dunye*; 1347 *Dinne*; 1589 *Dynney walke*.

A difficult name. Maybe OE **Dȳne-īeg* 'slope island' (i.e. raised land in marsh), though there is no obvious topographcal reason, and the original locus of the PN is not known. If at Denny Lodge, then there is marshland to the east and **Matley Bog** a mile to the north. Or **Dynne-īeg* 'Dynne's island'. The man's name *Dynne* seems to be found without the expected *-s* in *Dinton* (Bk and W), but the very fact of duplication invites scepticism.

Devils Dyke

See **Andyke**.

Dibden Liberty

1086 *Depedene*; 1165 *Diepedena*; 1201 *Dupedene*.

Apparently OE **Dēope denu* '(the) deep valley', with voicing assimilation of *p* to a following *d*. The historic village centre is on a slight hill just over 30 metres high, and the name is a distinct surprise. A better solution might be that it was the valley by the **Dēope* or zone of deep water in the Test estuary mentioned as *Deep Lake* on modern maps (e.g. 1866); or a similar, nearer, peril now obliterated by land reclamation. But there is no valley typical of the use of the word *denu* in the vicinity; there is a broadish but shallow pass leading across to Beaulieu Heath, but that is all.

Dibden Purlieu

1486 *Dibden in purlieu* ((?late) marginal note).

For *Dibden*, see previous entry. The *purlieu* (AN *puralé* 'perambulation') was an area around the nucleus of the New Forest. Technically it was land removed from the forest in the c14 when the forest boundaries as established by perambulations c.1300, reaffirmed 1327, were acknowledged (with more or less reluctance) by succeeding kings. In practice the king retained, or claimed, certain rights in the area, and the activities of the royal foresters in enforcing forest law there were a matter of great resentment. *Purlieu* as a PN element is also seen in the names of *Purlieu* in Sopley, *Holbury Purlieu* in Fawley, and *Brune's Purlieu* and *Ogden's Purlieu* in Ashley Walk, for example.

Dockenfield Presently in Frensham, Sr, previously assessed with Neatham
c.1150 *Docchenefeld*; 1586 *Dockenfelde*.
OE **Doccenafeld* 'open land marked by dock-plants'.

Dogmersfield
1106 *Dochemeresfelda*; c.1185 *Dokemerefeld*; 1206 *Dogmaresfeld*.
Spellings implying both [k] and [g] at the end of the first syllable alternate in the Middle Ages, with *g* forms coming to predominate in the early-mid c13. OE 'open land of/at **Doccanmere*', a place-name meaning 'dock pool' (from the plant), now lost. The pool mentioned may be an ancestor of Tundry Pond (origin unknown, cf. 1629 *Tundry greene*; from medieval French *tonderie* 'sheep- or cloth-shearing workshop'?), but I am not sure what effect the cutting of the Basingstoke Canal has had upon the local hydrology.

In Dogmersfield is *Ormersfield Farm*, which appears to be a deliberate revival of the corrupt DB spelling for the PN, *Ormeresfelt*.

Doiley Wood, bailiwick of Chute Forest, in Hurstbourne Tarrant
1155 *Digerlega*; 1196 *Digerle*.
OE **Digerlēah* 'thick wood'. The word *diger* is not on record, but it has good parallels in Continental Gmc languages. The expected modern form is **'Diley'*, which in Ha dialect would be *Doiley*; speakers of the prestige dialect have not corrected this Hampshirism back.

Downton Hamlet in Hordle
1164 *Dunchinton*; c.1200 *Doneketon, Duneketon*; 1280 *Doncketon*.
Most likely 'Dunneca's farm', and the more so if the form of 1164 can be seen as for **Dunnecingtūn*. Otherise OE **Dunnocatūn* 'farm of hedge sparrows'. The modern form (1691 *Downton*) seems to have been influenced by Downton in W, diametrically across the New Forest. *Estdonketon* (c.1200) may testify to this, though **South* would have been less surprising.

Drayton In Farlington
1242 *Drayton*.
Cf. *Houghton Drayton* in **Houghton**. Such names usually mean 'portage' or 'place for grounding boats'. The latter suits this place. The *Drayton* in Bighton (701, 956 (*to*) *dregtune*) must be 'farm at the steep ascent', as there is no water there. The essential original meaning of the first element is 'drag', applied to places where a special form of traction was required.

Droxford
826 (c12) *drocenesforda*; c10 (c12) *drocelesford*; 1086 *Drocheneford*; 1205 *Drokenesford*; 1236 *Trokenesford*.
Ekwall, in *DEPN*, suggests derivation from OE *drocen* 'a dry place', hence 'ford at the dry place'. I cannot improve on this. The c13 spellings with *T* remain unexplained. There was a (*to*) *þroc briggæ* '(at) plank or trestle bridge' in the bounds of Droxford (Sawyer 276), which Grundy (1924: 77) places where the modern A333 crosses a left tributary of the river Hamble, but despite the partial similarity of the name to *Droxford* no common origin can be suggested if we go on appearances; the forms in *D* appear in MSS. whose supposed archetypes are of the AS period. But there is sufficient doubt about the two MSS. in question to leave the matter open, the archetype of one being of uncertain date and the other MS. being spurious.

Dummer
1086 *Dunmere*; 1204 *Dummer*; c.1245 *Dummere*.
OE 'hill pond'. There is a small pond in the hilltop village, and present-day ponds fairly high on a hillside to the south of the village.

Dun Right tributary of the Test
No early forms. Back-formed from **Dunbridge** in Mottisfont.

Dunbridge Manor in Mottisfont
1086 *Denebrige*; 1167 *Denebrugge*; 1227 *Dunebrigge*; 1230 *Denebrigge*; 1256 *Donebrigge*.
The clear early tradition is OE *Denebrycg* 'bridge in The Valley' (cf. **Dean, East**; it is at the eastern end of this valley). Gover wonders if the first element could be a river-name (cf. **Dun**), but there is no support for this, especially given the unstressed medial syllable, which tells against an old river-name like *Don*; this would have compounded directly with *brycg*. The c13 transformation is unexplained. It would be very surprising if this major PN had been influenced by *Dun Wood* (no early forms; OS 1:50000) in the

adjacent parish of Sherfield English. This will be a late application of the river-name to the wood.

Durley

901 (e. c11) (*to*) *deorleage*; 903 (c16) *durlea*; 1086 *Derleie*.

OE *Dēorlēah* 'deer wood' or 'deer clearing'. The absence of an inflectional syllable in the first element may suggest that this is a meaningful compound, i.e. 'deer-wood' rather than simply 'wood where deer were found'. A further Durley is the DB manor of *Derleie* in Colbury.

E

Earlstone
See **Clere**.

East Aston Tithing(s) of Longparish
1256 *Esteton*; 1333 *Eston*.
Either OE (*be*) *ēastan tūne* 'east of the farm', presumably Middleton,
or **Ēasttūn* 'east farm'. The place was later recorded as two tithings,
1329 *Esteston* and c.1450 *Westaston*, but appearing in 1586 as
Ashton.

East Meon
873×888 (e. c11) (*æt*) *meone*; 1086 *Menes*; 1158 *Mienes*; c.1270
Estmunes.
The name comes from the river-name, q.v. East and West Meon
start being referred to separately in the later c13, but East Meon is
once (1203) *Kingesmeon*. The persistent final *s* may be due to the
unexplained Norman French peculiarity noted by Zachrisson (1924),
or may be a plural form due to the existence of the two villages,
for which cf. *Harting* in Sx.

East Stoke or **Eastoke** In Hayling Island
956 (c12) (*æt*) *east stoce, stoccæ*; 1327 *Estoke*; 1406 *Eststocke*.
Apparently OE '(at the) east tree-stump', i.e. east in South Hayling.
But it must early have been taken for **Eaststoc* 'east grange farm'
rather than *stocc* if the record and the present form are to be trusted,
distinguishing it from *Stoke* in North Hayling; a genuine *stoc* name
(1327 *Stoke*) for it was held by St Swithin's as an adjunct to its
Havant liberty. But this place is properly south of that Stoke.

Eastleigh Modern parish carved out of South Stoneham
932 (c13/c16) *east lea*; 1086 *Estleie*.
OE 'east wood or clearing' or perhaps better '[place] east of the
wood'.

Eastney In Portsmouth
The c13 forms *Esteney(e)* confirm that this is OE *ēastan īege* 'on
the east side of (Portsea) island'.

Easton
825 (c12) (implying) (*to*) *eastuninga* (*mearce*); 871×877 (c12) *eastun*.
OE **Ēasttūn* 'east farm'. The form of 825 occurs in a context
making clear that it means '(boundary) of the people of Easton'. It
is east of the lost place with an ancient type of name *Igtun*, on the

adjacent island in the river Itchen, as the OE bounds of Martyr Worthy make plain. More weakly, it is north-east of Winchester, which might explain the name.

Eastrop Former parish, now district of Basingstoke
1086, 1203 *Estrope*; 1272 *Estthrop juxta Basingestok*.
OE *Ēastþrop 'east village'. Places named *þrop* were often daughter settlements; the direction word suggests of Basingstoke in this case. Basingstoke has now swallowed it up again.

Ecchinswell
1086 *Eccleswelle*; 1172 *Echeneswolle* [*sic*]; 1176 *Egeneswell*; 1208 *Echeneswelle*; 1256 *Echeleswelle*; 1280 *Hykeneswelle*.
This name presents many problems. There is a stream here, a right tributary of the Enborne, which appears as 931 (c12) (*æt*) *eclesburna*, *ecelesburna*. The first of these forms appears to mean 'stream associated with a British church' (on the element *ecles see Cameron 1968). Of the second the most that could be said is that it might be the same. If the parish name has the same element, then DB unusually preserves the historically correct form in defiance of practically all later attestations. On these assumptions we have OE **Eclesiwielle/-wiella*, parallel to *Eccleswall* (He); and the later forms would show dissimilation of the first *l* to *n*. The fact that many of the *n* forms come from Winchester documents might lead us to suspect the analogical influence of the river-name **Itchen**, but that has uniform medieval *I*-, and *Y*- and never *E*-. All post-DB forms show a vowel between the *c* (or equivalent) and the *l/n*. This is hard to square with our first etymology, but some other names containing *ecles sometimes show the same feature. An unrecorded, but regular, man's name *Eccel* should thus be borne in mind; as should Ekwall's possible river-name *Ecel*, equally unrecorded. The pronunciation with [tʃ] is shown unambiguously from 1615 *Itchinswell*; this also does not support an origin in *ecles.

Efford In Milford-on-Sea
1236, 1242, 1290 *Ebbeford*.
OE/ME 'ford passable at the ebb' over Avon Water. The stream is not now tidal because of the sluice at Keyhaven. Morris identifies this with the DB manor of *Einforde*, but this does not square with the other spellings. It may be a bad form for the adjacent *Wainsford* (1365 *Wenefford*, 1461 *Wenford* 'wagon ford').

Egbury Hillfort in St Mary Bourne, tithing of Evingar hundred
1184 *Eggeburne* [*sic*]; 1248 *Eggebur'*; 1284 *Eggebury*.
OE *Ecganburh 'Ecga's fort'. Both its situation and the ME medial

syllable (if the second *e* indicates a pronounced vowel) speak against
Ecgburh 'steep slope fort'.

Eldon, Upper and Lower Farms in King's Somborne, extinct parish

1107 *Ellendune*; 1127 *Elledone*; 1167 *Elledena*, *Elledene*; 1205 *Elendone*.

OE 'Ella's hill' or 'Ella's valley' (*dūn* or *denu*). Since the church is at *Upper Eldon*, perhaps the first is the true origin. But perhaps there have always been two settlements, 'hill' and 'valley', and the two names have fallen together phonetically. Upper Eldon is on the chalk downs; *Lower Eldon* is at the head of a very marked valley. The first element is alternatively *elle* 'elder'.

Eling Parish, suburb of Southampton

1086 *Edlinges*; 1158 *Eling'*, *Elinges*; 1186 *Ailinges*.
The 1086 form may be a clue that a name like *★Æðelingas* lies behind this, in the sense of 'those associated with Æðel', possibly, and not 'princes'. (For a similar chain of spellings, cf. *Ellingsdean* (Sx; Gardiner and Coates 1987).) The preponderance of *E-* spellings may rather suggest a name like *★Edla*, which Ekwall inferred to have existed on comparative evidence from continental German. If DB is in error, the field is wide open for interpretation. Cf. **Ellingham**.

Ellingham

1086 *Adelingeham*; c.1165 *Haslingueham*; 1167 *Elingeham*.
OE *★Æðelingaham(m)*, either 'estate' or 'hemmed-in land' of the *Æðelingas*, cf. **Eling**. Maybe 'of the people of Eling'. The at first sight bizarre form of c.1165 appears to confirm OE *ð* by showing *s*; this would be a poor NF spelling for *ð*. (In addition cf. c.1240 *Elinkelond'* in Charford. There was a further PN, in Godshill bailiwick of the New Forest (about 6 miles N of Ellingham), which appears to contain the same element (1626 *Elinge Thornes* (*Hill*), 1670 *Island Thorns* (*Wood*)).)

The site is at the Avon water-meadows; possibly therefore a Dodgsonian *hamm-3*.

Ellisfield

1167 *Elsefeld*; 1219 *Ulsefeld*; 1236 *Ellesfeud*.
The first two forms are the typical ones, and the name may thus be OE *★Ielfsanfeld* 'open land of Ielfsa', as Ekwall suggests. *Ielfsa* would be a regular West-Saxon dialect form of *★Ælfsa*, a short-form of the common *Ælfsige*. The place is nowadays in a well-wooded area.

Elvetham

727 (c13) *elfteham*; 973×974 (c12) (*æt*) *ylfethamme*; 1086 *Elveteham*. OE **Ylfetahamm* 'swans' water-meadow'. *Hamm* here is either in the sense of a waterside meadow or of land between two streams, here a fork of the river Hart. The choice depends on whether the place is named from the site of Elvetham *Farm* or *Hall*. I assume the latter, since the church is by the Hall in the fork of the river.

Embley DB manor, house in Wellow

1086 *Emelei*; 1248 *Emmeleg'*. OE **Efnanlēa* '(at the) level clearing'. There is no bar in theory to its being 'Emma's wood/clearing', the name being that borne by Ælfgifu queen of Æðelræd II and of Cnut; though the status of this is an English name is open to doubt.

Emery Down District of Lyndhurst

1376 *Emerichdon*; c.1490 *Emeryesdowne*. The *Emmory* family is recorded here in 1389. The surname is of French origin, though goes back ultimately to a continental Germanic man's name.

Empshott

1086 *Hibesete*; c.1170 *Himbeset*; 1218 *Ymbeschete*; 1248 *Imbeshete*; 1270 *Imbeschate*; 1297 *Imbeshute*. OE **Imbanscīete* or **Imbascīete* 'corner of the bee-swarm(s)' (the continental Gmc. relatives of *imbe* could be strong or weak nouns). Probably an old corner of **Greatham** estate; the second element may in fact be *scēat* or its derivative *scīete*.

Emsworth

1224 *Emeleswurth, Emneswrth*; 1268 *Empnesworth*; 1304 *Emlesworth*. OE **Æmeleswyrð* 'Æmele's curtilage'. Spellings in *n* predominate in the later Middle Ages; this is the result of the assimilation of *l* to the preceding nasal consonant, a common type of change. There are sporadic forms without *s* in the thirteenth century.

Enborne River

749 (c12) (*on, andlang*) *aleburnan*; 931 (c12) (*on*) *alerburnan*. OE **Alorburna* 'alder stream'. The name has become confused (witness the c13 spellings *Aleburn, Aneburne*) with that of *Enborne* village 2 miles inside Brk, whose name is from OE **Enedburna* (1200 *Enedburn*) 'duck stream' (cf. **Andwell**).

Enham Two villages, one now a suburb of Andover, **King's Enham** and **Enham Alamein**

e. c11 *Eanham*; 1167 *Enham*.

Probably OE **Ēanhām* 'lamb estate'. The word **ēan* is not on record, but the verb *ēanian* 'to lamb' is found. Part of Enham was in the royal estate of Andover, hence King's Enham (1379 *Enham regis*), and the rest a separate manor, held by Matthew de Columbers who died in 1273 seized of a knight's fee and a half, hence Knight's Enham (1316 *Ennam militis*, 1389 *Knyghtesenham*). The curious form t. Hy III *Knytheneshenenham* is hard to explain, but may in a garbled way suggest *knight* in the plural (e.ME *knightene* in the genitive case), with a further *-s*.

Knight's Enham is now known as *Enham Alamein*. A rehabilitation colony for ex-servicemen was set up here after the Great War, and re-endowed after the Second World War as *Alamein Village* by the government of Egypt in gratitude for the defeat of the German army at El Alamein. The name of the place was changed accordingly on the wave of postwar national sentiment.

Ervills, Great Farm in Hambledon

c.1380 *Ereuelles*; 1397 *Ervelles*; 1557 *Arvilles*; 1586 *Erfildes*.

Obscure. Appears to be a surname of French origin. The manor is sometimes called *Ervelles Exton* (e.g. 1418), but no connection with **Exton**, 5 miles NW, is known, and the relation between the two parts of this name is unknown. We might hazard that the name is really OE **Eorðhyllas* 'earth hills', from the two barrows adjacent to the farm. But no exact parallel for such an early and permanent change of [ð] to [v] is known in Ha.

Eschetune DB manor, location unknown

Claimed by Hugh de Port to hold part of an unnamed hide in Somborne hundred. The name is presumably **Æsctūn* 'ash(-tree) farm'.

Eversley

1053×1066 (c13/c14) (*æt*) *evereslea*; 1086 *Evreslei*; 1236 *Evereslege*. OE *Eofreslēah* 'boar's wood/clearing' or possibly 'of Eofor', a man's name originally meaning 'boar'. The present place straggles from Eversley to *Eversley Centre* (c20) and *Eversley Cross* (1759 *Cross Green*).

Everton Village in Milford-on-Sea

c13 *Iveletona*; 1272 *Ivelton*; 1346 *Yevelton*; 1646, 1810 *Evelton*. OE **Gifltūn* 'farm on the (river) *Gifl*', a river-name and PN duplicated in *Yeovil(ton)* (So). The modern name appears to rely on the OE word *eofor* 'boar', but there are no such forms till the ModE period. It is perhaps suggested by the adjacent **Efford**, as if the name were *Efford-ton, with an easily understandable loss of *d*.

Ewhurst
1023 (c12) (*on*) *ywyrstæ* (*stigele*); 1086 *Werste*; 1185 *Ywersta*.

OE *Īwhyrst* 'yew wood' (on a hill; cf. Gelling 1984: 197–8). This is a common SCy name, especially on the Chalk. A wood called *Ewhurst Wood* is still in the parish.

Ewshot or Ewshott In Crookham
1236 *Hyweshate*; 1256 *Yweset*; 1305 *Iweshate*.

OE/ME *Īwscēat* 'yew corner'. *Scēat* often means an administrative 'corner', and Ewshot Hall is close to an indentation in the county boundary with Surrey (cf. **Aldershot, Grayshott**).

Exbury Hamlet in Exbury and Lepe
1086 *Teocreberie*; 1197 *Ykeresbir'*; 1212 *Ekeresbur'*; 1236 *Hukeresber'*; 1280 *Eukeresbir'*; 1291 *Eukesbiri*.

Ekwall suggests that the personal name involved is an OE form corresponding to ON *Íoarr*; this would be the regularly formed *Eohhere*. This is ingenious, but hard to square with the universal -*k*-. It is otherwise compatible with the DB form, which would show *T*- from a lost preposition *æt*. An alternative might be OE *iecere 'increaser', possibly used as a personal name much as *Strēona*, probably similar in meaning, is used as a by-name in OE for one *Ēadrīc*. The DB form does not support this. On the other hand, Gover suggests that *Agarton* in Milford-on-Sea (c12 *Elcreton* and always showing *c* or *k*) contains the name *Ealhhere*. If this is right, Ekwall's etymology for Exbury is supported.

Gover associates the second element with the earthwork on a low promontory at the mouth of the Beaulieu river, though this is at Lower Exbury and not near the putative parent village where the church is. Possibly, therefore, 'Eohhere's or Īecere's manor'.

Exton
940 (c12) (*æt*) *east seaxnatune, east seaxena tunes* (*boc*); 1086 *Essessentune*.

OE 'East Saxons' farm'. This must mean the farm was inhabited by people from Essex, but no historical light has been thrown on this yet.

Eyeworth DB manor in Ashley Walk, modern lodge and walk
1086 *Iuare*; 1365 *Iware*.

Probably OE *Īwwaru 'yew-weir or fishpond'. There is a pond near the lodge, recorded in the late c18 as *Ivory Lodge*. *Waru* is a form related to the *wer* which yields modern *weir*. If the modern name is not corrupt, it may indicate that an element *waroð* 'streamside meadow or marsh' survived, but this is less likely as *worth* is a common outcome of the corruption of various other elements.

F

Faccombe
863 (c12) (andlang) faccan cumbes.
OE *Faccancumb 'Facca's valley'. Facca is not recorded, but is the precise equivalent of the continental Gmc man's name Facco. Cumb usually denotes a bowl- or trough-shaped valley with three steep sides (cf. Cole 1982). Such valleys are common near the chalk scarp, and there is a **Combe** just across the county boundary in Brk (formerly in Hampshire). Faccombe village actually overlooks its valley from the top of a spur.

Fair Oak Modern parish carved out of Bishopstoke
1596 Fereoke (in decenn' de Stok').
ME or e.ModE 'beautiful oak'. No fair is known to have been held here, unlike in the case of the Fairlop Oak (Ess).

Fareham
964x975 (c12) fearnham; 1086 Fernham.
OE 'bracken estate'. A topographical description, for bracken can have had nothing to do with the function of the estate. The n between consonants begins to disappear – perhaps in French mouths – as early as the c12. Note though that the Millbrook charter of 956 (Sawyer 636) refers to fearninga broc 'brook of people associated with fearn' or with a person whose name descended from the Brit. *Sparno- (as represented in the name of the Welsh king Farinmail, slain in 577 according to the Ā and E texts of the OE Chronicle). There is room for a reappraisal of the relation between the names **Fareham** and **Farlington** and the Millbrook charter name in the light of this.

Faringdon
1086 Ferendone; t. Hy II Ferrendona; c.1200 Farendon; 1167 Ferninduna; 1207 Fernindon; 1280 Farndon.
Apparently OE *Fearndūn 'bracken-hill'. But the consistent two-syllable first element is most unexpected (ctrst the early spellings of **Fareham**). Instead the first element may be the related adjective *fiernen. The ecology is unclear as both parts of the modern village are on the chalk below hilltops capped with clay-with-flints.

Farleigh Wallop
1086 Ferlege; 1256 Farnlegh; 1291 Farlegh.
OE 'bracken clearing'. Known as Farleigh Mortimer from its feudal overlords between c.1297 and 1487 (cf. **Headbourne Worthy**),

when it passed to John *Wallop*, whose ancestors no doubt hailed from **Wallop**.

Farley Chamberlayne
1086 *Ferlege*; 1212 *Ferley*.
Probably OE *Fearnlēah* 'bracken clearing'. Cf. the forms on record for the many other Hampshire names in **Far(n)-**. The feudal specifier commemorates the family of *Chaumberleyn* (*Camerarius* in Latin); hence 1167 *Ferlega Camerarii*, 1297 *Farlegh Chaumberlayn*.

Farlington
1186, 1190 *Ferling(e)ton*; c13 onwards *Farlington(e)*.
Ekwall offers a solution bearing his own stamp: OE *Fearnlēa(g)inga-tūn* 'farm of those associated with a place called *Fearnlēah* ('bracken clearing'). No such place has been identified in this connection, and it is impossible to know whether it is to be associated in any way with **Fareham** (OE *Fearnhām*); though the supposed place-name is formally acceptable. The only alternative would involve guessing at the former existence of a man's name *Færla*. See further under **Fareham**.

Farnborough
1086 *Ferneberga*; 1230 *Ferenbergo* (Latin form); 1259 *Farenberwe*; 1284 *Farneburewe*; 1284 *Farnbureghe*.
OE *Fearnbeorg* 'bracken mound', with the second element later reinterpreted as if from *burh* 'fortification, manor, borough'. Farnborough lies on or adjacent to Barton and Bracklesham Sands, the sandy soils encouraging bracken. Cf. also the adjacent name *West Heath*.

Fawley
1086 *Falegia, Falelei*; 1194 *Faleleia*.
OE, either *Fealulēah* 'fallow(-coloured) wood/clearing' (i.e. the colour of vegetation which is no longer green), or *Fealglēah* 'clearing with land broken in for arable'. A further complication concerns a c10 charter form (*to*) *faleðlea*. It is not known whether it refers to this place. If it does, then the first element would appear to be OE *fileðe* 'hay', but in a form which is that of the Mercian dialect.

The name of *Fawley Hundred*, in E Ha, is as in the first sentence of this entry (1086 *Falelei*, 1158 *Falelea*).

Fernhill Gate Near New Milton
Probably the DB manor of *Fernehelle* in Rowditch hundred. S.-e., and not surprising on sandy soil (cf. *Fernhills Copse*).

Finchdean In Idsworth; also a hundred

1167 *Finchesdene* (hundred); 1248 *Finchesden'* (hamlet).

OE **Fincesdenu* 'Finc's valley', or just possibly 'finch valley'. The hundred was in DB called after Chalton (*Ceptune*). Alternative names for the hundred were 1168 *Wulpette* 'wolf-pit' and 1215 *Ulethorn* 'owls' thorn(-bush)'.

Finley's Row Lost manor in Ewhurst

1086 *Finlei*; 1248 *Fineleg'*.

The DB form is an interpolation in the entry for Wolverton. The name appears to be OE **Finlēah* 'woodheap clearing/wood' or **Finalēah* 'woodpeckers' wood'; unless, as Gover suggests, a form of 909 *þingleage* refers to the same place, in which case it is 'assembly clearing/wood'. For this to be plausible, we would have to show that this was the meeting-place of Kingsclere hundred.

Fleet Modern parish carved out of Farnborough, Yateley, Crookham, etc.

1313 *Flete*; 1505 *le Flete(brige)*, *Fletepondes*.

The town takes its name from the large natural pond called *Fleet Pond*, which contains OE/ME *flēot*. This usually means a creek or stretch of salt water, but is occasionally used of inland features like this. From the pond, the suburb of *Pondtails* is also indirectly named. *Pondtail Farm* (thus 1826) stood near the point of entry of the stream which feeds the pond. *Tail* is commonly used in this sense in the minor names of e.g. Sx. The character of the ground in the area, a large area of drift surrounded by soils of the Holidays Hill association, can be judged from these names plus *Blacklake Copse*, *Aunt's Pool Hill* and *The Flash* (ME *flasshe* 'swamp') in the same parish. Streams drain into Fleet Pond and do not escape again.

Fontley or **Funtley** Manor in Titchfield

1086 *Funtelei*; 1242 *Fonteleg'*; 1256 *Funtelegh*; 1316 *Fontele*.

OE **Funtanlēah* 'wood/clearing associated with a Romanized spring' (*funta*). On the hydrology of this area, see **Havant**. There is a copious spring here.

Fordingbridge Town and hundred

1086 *Fordingebrige* (hundred); 1227 *Fordingebrig'* (town); 1255 *Fordingebrug'* (town).

OE/ME **Fordingabrycg* 'bridge of the dwellers at Ford', this being the name of the place before there was a bridge (1086, 1242 *Forde*). The name survived as aliases for both the town and the hundred into the c15. In the last quarter of the c13 a short-lived tradition emerges with *Forth-*.

Four Marks

1548 *Fowrem'kes*.

EModE 'four boundaries'. It stands astride the boundaries of Medstead, Chawton, Faringdon and Ropley. The railway elevated this outlying spot to a position of some consequence.

Fox Lane Suburb of Farnborough in Hawley

Probably s.-e. But cf. *Foxlease Farm* (1516 *Foxleye corner* 'fox wood', used as a surname and appearing in the farm name as *Foxley's*). *Fox Lane* could be thought of as leading past Hawley Pond to Foxlease.

Foxcott or **Foxcotte** In Andover

The DB manor of *Fulsescote* has been identified with Foxcott(e) (1146 *Foxcote*, 1431 *Foscote*). But it cannot, as it stands, involve the same name; it would have to be a hypothetical OE, or anglicized Continental Gmc, man's name like *Fulcsige*. The present name is 'fox cottages', or maybe 'fox-earth(s)'.

Foxlease DB manor, house in Lyndhurst

1086 *Cocheslei*; 1300 *Cockesle*.

OE 'Cocc's clearing' or 'woodcock clearing'. It took a 'manorial' form with -s as early as the late c15 (c.1490 *Cokkesleys*), and this was reformed, perhaps in the early c19 (1826 *Foxleaze*), perhaps as a euphemism, as if it meant 'fox meadow'.

Fratton

982 (c14) (*æt*) *frodincgtune*, (*to*) *frodingtune*; 1086 *Frodinton*.

OE 'farm of Frōda', a man's name. The heavily contracted modern form appears in the c17.

Freefolk

1086 *Frigefolc*; 1245 *Frivolk*.

OE *Frēofolc* 'free folk'. This is the only village name in England with *folc* as the second element (ctrst *Norfolk*, *Suffolk*). The sense is unclear; *folcland* was land not exempted from providing foodrent to the king (Stenton 1970: 306–8), which goes ill with *frēo*.

Freemantle In Millbrook, suburb of Southampton

1336 (*land in Mullebroke called*) *Fremantel*.

See **Freemantle**, park in Kingsclere. Possibly an independent name or possibly copied from/associated with the other one. There is a common of the same name in Bitterne.

Freemantle Park in Kingsclere

1181 *Freitmantell*; 1205 *Fremantell*; 1214 (*apud*) *Frigidum Mantellum*.

A French name, 'cold cloak', latinized in the third form quoted. It is probably a transferred name, as there are several instances in N France of the form *Fromentel*. But it may have arisen as a joke or partial mistranslation. There is a common PN type *Caldecote* (e.g. in Bk) 'cold cottages'. There could have been an instance here which was mistakenly assumed to contain ME *cote* 'coat', itself of French origin. On the other hand the Norman sense of humour has not achieved wide recognition, and the first form is early enough to count against this view.

Frenchmoor Extraparochial area north of East Dean
1246 *Freschemore*; 1248 (*la*) *Frenshemore*.
The first form is isolated, the second typical. ME 'French moor'. Perhaps to be associated with *French's Wood* (OS 1:63 360; no early forms known) in East **Wellow**. Perhaps to be understood as distinct in some way from **Sherfield English**, 3.5 miles away.

Fritham In Bramshaw
1212 *Friham*; c.1280 *Frytham*.
Probably contains OE **fryhð(e)* from *fyrhð(e)* 'scrub on the edge of a forest' (Gelling 1984: 191–2). Possibly coincidentally, the site of the present village is heath surrounded pretty well on three sides by woodland. The second element may be *hamm* in Dodgson's sense 5a – a cultivated plot in marginal land.

Frogmore Hamlet and later suburb of Yateley
1567 (*marsh called*) *Frogmore*.
Names ending in *more* sometimes represent OE *mere* 'pool'; possibly therefore 'frog pool', or if s.-e. 'frog moor'.

Froxfield
975×971 (c12) (*æt*) *froxafelda*; 1207, 1245 *Froxefeld(e)*.
OE 'frogs' open land'. The presence of such a name on high ground a long way from streams is accounted for by the presence of clay-with-flints on the chalk downs here, providing a damp habitat for frogs. Cf. *Frogmore* in adjacent East Meon parish.

Froyle, Upper and Lower
1086 *Froli*; 1167 *Froila*; 1236 *Froyle*; 1199 *Frohill'*.
A difficult name. Ekwall and Gover both toy with the idea that it is OE 'hill of (the god) *Freō/Frīg*', which (1) is highly speculative; (2) does not account for the universal *o*; (3) does not really account for the morphology of the name – one might expect some c12 forms with three syllables; and (4) does not respect the fact that Upper Froyle is at the tip of a rather insignificant ridge, and closer

to the river Wey than to the more significant ridge to the north of it. Only a small group of forms like that of 1199 suggest 'hill'. Better perhaps an unrecorded ancestor of ME *frow* 'swift' and OE *wiell(e)* 'spring, stream'. The name would refer to the Wey, as there is no side stream here. There is plenty of support from other Gmc languages for an OE *frāw-*.

There is still the question of *Frobury* farm in Kingsclere, however (1184 *Frolebiri*, 1236 *Froillebyr'*, 1541 *Frowbery*, 1586 *Frolberry*). Ekwall considers this PN to contain that of Froyle (or one identical to it) as its first element. But *Froyle* shows lots of evidence for a medial *-i-*, whilst in *Frobury* only the form from 1236 has an *-i-*. The two are probably therefore unrelated. They are not really near each other (Froyle SU 755429, Frobury SU 512595). *Frobury* may contain *Fr(e)olla*, a short-form of the name *Freoðulāf* (*Friðulāf*).

Fryern Hill Suburb of Chandler's Ford
No early spellings found, but clearly ME 'friars' hill'. The element is also in *Fryern Court* in Fordingbridge (1541 *Freren courte*), where the reference appears to be to the Cistercian monks of Beaulieu, whom it was a mistake to call *friars*; but in 1541 nobody would have cared much.

Fulflood District of Winchester
961 (c12) (*to þære*) *fulan flode*; 1219 *Fulfloda*.
OE 'foul or muddy ditch or watercourse'. Appears as a FN in several Hampshire parishes.

Fullerton Hamlet and junction in Wherwell
1086 *Fugelerestune*; 1234 *Fughelerton*.
OE '(wild)fowlers' farm' (or better 'hamlet'). The forms implying a plural first element *fuglera* are in the majority. The fowlers must have got a good living by hunting at the confluence of the Test, Dever and Anton.

Fyfield
975 (c12) (*to*) *fif hidan*, (*æt*) *fif hidon*, *fif hida land* (*boc*); 1086 *Fifhide* (marginal note, contemporary).
OE *fīf hīda* '(the) five hides', cf. **Hyde Abbey**. The DB assessment of the manor is indeed five hides. The first distortion of the second element is 1535 *Fyfeld*. Thus also the same name in Brk, Ess, Gl, W, *Fifield* twice in each of O and W and *Fifehead* three times in Do. The frequency of the name is due to such an area being the standard holding of a thegn. Cf. **Toyd Farm**.

G

Gatewood In Exbury

1235 (*boscus de*) *Gatewod*.

OE *Gātawudu* 'goats' wood'. The attempt to identify it with the DB manor of *Gatingeorde* is philologically unsatisfactory on the face of it, because that would yield *Gattingworth*. Morris correctly points out that the DB scribe wrote *-orde* in **Otterwood**, undoubtedly a *-wood* name; but we would still have to assume that *Gatinge* was a lost PN – Morris does and translates it 'goat-place', on the model of supposed singular *-ing* names like *Ferring* (Sx) 'bull place' (Smith, *EPNE* I: 289). We are not told why the *-ing-* disappeared. Much is uncertain here.

Gerlei
See **Malshanger**.

Gilkicker Point Promontory

Thus in c17. Completely obscure. There is or was a field called *Gilkicke* in Whitwell (Westmorland), cf. *PNWe* I, 151. The point takes its name from a three-sided brick column, faced with stone, marking an underwater spit close to the site of 'Haslar Castle' (*Portsmouth Papers* 30). It had a partner, *Kickergill*, surely one of the most extraordinary PN pairs in the country.

Gliddon In Hambledon

1236 *Gleddon*; 1248 *Gliddon*; 1301 *Gluddon*; 1316 *Gluddene*; 1350 *Gliddene*.

OE, either *Glēodandūn* 'kite's hill' or *Glēodandenu* 'kite's valley'. The farm is in a valley, but the earlier forms imply 'hill'. The first element may be a personal name 'Kite'. The spellings do not suggest West Saxon *glīda*. The absence of any vowel between the two *d* is hard to account for.

Godesmannescamp Lost DB manor

This was in Rowditch hundred, but it has been thought, for no obvious reason, to be in Fordingbridge hundred; that is presumably why *Godmanes Cap* (*sic*) appears on modern OS maps as the name of the fortification above **Godshill**, whose own name has suggested the identification. The name means '*camp* of God's man', it seems. *Camp* in PNs originally meant 'uncultivated land on the edge of a RB villa estate', cf. Gelling (1988: 74–8).

Godsfield Extraparochial area of Bountisborough hundred
l. c12 *Godefeld*; 1305 *Godesfeld*.
Gover believes that this area was detached from Itchen Stoke and
granted to the Knights Hospitaller in the late c12; from which he
infers that the name is s.-e. But the earliest forms do not show the
expected -*s*. If the form is OE it could be 'Gōda's open land',
reinterpreted in the light of its being held by the Hospitallers.

Goodworth Clatford Formed out of South Clatford (see **Clatford,
Upper**) and Goodworth.
1086 *Godorde*; 1225 *Gudeworthe*.
OE **Gōdanwyrð* 'Gōda's curtilage'. The merged name is shown
for the first time on Saxton's map of 1579.

Gordleton In Hordle
c13 *Gorlitun, Golreton*; 1365 *Gorlington*.
Gover derives it from **Gorlēahingatūn* 'farm of those from *Gorley*'
(place in Fordingbridge whose name, however, means 'gore (wedge-
shaped) wood/clearing'), from OE *gār*. Against this is the late
appearance of the -*ing*- forms. Worse, however, is the absence of
any syllable between -*ing*- and -*tun*. But it is hard to countenance
the alternative, viz. a PN formed in -*tūn* from an earlier PN
*Gorlēahing, for that would be scarcely intelligible as an OE PN.
Much more likely it is an -*ingtūn* formation, but the first element
is obscure, perhaps the personal name seen in *Gorleston* (Nf). The
modern form has been influenced by the name of the parish.

Gosport In Alverstoke liberty
1251 *Goseport*.
Apparently a medieval name meaning 'town of geese' or 'port of
geese'. If the name dates from OE times one might envisage it
coming from a man's name **Gōsa*, analogous to *Horsa*.

Grately or **Grateley**
929 *greatteleiam* (Latin accusative case form); c.935 (*æt*) *greatanlea*.
OE *Grēatanlēa* '(at the) big wood/clearing'.

Grayshott Modern parish carved out of Bramshott and Headley
1184 (*boscus de*) *Grauesseta*; 1256 (*in bosco de*) *Graveshette*.
OE/ME **Grāfesscēat* 'grove corner'. The corner is an administrative
one, the piece of Hampshire surrounded on three sides by Surrey
(cf. **Aldershot**); the grove in question is referred to explicitly in
the two instances cited.

Greatham
1086 *Greteham*; 1167 *Grietham*; 1179 *Gretham*; 1235 *Grutam*.
OE *Grēothām* 'gravel estate', duplicating a name in Sx. The site of the manor is marked by the unusually named c19 house *Le Court* (t. Jas I *Lee Court*). However the geology suggests that the place is named from the present site of the village, on the occasionally pebbly Folkestone Beds, rather than from that of the manor, above the landslipped Gault on the sandy Upper Greensand.

Greywell
1167 *Graiwella*; 1236 *Greiwell*; 1253 *Grewell*; 1579 *Gruell*.
OE 'grey spring or stream'; or preferably the word *grǣg* applied in the sense 'badger', common as *gray* from Tudor times. The modern pronunciation is seen in Saxton's map form (1579).

Grims Ditch and **Grims Dyke**
See **Andyke**.

Gritnam DB manor in Brockenhurst
1086 *Greteham*; 1375 *Gretingham*.
Also mentioned in 1300 *Grettenhamdune* 'Gritnam down/hill'. OE *Grēotanhām* 'estate at the gravelly place', cf. Smith (*EPNE* I: 209).

Gundleton In Bighton
No early spellings have been found. Possibly ME 'Gunild's farm', this being a well-known Anglo-Scandinavian female name, found in 1324 in *Gunnildcroft*, 1365 *Gonyldegate* in the New Forest. Or it may be related, due to a misreading of some earlier MS., to the minor local name (*Edney's*) *Girdledon* in Bighton, cited (unlocated) by Grundy (1921: 109). But the name may not really be ancient.

H

Hackwood Park Park in Basingstoke
1228 *Hagewod*; 1236 *Hacwde*, *Hacwud*.
The first form suggests 'haw(thorn berry) wood' (a rather curious way of expressing the idea), but all others superficially suggest ME *Hacchewude* 'gate wood', in the sense of 'forest gate'. A licence to empark was granted in 1223, and, given the date of the earliest mention, we could conclude that the name dates from then. However, *hacche* appears as *hack* and the like only in NCy; we would expect *Hatchwood* here. It could rather contain ME *hake*, whose OE ancestor meant 'hook, door-fastening', as possibly in *Hackpen* (W) 'boltable enclosure'. *Hakewude* would mean therefore 'wood which could be securely closed off'. The grant of 1223 speaks of denying the king's deer free access and exit (*VCH* IV: 122). Against this attractive solution is the dearth of forms with a medial *e*.

Hale
1158 *Hala*; 1219 *la Hale*.
OE *healh* 'nook, angle', often of an administrative area. Gover notes that Hale was in the NW corner of the county (seen from the New Forest) until Whitsbury and Martin were absorbed from Wiltshire in 1895; but the Charfords and Breamore were beyond it. Rather, the eastern end of Fordingbridge hundred, up against the western limit of the New Forest.

Halterworth Hamlet, now suburb, of Romsey
1256 *Haltreworth*.
Gover suggests OE *Healdtrēow-worð* 'shelter-tree curtilage'. An expression *healde treow* is found in an AS period (901 (e. c11)) document. Possibly the element is really *heald* 'leaning, sloping'. Otherwise uncertain.

Hamble (officially Hamble-Le-Rice)
1165, 1175 *Hamele*; 1368 *Hamele de Rys*; 1391 *Hamele in the Rice*.
The village is named from the river (c.750 *homelea*, 900 (e. c11) *hamele*), which is OE *Hamelēa* 'crooked (literally 'mutilated') river'. The allusion must be to the big bend at Bursledon. The qualifying phrase means '(in) the brushwood or undergrowth' (OE *hrīs*)).

Hambledon
956 (c12) (*to*) *hamelandunæ*; 1086 *Hamledune*.

There are a number of names of this or a similar form in England (Sr, Du, YNR (×2), R, Do, Nb, La, YWR). They are generally assumed to mean 'crooked hill' or 'scarred hill', the first element being OE *hamel* 'maimed'. (Cf. OHG *hamalscorro* 'collapsed cliff'.) The site of the village church suggests that Windmill Down is intended. Not connected with the river **Hamble**.

Hammond's Green District of Totton
On the site of *Hammond's Farm*. William *Hammon* lived in Eling in 1588.

Hampage Wood In Avington
1256 (*in bosco de*) *Hanepinge*; 1374 *Hampyng*.
A singular -*ing* derivative (possibly in an old locative case form) of OE *hænep* 'hemp', thus 'hemp-place'. It is not known whether other plants than hemp could be called by this name; hemp itself is an ancient introduction. For the variable application of plant-names, see Grigson (1959).

Hanger DB manor in Netley Marsh
1086, 1242 *Hangre*.
OE *hangra* 'sloping wood'.

Hannington Parish, and manor in Kingsclere
1023 (c12) *hanningtun*; 1086 *Hanitune*; 1164 *Hannintun*.
OE *Haningtūn* 'farm of Hana', an OE man's name meaning 'cock'. (There was a manor in adjacent Kingsclere called 1333 *Hannington Lancelevy*, 1586 *Hanyton Launces*, from the name of the tenant in 1333, John *Lancelevy* 'raised lance (AN)' (*VCH* IV: 258–9). There is a *Lance Levy Farm* in Sherfield-on-Loddon.)

Harbridge Shrunken village, parish united with Ibsley
1086 *Herdebrige*; 1236 *Hardebrigge*; 1248 *Harding(e)brigge*.
OE *Heardanbrycg* or *Heardingbrycg* 'Hearda's bridge'.

Hardley Farm/hamlet in Fawley
1086 *Hardelie*; 1324 *Hardele*.
OE *Heardan lēa* '(at the) hard wood/clearing', presumably as distinct from the marsh to the E and W of the site.

Harestock Hamlet in Littleton, now suburb of Winchester
854 (c12) (*to*) *heafod stoccan* (in bounds of Headbourne Worthy); 909 (c11) (*to*) *heafod stoccum* (in bounds of Chilcomb); 961 (c12) (*of þam*) *heafod stoccam* (in bounds of Easton).
These are all boundary marks in adjacent parishes; clearly something very conspicuous is denoted. We probably have OE *hēafodstoccas*,

once said to mean 'posts on which criminals' heads were exposed'. Gallows and similar gruesome objects give rise to parish names in e.g. *Worgret* (Do), *Warter* (YER, from *weargrōd, weargtrēow* 'gallows').

Harewood Forest
1198 *Harewode*.
Probably OE **Haranwudu* 'hare's wood', specifying the main object of the hunt. But in 1238 we have (uniquely) *Horwud'*, suggesting 'hoar (grey, lichen-covered) wood'.

Harford or Hartford DB manor in Beaulieu
1086 *Hariforde*; 1247 *Hareford*.
Perhaps OE **Hāranforde* '(at the) grey ford', but *hār* appears only to mean 'lichen-covered'. Otherwise **Haranford* 'hare's ford'.

Hartford Bridge Hamlet in Elvetham
1327 *Hertford(brigge)*.
ME 'bridge at *Hertford*', meaning 'hart (mature male red deer) ford'. The bridge presumably superseded the ford. The name of the river *Hart* is a modern back-formation from either this name or **Hartley Wintney** nearby.

Hartley Maudit or Mauditt
1086 *Herlege*; 1212 *Hertlie*; 1242 *Hurtlye*.
OE **Heorotlēah* 'hart (mature male red deer) wood/clearing'. The feudal specifier appears in the late c13, but William *Maudoit* ('badly brought up') held land here as early as DB. It distinguishes this place from **H. Wespall** and **Wintney**.

Hartley Wespall
1156 (*apud*) *Heortlegam* (preserving an archaic spelling); 1086 *Herlei, Harlei*; 1236 *Hertlegh*.
OE **Heorotlēah* 'hart (mature male red deer) wood'. Distinguished from **H. Wintney** and **Maudit** as c.1270 *Hertlegh Waspail*, from the AN family name of the tenant in 1236.

Hartley Wintney
1218 *Hertlega*; 1228 *Hurtlegh*.
OE/ME 'hart (mature male red deer) wood' (cf. **Hartley Maudit** and **Wespall**). Early in the c13 the place is distinguished as 1236 *Minechenherteleye* 'nuns' Hartley', 1270 *Hurtle Monialum* 'clerical Hartley', from the nunnery Wintney Priory in the same parish. The name of the priory was later applied instead. *Wintney* (1139x1161 (1337) *Winteneia*) appears to mean 'Winta's island', i.e. 'Winta's raised land in marsh'.

Haslar

1292 *Haselhorde*; c.1400 *Hasilhorde.*

OE **Hæselord* 'hazel point'; the point (cf. **Spithead**) juts into Portsmouth Harbour. Later spellings show confusion with ME *worth* 'curtilage'; some SCy dialects lose *w* before round vowels and show *d* for ME *th*.

Hat or **Hatt**

Found in several names in the New Forest for a small tree-crowned hill, e.g. *Kings Hat Inclosure* and *Crabhat Inclosure* in Dibden Purlieu (1789 *Crabtree Hat*); a list is given by Sumner (1972: 69). Beyond the Forest there is also *Hatt Hill* in Mottisfont. For another New Forest term see **Inclosure**.

Hatch Warren DB manor in Cliddesden

1086 *Heche*; 1212 *Hache*; 1302 *Hacche.*

OE *hæcc* 'gateway', to what is uncertain. The nearest PN hinting at forest is **Waltham**, **North** just over 3 miles to the SW.

Hatherden Hamlet in Andover

1193 *Heðerden*; 1269 *Haytherdene*; 1280 *Hetherdene.*

Perhaps OE **Hægþorndenu* 'hawthorn valley', i.e. the dry valley debouching at Charlton. ME *hethere* 'heather' can hardly be envisaged on the chalk here.

Havant Liberty

935 (c12) (*æt*) *hamanfuntan*; 1086 *Havehunte*; c.1170 *Hauunta*; 1256 *Hafhunte.*

'Hāma's spring'. OE *funta* usually means a spring in some way Romanized; the word is, indirectly, a borrowing from Latin *fontāna*. Havant, along with **Fontley** and **Boarhunt**, is in a hydrologically remarkable area. The chalk which forms the ridge of Portsdown is here overlain by Eocene Beds, and when the chalk is bored into through these beds artesian fountains may occur (Cole 1985: 6). One such fountain, or one of the copious springs in the area, may be referred to by the name. It may be the *Home Well*, whose name may be related to the place-name. *Hāma* is a derivative of the element *Hām-* or *Hæm-*, frequent in personal names.

Hawkley

1207 *Hauecle*; 1234 *Haveclige*; 1248 *Hauekele.*

OE/ME *Hafoclēah* 'hawk clearing or pasture'. Hawks hunt in open land rather than woods, thus less likely 'hawk wood'.

Hawley Modern parish carved out of Yateley

1248 *Halely*; 1248 *Hallee*; 1280 *Hallegh.*

In view of the absence of early spellings, what follows is uncertain. Perhaps OE/ME *Healhlēah or *Hēalalēah 'clearing or meadow of the nook(s)'. The word *healh* was often used of an outlying end of a parish; the situation of Hawley in relation to Yateley is comparable to that of *Tottenham Hale* in relation to Tottenham (Mx). This fact also makes it eligible to include *hēalas* in the sense of 'dry ground in marshes' (of the river Blackwater). It is also adjacent to the long-established county boundary between Hampshire and Surrey, a further application of the term *healh* being 'projecting corner of an administrative unit'. There is a slight blip in the river boundary near Hawley Park. On all this see Gelling (1984: 100–11).

Hayling Island, North and South Hayling

956(c12)(to) heglingaigæ,(to) hæglingaiggæ; 1086 Helingey, Halingei; 1139x42 Hailinges; 1242 Heling, Heyling'; 1261 Helinghey; 1316 Hayling.

The island was originally OE *Hægelinga īeg 'island of the Hægelingas'. This seems to have been a folk-name based on an unattested, personal name *Hægel*. (This, if real, might have been a pet-form of one of the men's names in *Hēah-*.) The form *Hailinges* suggests either that the folk-name denoted the place, as in the case of *Hastings* (Sx); or that the place was named in the plural in ME for the two parishes of Hayling, called in medieval times *Northwode* and *Southwode*. The disappearance of the woodland may account for the modern replacement names *North* and *South Hayling*.

Hazeley and Hazeley Heath Hamlets in Mattingley

1167 Heyshulla; 1317 Hayshull; 1506 Heysull hethe; 1586 Hesill.
OE/ME 'brushwood hill'. OE *hēse* 'brushwood' is well attested in the SCy. The universal early *u* forms in the second element are rather unusual; some *e* and *i* forms are expected. The modern *-ley* ending is a rationalization of c17 spellings in *-le*, presumably really representing the sound in *handle*.

Headbourne Worthy
See **Worthy**.

Headley

c.1190 Hetliga; 1242 Hetle; 1248 Hedlegh; 1269 Hethleghe.
OE *Hǣðlēah 'heath clearing'. The place is on the sandy Bagshot Beds and there is heather enough here still. *Headley Down* is on the hill east of the village.

Headley Common and hamlet in Kingsclere
1759 Headley Common.

See **Headley**.

Heath End In Baughurst and Tadley
OS 1:50000. S.-e. There are several *heath* names adjacent, e.g.
Headley and *West Heath* in Baughurst. The place lies at the N
extremity of the Bagshot Sands.

Heckfield
1207 *Hechfeld*; 1208 *Hecfeld*; 1272 *Heghfeud*; 1280 *Heggefeld*.
This name has been subject to alternative, and parallel, developments.
It could be (and was taken in 1280 to be) 'hedge open land', but
that does not make good sense. Many medieval and later forms
suggest OE **Hēahfeld* 'high open land', which does. But there are
persistent spellings suggesting that the final *h* ([x]) of the first
element became [k], and that *Heckfeld* and *Highfield* competed
right down to modern times. Today the village is *Heckfield*, but
we find *Highfield House* (possibly a revived name) right in its
historic centre.

Hedge End Modern parish carved out of Botley
1759 *Cutt Hedge End*; 1826 *Hedge Ends*.
S.-e. The oldest record suggests a hedge trained, or laid, as a
boundary.

Hengistbury Head West arm of Christchurch Harbour
t. Hy I *Hedenesburia*; t. Hy VII *Ednesbury*.
OE **Heddinesburh* 'fort of Heddin'. The same name is found in a
document of 877 (c12) (Sawyer 1277), from Nursling, in the PN
hedenesdene. A continental relative also appears in the name of the
Baltic island *Hiddensee*, for which there is Norse saga evidence.
Renaissance antiquaries preferred *Hengest*, a relatively known
quantity (1611 *Hengestbury heade*).

Hensting Farm in Owslebury (and now hamlet in Colden
Common)
970 (c12) *hefesylting*; 1208 *Hevenstigge*; 1231 *Hevelesting*'; 1350
Havelestyng, Hevelestynche.
The OE form is out of line with later ones. That of 1231 is typical,
suggesting that *l* and *s* have been transposed in Sawyer 827 in the
act of copying. Ekwall (1962) tries to derive the name from **sielting*
'salt-place, salt-lick', which is topographically highly unlikely (the
place is not adjacent to tidal marshes) and leaves the first element
unaccounted for (Ekwall flounders about with a supposed personal
name). Gover leaves the question of interpretation severely alone.
   Although one might have expected more medieval spellings with

a in the first syllable (the form of 1350 is unique), it appears to be a singular *-ing* derivative of OE *hæfelēast* 'want, poverty'. It is therefore conceivable that it is the last trace of a lexicalized derivative showing double *i-* umlaut caused by the *-ing* suffix (cf. *Swaythling* below), i.e. **hefelīesting* 'poverty-place', in which case the first vowel would be expected to be *e*, and the vowel of the penultimate syllable of the OE record acquires extra significance: perhaps we have West Saxon *y* for *ie*. The later spellings with *n* for *l* are due to assimilation to the nasal consonant in the final syllable. Reduced forms akin to the shape of the modern name are found from the sixteenth century onwards: 1534 *Henstyng*, 1759 *Henstead*.

The name is therefore highly unusual; such derivatives of abstract nouns are all but unknown in English toponymy. The original farm is in Owslebury on the soils of the Andover-1 association. These soils are thin and fertile but potassium-deficient when newly broken in; barley may suffer from magnesium deficiency too (Jarvis *et al.* 1984: 84). Their agricultural quality may be further indicated by the fact that much of the parish in medieval times was episcopal rabbit-warren, and therefore not prime arable land. These soil characteristics may account for the name.

Herriard

c.1160 *Herierd*; 1236 *Hereyerd*.

There are occasional spellings with *h* in the second element (1269 *Hereyherd*), but the name is fairly clearly OE **Heregeard* 'army yard or enclosure'. Although in use as a personal name element, the word *here* was not a flattering one by later OE times; the *Laws of Ine* define it as a band of more than 35 robbers, and it is the normal word for the dreaded Danish host. What events are commemorated by this PN is not known for certain. But intriguingly, the *OE Chronicle* (Ā and E versions) records that in 851 [850] '[the heathen, i.e. the Danes] went south over Thames into Surrey; and king Æthelwulf and has son Æthelbald, with the West Saxon levies, fought against them at *Āclēah*, and there was the greatest slaughter of a heathen host that we have ever heard tell of, and there won the victory' (Garmonsway's translation of the E-text). Recent historians have declined to identify *Āclēah*; it is certainly not Ockley (Sr), as once thought. There is an **Oakley** about six miles NW of Herriard, and it is tempting to wonder whether we should look beyond Surrey, into north Hampshire, for the site of Æthelwulf's famous victory, as argued by e.g. Baring (1907). (Not too much should be read, however, into the existence of *Battle Down Farm* in East Oakley, on record since the c14. This contains a French word, and probably refers to the site of juridical battles (cf. *Battles Piece*, a field in Bishop's Sutton). It is not likely to allude to a memory of the c9 battle.)

If Herriard was not the site of the Danish or English camp in 851, it may have been that of 871 [870], when the Danes defeated the Saxon levies at Basing, about 6 miles away (cf. **Lickpit/Lychpit**)

Highclere
See **Clere**.

Highcliffe Modern parish carved out of Christchurch
1759 *High Clift*.
S.-e. Referred to earlier as 1610 *Black Cliffe*. In the same area was 1575 *Cliffe parke*.

Highfield In Southampton
Takes its name from an c18 mansion.

Hill In Southampton
Hulle in 1358, *Hill* in 1488x1490. A s.-e. name for the long climb up to Southampton Common, which is followed by *Hill Lane*.

Hill Brow In Liss
S.-e. The place is on an elongated ridge followed by the Sx boundary.

Hill Head In Stubbington
Neither the hill nor the head are very obvious. There are l. c14 mentions of hills in the parish, however.

Hilsea
1236 *Helesye*; 1248 *Hulleseie*; 1259 *Heleseye*.
Ekwall is probably right in suggesting that this is OE *Hylesieg 'holly island', though relatives of the supposed word are known only in the continental Germanic languages. Since holly (*Ilex aquifolium*) prefers chalk, there may be a reference to sea-holly (*Eryngium maritimum*). *Īeg* may also mean 'raised land in marsh' which would suit here though the rise is not large.

Hiltingbury Suburb of Chandler's Ford
1233 *Hiltyngebury*; 1280 *Heltyngbur'*; 1447 *Hultyngbery*.
Apparently OE *Hyltingaburh 'fortification or manor-house of the Hyltingas', a tribal name meaning 'dwellers at the *hylte* or woodland. This is highly doubtful both topographically and histori-cally, but the rare element *hylte* is found also in **Shirrell Heath** A safer etymology might involve a ME formation meaning 'manor-house (i.e. the former *Hiltonbury*, OS 1:63 360) at *Hyltinge*' a PN

fossilized in the dative case and meaning 'at the woodland'.

Hinchelsea or **Hincheslea** Pre-DB manor, house in Rhinefield
1086 *Hincelveslei*; 1331 *Hinchalvesle*.
OE **Hindcealfes lēah* 'hind-calf (immature female red deer) wood/
clearing'. Ekwall pointed out in a letter to Gover that the skins of
these animals were once highly prized.

Hinton Admiral In Christchurch East
1086 *Hentune*; 1242 *Henton*; 1379 *Henton Aumarle*; 1412 *Henton Damarle*.
OE (*æt þām*) *hēan tūne* '(at the) high farm', possibly as seen from
Burton. It is on ground which falls gently away to the west. The
manorial specifier is in fact the surname *Albemarle*; Reginald de
Albemara held the manor in 1242. The modern perversion is first
seen in 1592 (*Hynton Admyral*). It is distinguished from **Hinton
Ampner** and **Hinton Daubeney**.

Hinton Ampner
1045 (c12) (*to*) *heantune*; 1086 *Hentune*.
OE 'high farm', in an oblique case-form. The place is on the western
end of a ridge overlooking the source of the river Itchen near
Cheriton. *Ampner* is added in Tudor times (1544 *Amner*), which
is a form of *almoner*. The manor was held by, and paid the expenses
of, the almoner of St Swithin's, Winchester.

Hinton Daubeney or **Daubnay** In Catherington
1167 *Hentona*; 1316 *Henton*.
For *Hinton* see **Hinton Admiral**. *Daubeney* is from the surname
d'Aubeney, likely to derive from the village of *Aubigny* near Falaise
in Calvados, Normandy (though this PN, from RB **Albiniacum*,
is common in France).

Hoburne DB manor in Highcliffe
1086 *Hoburne*; 1169 *Hoburna*; 1333 *Houburne*; 1810 *Hubborn*.
All spellings except one suggest OE *hōh* 'spur of land' as the first
element. Since there is no marked hill there, we should consider
relying on 1552 *Woburne*, a common stream-name representing
OE **Wōhburna* 'winding stream', as in *Woburn* (Bd). However,
there are no remarkable bends in the Bure Brook here.

Hoddington Domesday hundred, now house in Upton Grey
1046 (c16) *hodingatun*; 1204 *Hodingetun*.
OE 'farm of those associated with Hōda'.

Hoe Tithing of Meonstoke hundred in Soberton
In 1086 *Hou*; OE *hōh* 'heel, hillspur', i.e. the bold bluff above the
B2150.

Hoe, East DB manor in Soberton
1086 *Hou*; 1236 *Ho*.
OE *hōh* 'heel, spur of land'. The slight eminence separated by a
valley from Windmill Down in Hambledon must be meant.

Holbury Manor, now estate in Fawley
1186 *Holeberi*.
A moated site. The name, apparently OE (*æt ðǣre*) *holan byrig*, means
'(at the) hollow fortification', not clear in relation to what feature.

Holdenhurst
t. Hy I *Holeherst*; 1169 *Holehurst*; 1397 *Holnhurst*; 1409 *Hulnhurst*.
The later forms suggest OE **Holegnhyrst* 'wood(ed hill) marked
with holly'; but it is strange that there is no trace of the medial *-n-*
till the end of the c14. Perhaps the modern form of the word
without *-n-* was current early, and the two forms were in dialect
competition at some period. The forms with *d* do not appear til
the l. c18.

Holdshott Farm in Heckfield and hundred
1086 *Holesete* (hundred); 1167 *Holessieta* (hundred); 1209 *Holesset*
(farm).
OE *holan scīetan* '(at the) angle or nook in a hollow'. At the far
eastern end of Heckfield parish, but there is no obvious reason for
the first element. One might imagine the bed of the river Whitewater
as running in a slight hollow or gate between rising land in Heckfield
and Hazeley.

Holmsley Walk or **Holmesley Walk** Forest walk in Burley
The *holm*-names are a notorious problem, but often include ME
holm, a development of OE *holegn* 'holly', as is certain here (1371
Holneslegh, 1665 *Holmesley*). ME 'wood of (the) holly(-tree)'. The
nearby *Thorn Hill Holms* are dense holly-groves.

Holybourne Parish, suburb of Alton
1086, 1236 *Haliburne*.
OE **Hāligburna* 'sacred stream'. The stream rises by the church. In
medieval times it divided the two manors from each other
and they were known as 1333 *Halebourne Estebrouk* and 1390
Halibourne Westbrouk (cf. **Alton**).

94

Hook Modern parish carved out of Nateley Scures, Newnham and Odiham

1223 *Hoc.*

Originally applied to a wood, as often in Sr, this is OE *hōc*/ME *hōk* in a topographical sense like 'angle, nook'; Hook is on land between two left tributaries of the Whitewater. It grew around the site of the LSWR's station for Odiham.

Hook Parish near Titchfield

1086 *Houch*; 1236 *la Hok'*; 1242 *Hok.*

OE *hōc* 'spur of land', i.e. the one projecting into the marshes; or with reference to the small promontory at the mouth of the river Hamble.

Hordle

t. Hy I *Hordella*; t. Ste *Hordhulle*; 1331 *Hordehull, Hurdhill.*

OE **Hordhyll* '(treasure-)hoard hill'. The events which gave rise to this name are lost for ever. In English PNs, *hord* may be associated with words for barrows and supposedly haunted places. *Hyll* never appears to mean 'barrow'. More prosaically, there was an OE word *hordærn* 'storehouse'; this name may be elliptical for **Hord(ærn)hyll*, but that is pure speculation.

The name *Golden Hill* (OS 1:63 360) in the same parish is tantalizing, and its relation to the parish name is unknown. It may be a deliberate allusion to the fruits of PN research.

Horndean

1199, 1287 *Harmedene.*

OE **Hearmandenu* '(dor)mouse valley' or the valley of a person so called. The *Horn-* form is a modern rationalization; it is preceded by some Tudor/Stuart spellings with *-md-* assimilated to *-nd-*.

Hotlop Lost DB manor in Broughton hundred

Identified by *VCH* with Oakley in Mottisfont, but there are scarcely any linguistic grounds for this. Unexplained.

Houghton

982 (c12) (*be*) *hohtuninga* (*mearce*); 1171 *Hoghtone.*

OE **Hōhtūn* 'farm by the heel or spur', a common name-type. The projecting feature at Houghton church does not look significant, but there is a tongue of land jutting NE in the N of the parish towards Stockbridge. *Houghton Drayton* (1267 *Drayton*) contains an element, OE *dræg*, sometimes meaning 'portage'. A well-marked route, now with bridges, crosses the three branches of the Test here to King's Somborne where the hundred met. No ford is on record here, so goods would have to be manhandled to King's Somborne, not taken by cart, if the route via Horsebridge was to be avoided, twice the distance, round the far side of John of Gaunt's Deer-park. *Dræg* may, however, mean 'place where boats can be dragged up out of the water'. There is a further *Drayton* (995x1006) (c14) *Drægtune*) in Barton Stacey, where again the Test flows in several channels.

Hound

1086, 1176 *Hune*.

OE *hūne* 'hoarhound (Marrubium vulgare)', elliptically for a place where this plant grew. Cf. *Arundel* (Sx) 'hoarhound dell'. The headquarters of the Hampshire Police dog-handling squad are adjacent.

Houndmills District of Basingstoke

VCH (IV: 135) relates that one of the three Domesday Book mills of Basingstoke gave its name to the prominent landowning family of *Houndsmill*. On some maps the old name has been altered to the form shown in the heading, now appropriate in the sense that the area is an industrial estate.

Howe, East and West Locations in Kinson, now in Do

There is a dialect word *howe* 'enclosure', common in the eastern parishes of Do, and both these late names (1811) derive from it. (Cf. *PN Do* II: 8).

Hunton

909 (c11) (*in, to*) *hundatun*; c.965 (c12) *hundetun*.

OE 'dogs' farm', or possibly 'hounds' kennels' for the hunt in e.g. Harewood Forest. From Hunton to the forest is an easy ride on established (mainly Roman, Margary 422) roads.

Hurn Modern parish carved out of Christchurch, airport

1086 *Herne*; 1256 *Hyrne*; 1367 *la Hurne*.

OE *hyrne* 'angle, nook'. The vilage was in the NW of old Christchurch parish. The name has been prettified in the house-name *Heron Court* (1759 *Hern Court*).

Hursley

1167 *Herselega Episcopi*; 1171 *Hurseleye*.

Smith (*EPNE* I: 276) accepts Ekwall's suggestion that there was a lost OE form **hyrse* 'mare', which would account for this PN far better than *hors* 'horse'. Probably therefore OE **Hyrsanlēah* 'mare's clearing/wood'. It was part of the Bishop of Winchester's Merdon manor, hence *Episcopi*. *Merdon* (note also *Merdon Castle*) was 1138

Merdona, 1184 *Meredon*, apparently 'Mæra's hill' according to Gover, because it is on no known boundary (*gemære*) and there is no pond (*mere*) there. But why not from *miere* 'mare', confirming the parish name (the reason for the duplication being obscure) and accounting for the 1167 form *Merendon(a)* from *Mierenadūn 'hill of mares'?

Hurst Castle Fort in Milford-on-Sea

1543 *castle or fortress of Hurst.*

This Tudor fort stands on a spit of land which is likely to be referred to 1434 (*wreck off*) *Hurst*, 1539 (*an herd sand called*) *the Hurst*, this expression containing the dialect word *hurst* 'sandbank' which may be a partial assimilation of ON *hestR* in the same sense. Or it may be the common OE *hyrst* 'wooded eminence', originally applying to an adjacent coastal feature.

At the landward end of the split is *Sturt Pond*, which appears to contain an old name for a coastal feature here, OE *steort* 'tail, point of land', as in *Start Point* (D).

Hurstbourne Priors and Hurstbourne Tarrant Two parishes/ manors

786×793 (c13) (*juxta*) *Hissaburnam* (H. Tarrant) (Latin form); 873×888 (c11) (*on ðam*) *neoðeran hysseburnan* (H. Priors), (*æt*) *hysseburnan* (H. Tarrant); 900 (c11) (*be*) *hysseburnan* (H. Priors), (*to*) *hysseburnan* (H. Tarrant).

Either OE *Hysseburna 'tendril stream' (in relation to some unidentified water-plant, ?water crowfoot) or *Hyssa burna 'stream of the sons/youths'. Hurstbourne Priors is distinguished in AS times as 'Nether Hurstbourne', from being lower down what is now called the **Bourne Rivulet**. It is *Hurstbourne Priors* in 1167 (*Hesseburna Prioris*); it belonged to the prior of St Swithin's, Winchester. From 1602 it appears as *Down Hursborne*, 1707 *Down Husband*. Hurstbourne Tarrant is 1242 *Huphusseburn'*, and this name is current again later (1719, 1822 *Up Husband*). In the Middle Ages it was *Hurstbourne Tarrant*, as it is now, from being granted to Tarrant Abbey (Do) by Henry III. Its former royal ownership is remembered in 1291 *Husseburne Regis*, 1628 *Kings Hursborne*. The DB spelling *Esseborne* is revived in the name of a local hotel.

Hyde Abbey In Winchester

901 (e. c11) *monasterio Sanctae Trinitatis quod ... Novumque appellatur*; 964 (*of*) *niwan mynstre*; 1156 *Hida*; 1219 (*abbacia de*) *la Hyde*.

Originally in Latin *Novum Monasterium* and in English *Nīwe mynster* '(the) new monastery', the old one being the old St

Swithin's cathedral. The monastery was moved outside the city walls in the mid c12 and took its new name from a pre-existing PN. *Hīd* is a land-measure term of variable application (usually 100–120 acres) considered suitable for the upkeep of a (free) family. There may be some relation between this name and that of **Headbourne Worthy**.

Hythe Hamlet in Fawley, later in Dibden, now town
1248 (*la*) *Huthe*; 1422 *Heothe*.
OE *hȳð* 'landing-place, hythe, staithe'. It is on Southampton Water.

I

Ibsley Parish, united with Harbridge
1086 *Tibeslei*; 1166 *Tibesleia*; c13 *Ibeslehe*; 1236 *Ibbesleg'*.
OE 'Tibb(i)'s wood/clearing'. The man's name involved is unattested but corresponds regularly to *Tibba*, which may be a short-form of *Tīdbeorht*. The loss of *T-* is due to misdivision of the expression *at Tibsley*.

Ibthorpe Hamlet in Hurstbourne Tarrant
1236 *Ebbedrope*; 1269 *Ybethrop*, *Ebethrop*.
OE **Ibbanþrop* 'Ibba's secondary settlement'. The same personal name is found in **Ibworth** in Hannington.

Ibworth Hamlet in Hannington
1233 *Hibbewrth*; 1245 *Ibbewrth*.
OE **Ibbanwyrð* 'Ibba's curtilage'. It is 1650 *Ebworth Deane* from being close to **Deane**. Ibworth itself is on a hill.

Ickland Road
The Roman road from Winchester towards Cirencester (Margary 43) appears in some medieval records as c14 *Ikenyldewey* and the like, the name being borrowed from the real *Icknield Way* (partly Margary 333) in East Anglia, whose name is highly obscure. That name may have been purloined in the hope that the privileges of the latter, one of the royal highways, might accrue to the former. The modern name, corrupt, is found in 1795.

Idsworth
c.1170 *Hiddeswrthe*; c.1200 *Iddesworthe*; 1204 *Idesworð*.
OE **Iddeswyrð* 'Iddi's curtilage'. In 1256 we find the curious error *Iddlesworth*.

Inclosure
There are numerous places in the New Forest containing this element, always spelt with an *I-*; e.g. *Appleslade Inclosure* (Ellingham), *Wilverley Inclosure* (Rhinefield) and *Irons Hill Inclosure* in Denny Lodge parish. The inclosures themselves are unusual. The typical enclosure in the landscape is a marked-off piece of agricultural land with the woodland beyond the fence. The New Forest inclosures are pieces of managed woodland fenced off to keep the commoners' animals from grazing seedlings or browsing young growth. Enclosing portions of the royal forest was illegal for any reason till 1488, but Acts of that year, of 1698, 1808, 1949, etc.,

established and confirmed the practice in the interests of timber provision. Many inclosures were made especially after 1808 and in 1850–65, amounting to the legal maximum granted to the Crown of 16,000 acres. For another New Forest term see **Hatt**.

Inhurst In Baughurst
1236 *Hyneshurst*; 1256 *Ineshurst.*
Probably OE **Ineshyrst* 'Ine's wooded hill'. This name was borne by a king (688–726) of Wessex whose reign is documented in the *OE Chronicle*.

Ipley In Colbury
c.1210 *Huppeleia*; 1236 *Yppele, Ipelegh.*
OE **Yppelēah* 'dais or hunting-platform clearing'; it is in forest land. See Coates (1986).

Isington In Binstead
1269 *Esinton*; 1272 *Isynton.*
A medieval name apparently having its source in an OE personal name, but we cannot decide between *Ēsa* and *Īsa* on the evidence available. 'Ēsa's or Īsa's farm'.

Itchell Manor In Crondall
973 (c12) (*on*) *icæles* (*æwilmas*); 1086 *Ticelle*; 1165 *Hichelle*; 1208 *Ichulla*; 1236 *Ichille*; 1272 *Echehulle*; 1320 *Ychhulle.*
Later spellings suggest a compound involving 'hill', but the earliest form, '(to) the sources of *Icæl*', suggests a river-name, i.e. that of the stream that rises N of Itchel Home Farm. Whatever the origin of this, which is quite uncertain, it seems to share a root with **Itchen**. The name is pre-English, and must have passed through a PrW form **īgel.*

Itchen River, and modern parish carved out of St Mary Extra and others
1372 *Ichene juxta Southampton.*
The place is named from the river (701, 854 etc. (various prepositions) *icenan*)), which may appear as *Cenio* in the *Ravenna Cosmography* (cf. Coates 1981). The origin and meaning of this are unknown; it is pre-British. Cf. **Itchell Manor**.

Itchen Abbas
1086 *Icene*; 1167 *Ichene Monialum*; 1539 *Ichyn alias Abbesse Ichyn.*
The village takes its name from the river (q.v.). Historically it is *Abbess* Itchen; the manor was held by the superior of St Mary's Abbey, Winchester, in 1086. (Cf. **Leckford Abbas**.)

Itchen Stoke

1086 *Stoche*; 1185 *Ichenestoke.*

Itchen is absent in the earliest form, which arouses the suspicion that the place was originally a *stoc* or dependent farm of **Itchen Abbas**, which was merely *Icene* in DB.

J

John of Gaunt's Deer Park In King's Somborne
See **Danebury Hill**.

Jumpers Common Suburb of Christchurch
OS 1:63 360. No early spellings found. Apparently from a surname.

K

Kempshott Submember of Dummer parish, now district of Basingstoke

1086 *Campessete*; 1269 *Kembeschete*; 1280 *Kempeschotte*; 1346 *Kembeshute*.

Apparently OE **Cempan scēate* 'warrior's corner', with some c14 and later forms suggesting *sciete*, with the same meaning. It is common for *-shot* PNs in Hampshire to contain a plant-name as the first element (**Aldershot, Bramshott**), and this is what persuades Ekwall to suggest the first element is really OE *cenep* 'moustache' used as a plant-name. That is quite clearly what appears in the name of *Kempley* (Gl). The plant-name in question may alternatively be a loan from Latin *cannabis* 'hemp'. *Scēat* often means 'corner' in the sense of a projection of one administrative unit into another (**Aldershot, Grayshott**).

Keyhaven In Milford-on-Sea

c1170 *Kihavene*; 1228 *Kyhaven*.

OE **Cȳhæfen* 'cow('s) haven'. Precise implication unknown; a point of (dis)embarcation to/from the Isle of Wight for animals bound for markets?

Kilmeston or **Kilmiston**

961 (c12) (*to*) *cenelemestune*, (*æt*) *kenelmestune*.

OE 'Cœnhelm's farm'. *Cœnhelm* is an ordinary AS-period name, but there may be a connection with the cult of the boy-saint Kenelm. The modern pronunciation is indicated in the 1586 spelling *Kimpston* (1611 *Kimston*).

Kimbridge Hamlet in Mottisfont

1202 *Kinbrige*; 1218 *Kinebrige*; 1611 *Kimb bridge*.

Almost certainly contains OE *cyne-* 'royal'. Accordingly transformed to *King-* in the c13 (1236 *Kingebrigge*), but the historically authentic form prevails in the modern PN. Mottisfont was a pre-1066 royal manor.

Kimpton

1086 *Chementune*; 1167 *Keminton*; t. Hy III *Kumynton*; 1256 *Cyminton*.

OE **Cȳmantūn/*Cȳmingtūn* 'Cyma's farm'.

King John's Hill (1) in East Worldham, (2) in Kingsclere

Both these places are associated by tradition with John's hunting.

He is recorded as being at East Worldham twice in the first decade of the c13 (*VCH* II: 518), and certainly hunted in Freemantle Park, Kingsclere, where folklore places his lodge on the S slope of this hill. It is, or was, otherwise known as *Cottington Hill* after Lord Cottington of Hanworth, whose estate here was sequestered by Parliament in the Commonwealth (*VCH* IV: 252–3).

King's Enham
See **Enham**.

King's Furlong District of Basingstoke
1231 *Kyngesforlang*.
Basingstoke was a royal manor before and after 1066. Why a particular furlong of an open field should be so called is not known.

King's Garn Gutter Stream in Bramshaw
King's Gairn strem in 1670. The clue resides in *Hive Garn Gutter* in Fordingbridge. Sumner (1972: 23–4) recounts that Forest bee-keepers used to send their hives into the heaths during the time the heather was in flower, and these hives were ranged up in embanked enclosures so that the ponies would not disturb them. These enclosures Sumner calls *bee-gardens*. It becomes clear that *garn* is simply a reduced form of the word *garden* (cf. Cope 1883: 36). An **Inclosure** was planted at King's Garn in 1860. *Gutter* is a usual word in the north of the Forest for a stream. The form of 1670 suggests this is a fairly recent development.

King's Somborne and Little Somborne Two parishes
909 (c12) (*to*) *swinburnan*; 1086 *Sunburne*; 1155 *Sumburna*.
OE 'pig stream', a left tributary of the Test. A royal manor before and after 1066, distinguished as 1256 *Kynges-*, 1204 *Parva Sunburn'*. Higher up the valley is the hamlet of *Up Somborne* in King's Somborne (1167 *Opsunburna*).

King's Worthy
See **Worthy**.

Kingsclere
See **Clere**.

Kingsley
c.1210 *Kyngesly*; 1256 *Kyngesle*.
OE/ME 'king's wood'. It is not mentioned in DB, but it may be worth noting that the adjacent East Worldham was held by Alwin of King Edward before 1066.

Kingston In Ringwood
1280 *Kyngeston.*
'King's farm'. Ringwood was a royal demense in DB. There is
another Kingston in Portsmouth (1202 *Kingest'*, 1586 *Kinkeston*),
but its royal connections are uncertain in its manorial history.

Kinson Suburb of Bournemouth, formerly in Do, now returned
to Do
1086 *Chinestanestone*; 1230 *Kenstaneston.*
OE 'Cynestān's farm'.

Knapp DB manor in Christchurch
1086 *Chenep*; t. Hy II *Knep*; 1227 *Cnappe.*
OE *cnæpp* 'hillock'.

Knight's Enham
See **Enham**.

Knowl or **Knowle** Farm, DB manor in Kingsclere
1086 *Chenol*; 1272 *Knolle.*
OE *cnoll* 'mound, rounded hill', i.e. with reference to *Great Knowl
Hill*, NE of Kingsclere. See also **Sandford**.

L

Laffan's Plain Parade ground in Aldershot
Named after Lt.-Gen. Sir Robert Laffan (1821–82), former Commanding Royal Engineer of Aldershot, who was responsible for some landscaping at the Camp. The spot was formerly called *Queen's Birthday Parade.*

Lainston House in Sparsholt
1252 *Layneston*; 1256 *Leneyston*; 1280 *Lewyneston.*
Possibly OE/ME 'Lēofwine's farm', but the spelling of 1280 pointing in this direction is isolated. Otherwise maybe contains ME *leyne* and amounts to 'farm of the (arable) great field', but the implications of that are unclear. *Leyne* is found in K and Sx.

Landport In Portsmouth
The area beyond the old town walls to landward was reached through the (1745) *Land Port Gate*, either the 'landward town-gate' or the 'gate called Land-Gate'.

Langley DB manor in Fawley
1086 *Langelie.*
OE 'long wood', in view of 1298 *boscus de Langele*. There is another *Langley* in Colbury (1236 *Langele*).

Langrish Modern parish carved out of East Meon
1236 *Langerishe*; 1245 *Langrix.*
OE *Langa--risc* '(the) long rush-bed', the word for 'rush-bed' appearing in the c13 in either of the dialect forms *rish, rix* from OE *risc, rix* (cf. *Sharprix*, under **Lisle Court**). The rushes grew in a headwater of the river western Rother.

Langstone Harbour
Named from *Langstone* in Havant (1307 *Langestone*), 'long stone'. The reason for the application of this name is unknown.

Lansdowne Hill In Southampton
Commemorates the second Marquis of Lansdowne (held the marquisate 1805–9), who developed the old castle site with a sham Gothic affair pulled down after his death. This event was among those marking the end of the pretensions of Southampton as a select spa; cf. **Polygon**.

Larkwhistle
See **Laverstoke**.

Lasham

1174 *Lasham*; 1195 *Lessham*; 1200 *Lesham*; c.1270 *Lassham*.
I cannot improve on Ekwall's alternative suggestions (1) OE *Læsshām* 'smaller estate', (2) *Lēaxanhām* 'estate of Lēaxa', the man's name appearing in a pet-form *Lēassa*. Against (2) is the frequency of forms with no medial syllable. Suggestion (1) is plausible from the viewpoint of Odiham, because Lasham is a detached part of Odiham hundred. Like Odiham, it was a pre-Conquest royal estate.

Laverstoke

1086 *Lavrochestoche*; 1155x1158 *Laverchestoch*; 1219 *Laverstok*; 1236 *Laverkestoke*; 1378 *Larkstoke*.
OE *Lāfercestoc* 'lark dependent farm'. In OE the word for 'lark' unaccountably varies between *lāferce*, *lǣwerce* and *lāwerce*. We have the first here. A *stoc* was a secondary or dependent settlement, sometimes having religious connections (cf. Ekwall, *DEPN*: 443, Smith, *EPNE* II: 153–6), and in ME at the latest developing the more general meaning '(inhabited) place'. It is not known precisely what sense of *stoc* is intended here. It is remarkable that the name seems to recur three further times: *Laverstock* (W), *Laverkestoke/- stou* (now *Langley* (Bk)) and *Lark Stoke* (Gl). One would expect the present name to be like the Gl one (cf. the form of 1378); the pronunciation of the modern name seems to derive from the written tradition. There are several minor places called *Larkwhistle* in Hampshire, e.g. in Wonston; the name is said to signify a lonely spot.

Leckford

947 (c14) (*to*) *leahtforda, leghford*; 1086 *Lechtford*.
Ekwall, following Bradley (1928), guesses that there was an OE word *lēaht* 'irrigation channel, side-channel', using comparative evidence from Flemish (cf. the Belgian PN *Anderlecht*). As such it would probably be the ancestor of ModE *leat*. The change of [x] to [k] before certain consonants is met elsewhere; cf. e.g. **Heckfield**. The Test flows in multiple streams here, and flooding is held in check by a complex array of sluices. It may well have been artifically controlled from a very early date. Probably therefore 'leat ford'.

A farm in the parish is occasionally referred to as *Leckford Abbas*. This was a grange of St Mary's, Winchester, here (1563 *Lecforde Abbisse*). The masculine form *Abbas* is misleading (cf. **Itchen Abbas**).

Lee Tithing of Romsey

Since *Lee* PNs are scattered for quite some distance S of Romsey, *la Legh* of 1256 is probably to be taken as 'wood' rather than 'clearing'.

Lee-on-the-Solent In Crofton
1242 *la Lye.*
Cf. **Leigh** in Havant. See also **Solent**. The last three words were only added when the resort developed about a century ago.

Leigh In Havant
1236 *la Lye*; 1280 *la Lygh.*
OE *lēah*, here possibly in the sense 'tract of ancient woodland', i.e. part of Bere Forest, or in the sense 'clearing-settlement' within it. The element *lēah* is discussed at length by Gelling (1974 and 1984: 198–207), Johansson (1975); see introduction.

Lepe Hamlet in Exbury and Lepe
1277 *Lepe*; 1280 *Lupe*; 1324 *Leope.*
OE *hlīep(e)* 'leaping place', especially for deer; a fence to allow deer to jump where other animals are restrained, i.e. kept out of deer reserves. A common name-type in forest areas. Possibly a jumpable stream, or other such crossing-place.

Lickpit or Lychpit Farm in Basing
945 (c14) *licepyt*; 1086 *Lichepet*; 1236 *Likeputte.*
From OE *līcapytt* 'corpse-pit'. Early spellings point to an analogical palatalized genitive plural of *līc*, viz. **līcea*, unless the *e* simply marks the palatality of the *c* in the nominative case form *līc*. The source of the corpses is unknown; Gover suggests it was a plague-pit, but local tradition associates it with the aftermath of the Danish victory at the battle of Basing in 871.

Lindford In Headley
1269 (*pontem de*) *Linford*; 1298 *Lyngfordes(brygge)*; 1300 *Lymfordes(brigge).*
Uncertain because of the variability in the first element. Maybe 'ford associated with *Linstead*', another small place in Headley, which is (1280 *Lindsted'*) 'lime-tree place'.

Linkenholt
1086 *Linchehou*; c.1145 *Lynkeholt*; 1289 *Lynkenøld.*
OE **Hlincenholt*. This seems to mean 'managed woodland on a terrace or bank' (**hlincen* 'of terraces'). DB explicitly mentions that the manor has woodland for fencing (*silua ad clausuram*). There are some strange Tudor-period instances of assimilation of *l* to *n* (e.g. 1579, 1593 *Nyncknoll, Ninckenholt*) reminiscent of early medieval French renderings of the name of *Lincoln*.

Grundy demonstrated (1927: 281–3) that Linkenholt was probably included in the place called *Æscmere* in a document of 866×867.

Liphook Hamlet of Bramshott, now village
1364 *Leophok*; 1404 (*atte*) *Lepok*; 1421 *Lepook, Lippuck*.
Gover suggests on the basis of personal names found in the manorial rolls of Chiltlee that the place had, in the c14, the alternative names *Lepe* and *Lepehoc* 'the leap' (cf. **Lepe**) and 'spur at the leap'. If this is right, the 'leap' would have been over the headwater of the Wey at or near where the modern A3 crosses it; he takes the 'leap' to have been a stream-crossing. Ekwall suggests the same elements but translates 'deer-leap enclosure', citing ME *inhoc* 'enclosure'. The detailed interpretation is thus still uncertain. cf. also **Hook**

Lisle Court House in Boldre
So called 1759, an antiquarian revival of the name of the family who held it in 1331. The place was earlier *Sharprix* (t. John *Scherperyxe*, 1306 *Scherperishe*, 1242 *Sharprixe*), OE **Scearpan risce/rixe* '(at the bed of) sharp rushes'.

Liss or **Lyss**
1086 *Lis*; 1174 *Lissa*; 1175 *Lisse*.
A Celtic name, Brit. **lisso-* or PrW **lis* (W *llys*) 'palace, large estate, main place in a district' (cf. Jackson 1953: 285). It is not known what administrative set-up is referred to. The spelling in *y*, common into the c19, is now obsolete, but preserved in the name of *Lyss Place*. The tithing *Lisse Torney* recorded in 1586 represents a misdivision of **Liss Sturmy*, from the family of the holder of part of the manor in 1323. Liss Abbots (1413 *Lysse Abbatisse*) recalls that the nunnery of St Mary's, Winchester, held the manor before 1066 and subsequently.

Liss Forest District of Liss
Occupies the SW corner of **Woolmer Forest**.

Litchfield
1168 *Lieueselva*; 1212 *Livesulve, Lidesull'*; 1219 *Lidescelve*; 1238 *Lidesulve*; c.1270 *Ludeshulve*; 1291 *Leveshulle*.
The second element is clearly OE *scylf(e)* 'terrace, shelf'; *field* is not found till 1539 (*Lychefeld*). What the shelf might be topographically is unclear, for Litchfield is in a rather narrow dry valley debouching into that of the upper Test. The valley broadens a little just above the church. The first element can scarcely be OE *hlīf* in any sense derived from *hlīfian* 'to overhang'; a vaguer sense of 'protection' may be appropriate to the site, if the fact of its being

in a valley is sufficient. The spellings in *d*, more frequent but on the whole later than those in *v*, suggest OE *hlid*, *hlið* 'slope', but we may have *hlid* 'lid' in the application 'gate', for the valley mentioned in the pass connecting the Kennet and Test valleys.

Having said all this, though, the first element appears to descend from *(h)lȳf-*, not a form in *-i-*; no element of this shape is known. Maybe we have the *hlȳwe* found in two AS charter boundaries from Ha (Sawyer catalogue nos. 944 and 1013 (South Stoneham and Hoddington)). It is held to mean 'sheltered place' (Smith, *EPNE*: I, 254). Either it shows the same alternation that is seen in *lāwerce*, *lāferce* 'lark' (see **Laverstoke**); or the *u/v* actually represents [w] not [v]. Possibly this most problematic name is thus *Hlȳwanscylf(e)*, *Hlȳfanscylf(e)* 'shelter shelf', with later reinterpretation of the obscure first element. A further possibility would be *Lēofesscylf(e)* 'Lēof's shelf', though this does not explain the early *i*'s so well. The modern name appears, unaccountably, to have been influenced by that of *Lichfield* (St).

Seven miles away in Ashe is *Litchfield Grange*. The original name of this place is 1033 *wutinga scylf*, 1147 *Nutesceolvam* (Latin form), t. Ric I *Nuttesself*, i.e. OE *Hnutuscylf(e)* 'nut(-tree) shelf'. The first form is corrupt. It is curious that its modern name has been influenced by the only other *scylf(e)* name in the district, after it was no longer recognizable as such. See further under **Nursling**.

Litchfield Grange Farm in Ashe
See **Litchfield** and **Nursling**.

Little Ann
See **Abbot's Ann**.

Littleton
1171 *Litletone*; 1205 *Litleton*.
OE/ME 'little farm', probably by contrast with the nearby Worthy and Barton estates in royal and episcopal ownership. A DB manor of the same name is recalled by *Littleton Copse* in Kimpton.

Lockerley
1086 *Locherlega*; 1194 *Lokerlay*; 1271 *Lockerleye*.
Probably contains the OE ancestor of ME *lōkere* '"looker"', i.e. 'keeper/shepherd'; thus maybe 'shepherds' clearing/wood'.

Loddon River
1227 (*aqua de*) *Lodene*; 1272 *Ledene*; 1279 *Lodre*.
Since Ekwall (1928), said to be from a British *lutnā* (*abonā* 'river' understood) 'muddy'. There are fair Celtic parallels, but no RB

name certainly contains such a word and it has no existing derivatives in Welsh. If the 1272 spelling were correct, we would not hesitate to derive it from PrW *lidā̆n 'broad', topographically not unreasonable for parts of the river. But this spelling is isolated.

Lomer Farm, DB, manor in Exton

802×839 (c12) (to) lammæres (geate); 959×975 (copy) (to) lammære; 1086 Lammere.

Probably OE 'loam pond', despite the AS-period æ in the second element.

Long Sutton

979 (c12) suðtun; 1086 Sudtone; 1234 Lang Sutton.

OE 'south farm', from being south of the ancient royal manor of Odiham. Long distinguishes it from **Sutton Scotney** and **Bishop's Sutton**. It may suggest that the hamlet first straggled along the road from Four Lanes' End to Well.

Longham Hamlet in Hampreston (Do), formerly a detached part of Ha

OE/ME 'long hemmed-in place'; it is a hamm-1 site in a bend of the river-Stour. Returned to Do by the Act of 1844.

Longmoor Army camp in Greatham

1298 Longemore.

OE/ME *Langmōr 'long moor or marsh'. The area is marked by streams in shallow valleys, and there is a marshy area at Woolmer Pond nearby (cf. **Woolmer Forest**).

Longparish

1389 Langeparisshe.

The place was originally Middleton, first mentioned 1019 (c14) (be) middel hæma (mearc) 'near the boundary of the people of Middle(ton)', whose name survives as that of a hamlet in the parish. Three hamlets called tūn are strung out along the river Test: Easton (1256 Estetun) 'east of the farm' or 'east farm', Middleton and Forton (1228 Forton) 'ford farm'. The old name is thus s.-e. Considering all this, the modern name is also s.-e.

Longstock

982 (c12) (æt) stoce; 1086 Stoches; 1233 Langestok.

Originally OE stoc 'dependent farm'; it is not known where it was dependent upon (Stockbridge?). It straggles along a road closely following the 40m contour line. There is no other Stoke name close by, but there are numerous others further afield in Hampshire, and the later name looks like one devised by central administration (the first record of the longer name is in a Close Roll).

Lordship Tithing of Kingsclere hundred
See **Parsonage**.

Lovedean
c.1350 *Levedene*; 1422 *Loveden*.
OE/ME *Lēofandenu* 'Lēofa's valley'. If the first spelling is a mistake for *Love-* (two other c15 mentions show *o*), possibly 'love valley', a name for a suitably secluded place. The place is at the mouth of a narrow notch in the 250ft contour-line.

Ludshott DB manor, common in Bramshott
1086 *Lidessete*; 1230 *Ledessete*; t. Hy I *Ludeschate*; 1356 *Lydshute*. Smith (*EPNE* I: 254) conjectures an OE word or name for a stream *hlȳde* 'the loud one' (cf. **Lyde**); a form of this shape will account for the first element. The second is *scēat* 'nook, angle'. But no other case is known of *scēat* preceded by an ancient PN. The typical name has a tree- or plant-name in first place. No plant-name (*h*)*lȳde* is known.

Lunways Inn In Micheldever
Enshrines the medieval name of the Winchester to London Roman road, Margary 42a, by which it stands, viz. *Lunden*(*e*)*weie*.

Lyde Stream, right tributary of the Loddon
1262 *la Lude*.
Probably from OE *hlȳde* 'torrent', according to Ekwall; a derivative of *hlūd* 'loud'. (Cf. **Ludshott**.)

Lymington Borough
t. Hy I *Lemynton, Limneton, Limenton*(*a*); 1185 *Limington*; 1196 *Liminton*; c.1210 *Lemeton*.
Appears to have as its first element the river-name found in that of the eastern Rother (Sx; 697 *liminaea*) and others (see *Leam, Lymn* in *DEPN*). The river in question has been known as the *Boldre* for probably 600 years or more (see **Boldre**), but there is no bar to an older label of this type. Thus OE 'farm by the river Limen' (or the like). This river-name has excited some controversy (Rivet and Smith 1979) about whether it derives from PrW *lēm*, the source of Welsh *llwyf* 'elm'. This, the traditional view, still seems best, but Jackson (1953) guardedly gives no translation of the element seen in *Limen*. Association between words for trees and river-names are commonplace, e.g. the various *Derwents* and PrW *derw-* 'oak'.

Lyndhurst

1086 *Linhest*; 1165 *Lindeherst*; 1196 *Lindhurst*.

OE *Lindhyrst 'lime wood'. Other references to the tree can be found in this district, e.g. *Linwood* in Broomy Walk (c.1170 *Lyndewode*), *Linford* in Ringwood (961 (*on*) *lind ford*). The native limes are 'almost absent from southern England' (Rackham 1980: 237), and have disappeared from Lyndhurst because of soil impoverishment or wood-pasture effects in forest areas (Rackham 1980: 242). Lime tends to form stands, and Lyndhurst probably therefore had a lime wood rather than a wood with a prominent lime.

M

Malshanger House in Oakley
1390 *Mailleshangre*; 1399 *Maleshanger*.
The first element appears to be a ME surname of AN origin; the second is from OE *hangra* 'sloping wood'. The site is that of the DB manor *Gerlei* (1167 *Gerdelai*, 1272 *Yerdeley*, from OE *Gierdalēah* 'wood where yards or spars were got').

Mapledurham DB manor in Buriton
1086 *Malpedresham*; 1217 *Mapeldereham*.
OE *Mapuldorhām* 'maple-tree estate'. Maple is widespread but not common in unmixed woods (Rackham 1980: 207), and prefers clay soils (cf. **Mapleham** and **Mapledurwell**), though Rackham says it is 'unusually and significantly abundant in the coppices of those few forests that are on calcareous soils'. Buriton on the Chalk. It is 'near its climatic limit' in present-day England. Its botanical record in ancient times is very thin, despite often occurring in the charter and PN record. This PN recurs in O.

Mapledurwell
1086 *Mapledrewell*; 1183 *Mapeldurewelle*.
OE *Mapuldorwiell(e)* 'maple-tree spring'. The river Lyde rises close to the church. Gover points out that the tree may be mentioned in the OE bounds (1046) of the adjacent parish of Upton Grey, where we meet the phrase *on mapoldre get* 'to mapletree gate'. However this does not square with Grundy's topographical description (1927, under *Upton Grey*). Cf. previous entry.

Mapleham Lost DB manor in the New Forest
Clearly OE *Mapulham(m)* 'maple estate or hemmed-in land'. Location not known. Cf. **Mapledurham**.

Marchwood
1086 *Merceode*; 1254 *Merchewude*.
OE *merecewudu* 'smallage (wild celery) wood' seems more likely than *Mierc(e)a wudu* 'wood of Mercians'; but note the problem concerning the not far distant parish of **Fawley**. Smallage prefers wet ditches, usually near the sea; Marchwood is appropriately placed.

Martin Formerly in Wiltshire
944x946 (c14) *mertone*; 1225 *Meretun*.
OE *(ge)Mǣretūn* 'boundary farm' seems the most likely, given the proximity of the county boundary, but *Meretūn* 'pond farm' is formally quite acceptable.

Martyr Worthy
See **Worthy**.

Marwell Hall In Owslebury
1182 *Merewelle*.

OE *(ge) Mǣrewiell(e)* 'boundary stream', from the left tributary of the Itchen which partly formed the boundary between Bishopstoke and Owslebury. The name first applied to *Marwell Manor*, which is right next to the stream.

Matley Bog In Denny
A peat bog in a valley cut into the Barton Sands. Named from *Matley Wood* (1270 *Mattele*). Perhaps 'Matta's wood', as Gover suggests, but possibly containing OE *meatte/-a* 'mat', thus 'wood where rushes (for mats) were got'.

Mattingley Modern parish carved out of Heckfield
1086 *Matingelege*; 1242 *Mattingele*.

OE *Mattingalēah* 'wood/clearing of those associated with *Matta', a man's name not recorded in English but with good continental Gmc parallels. The same name may be responsible for *Matt's Copse* in Herriard (1338 *Mattecrofte*).

Maybush In Millbrook, suburb of Southampton
Maybush Farm (i.e. 'hawthorn bush') is found in the 1840 TA.

Medstead
1202 *Medested*; 1262 *Medestede*.

OE *Mǣd(we)stede* 'meadow-place'. For the difficulties involved in interpreting the element *stede*, see Sandred (1963).

Melchet Park Estate in Melchet Park and Plaitford, originally in Wiltshire
1086 *Milchete*; 1236 *Milcet*; 1244 *Mulset*.

According to Ekwall, probably PrW *Mẹlcẹ̄d* 'bare-hill wood'. (Cf. Jackson 1953: 326–7.) It was ancient forest (part of Clarendon forest), and passed through several periods of afforestation till its final enclosure in 1577 (*VCH* IV: 540). It was extraparochial, and the manor of **Plaitford** was held by the keeper of Melchet.

Mengham In South Hayling
1272 *Mongeham*; 1327 *Meyngham*; 1352 *Mengham*.

The first spelling may well contain *o* in error for *e*; in which case we probably have OE *Mǣgingahām* 'estate of the people associated with *Mǣg(a)*' (a man's name); or possibly their *hamm* or 'hemmed-in land' (though the site does not clearly suggest this).

Meon River, and hamlet in Titchfield

786×793 (c13) *flumen quod appelatur Meonea*; 824 etc. (various prepositions) *méone*.

The river-name is obscure in origin, but probably related to that of the *Main* in West Germany. The river gave its name to a *provincia* of the early English invaders (c.750 *meanuarorum prouincia*; *Meonware* meant 'dwellers at/by Meon'). The historical significance of this people has been much debated, as has their apparent affinity with Sx.

Meonstoke Parish and hundred

1086 *Menestoche*; 1156 *Mienestohc hdr'*; c.1200 *Meonestok*.

OE 'dependent farm (*stoc*) by the river Meon', or 'farm dependent on Meon' (i.e. **West** plus **East Meon**).

Merdon Castle In Hursley

See **Hursley**.

Merritown Farm in Hurn

A name found in 1682 (*Merrytown*) replacing earlier c.1300 *Fonketone*, 1682 *Funk Towne*, apparently regional ME 'pong farm or town', for euphemistic reasons. The new name may be s.-e., or may contain the familiar dialect word for the wild cherry. There are *Merry Fields* in Durley and Froxfield, and a *Merry Orchard* in Winchfield (Field 1972).

Micheldever

862 (c12/c13) *mycendefr*; 901 (e. c11) *myceldefer*; 984×1001 (c12) *myceldefer*; 1086 *Miceldevere*.

To judge by the mention of 901, the name is originally that of the river *Dever*. If the name is English and means 'big Dever' (OE *mycel, micel*), then the little Dever could be the little stream rising today near **Preston Candover**. But probably Ekwall is right to draw attention to the earliest form, with *n*, which suggests a PrW name *★Mïgndiβr* from Brit. *★Micnodubrī* 'bog-waters', perhaps from the fact that the river flows into the marshes of the Test. In later times the name was certainly understood as containing OE *mycel* (1195 *Muchelediure*). The manor was held by Hyde Abbey, from 901, hence 1167 *Micheldeura Abbatis*.

Michelmersh

985 (c12) (*æt*) *miclamersce*; 1213 *Michelmerse*; c13 *Muchelmersh*.

OE *★(se) mycla mersc* '(the) big marsh', referring to the wetland at the confluence of the Test and Dun. In the same parish is *Stonymarsh* (OS 1:50 000). Winchester documents of the l. c12/c13 show French-influenced spellings like 1171 *Muchelmareis*, 1243 *Mychelemarays*, where OF *mareis* 'marsh' is substituted for the related English word. The name is most unusual in not having become *-marsh* in ModE, though this form is recorded sporadically (e.g. 1817).

Midanbury District in Bitterne

Perpetuates the house-name *Midanbury Lodge* (thus 1791). Origin unknown.

Midgham Manor in Fordingbridge

1175 *Migham*; 1227 *Migeham*.
Probably OE **Mycghamm* 'midge hemmed-in land', a Dodgson *hamm*-3 or watermeadow site. It overlooks the dividing Avon.

Milford-on-Sea

1086 *Melleford*; t. Hy I *Melneford, Mulneford*; 1152 *Milneford*.
OE **Myl(e)nford* 'mill ford', over Danes Stream. *On-Sea* is a purely modern addition with the intention of exploiting the c19/c20 holiday trade.

Millbrook

956 (m. c10) (*æt*) *melebroce*; 1045 (c11/c12) (*on*) *mylebroces* (*ford*).
OE 'mill stream' (more likely) or 'mill marsh/watermeadow', despite the absence of *n* expected in OE spellings of a derivation of OE *mylen*. The mill was driven by the last tributary on the left bank of the river Test.

Milton

1086 *Mildeltune* [*sic*]; 1242 *Middelton*.
OE 'middle farm', from its situation between **Barton(-on-Sea)** and Chewton (see **Chewton Bunny**). *New Milton* grew up around the station on the L&SWR's Bournemouth branch and the company changed the station name from *Milton* to *New Milton* in the late c19, after Mrs Newhook's sub-Post Office, leaving the original settlement to be called *Old Milton*.

Milton In Portsmouth

Found as *Middelton in Porteseia* in 1186; like *Middleton* in **Longparish**. So-called perhaps for being between Eastney and Fratton.

Minley DB manor in Yateley

1086 *Mindeslei*; t. Ric I *Mundeleya*; 1236 *Mundele*; 1280 *Mendeley*.
The forms, with the exception of DB, suggest OE 'Mynda's wood/clearing'. Such a man's name would be a regular derivative of a name in *Mund-*.

Minstead

1086 *Mintestede*; 1248 *Minstede*.

OE **Mint(an)stede* 'mint place', i.e. 'place where mint grew'. The village is associated with two patches of sand in the Barton Clay. Whether the name implies cultivation is unclear. The name is also found in Sx.

Mirabyll Lost place in Titchfield

May have been named after Queen Eleanor's castle of *Mirabel* in Poitou. It is first recorded in Edward I's reign, which strengthens the likelihood.

Mockbeggar A common house/farm name

First found in 1622 in a poem by Taylor the Water-Poet as a name for a place where no welcome could be expected. Very fashionable from then onwards, though the names may not have been bestowed with the occupiers' consent. There is one just east of Ibsley, for instance.

Monk Sherborne

1086 *Sireborne*; 1255 *Shireburna*.

OE 'bright stream'; but see the discussion under **Sherborne St John**. A priory was founded here t. Hy I, and the monks are commemorated in the feudal specifier in Latin, Middle English and French: 1278 *Syrburne Monachorum*, 1306 *Monkeneschirbourne*, 1332 *Shirebourn Moygnes*. At the turn of the c13/c14 it is found as Dean's Sherborne (*Schirebourne Decani*). All these devices, and the form 1330 *Westshyrebourn*, are to distinguish it from **Sherborne St John**, from which it is divided by the Roman road (Margary 42a) from Silchester to Winchester. The two may have once formed a single unit.

Monkwood Settlement in Ropley

Recorded as *Munckwodd* in 1548. There is a spot called *Abbots Croft* (1840) in the same parish.

Monkton

t. Ed II *Monekeston*.

Takes its present name from the family (?) of Walter *le Munek* 'the monk' who held the manor in the c13. Like **Sarson**, therefore, a late name including ME *tūn* 'farm'. It was earlier called 1269 *Anne de Bek*. It was one of the manors of the very large royal domains at and west of Andover (see **Abbot's Ann**), and was by the e. c13 granted to the abbey of Bec-Hellouin in Normandy, which also held the manor of *Tooting Bec* (Sr).

Moordown Suburb of Bournemouth, now in Do

c.1300 *Mourdene.*

Apparently OE/ME 'moor valley', but the topography suggests 'moor hill', as does the modern form of the name. It is not possible to decide whether the local word *moor(e)* 'tree-stump' (cf. Cope 1883: 59) is involved.

Morestead or **Morested**

c12, c13 *Morsted, Morstede.*

Morestead is at the head of a dry valley, and the sense of OE *mōr* here must be 'barren upland'. A large section of the NE part of the parish was given over to *Longwood Warren*; its use as warren testifies that it was not prime agricultural land. OE *stede* has been fully investigated by Sandred (1963). It appears to mean 'site of something', 'site of something no longer there'. No better translation than 'moor place' can be offered. The other sense of OE *mōr*, 'marshy area', is in evidence close by in the watermeadows of *Twyford Moors*, but these are not close enough to give rise to the present name. A deceptively simple name.

Mortimer West End Formerly in Berkshire

The former west end of Stratfield Mortimer parish in Brk. Gelling, in *PNBrk*, reports that the local name is just *Mortimer*, and this accounts for the form of the Ha portion's name and that of a large secondary settlement in the Brk place itself. The manor was held by Ralf *Mortimer* in 1086. The area called *Stratfield* clearly straddled the present line of the county boundary; the Mortimer manor is in Brk, **Stratfield Turgis** and **Saye** are in Ha. For comparison, note what is said under **Clere** and **Sherfield-on-Loddon**.

Mottisfont Village and priory

1167 *Motesfont*; 1170 *Motesfonte, Motesfunt.*

Most likely OE *(ge)mōtes funta*, either 'spring near the confluence' (of the Test and Dun), or 'spring of the moot'. No evidence has been produced to support Ekwall's and Gover's conjecture in favour of the second; the meeting place of the hundred (Thorngate; 1086 *Brocton* (Broughton)) is not known, so little can be built on this. *Funta* is nowadays (Gelling 1988: 83–6, Cole 1985) taken to denote a spring bearing marks of Roman activity. The spring alluded to by the PN is no doubt the one on the lawn of Mottisfont Priory, described as 'full of water as clear as crystal, ever flowing and yielding perhaps 2 million gallons of water daily', situated at the junction of the Chalk and the Reading Beds. A further spring in the parish is *Spearywell* (1540 *Spyrewell* 'spring where thatchers' canary-grass grows', i.e. *Phalaris arundinacea*; cf. Cope 1883: 87).

The DB spellings, *Mortelhunte*, *Mortesfunde*, appear corrupt. But a man's name *Mort has been inferred from *Mosterton* (Do) and *Morta* is on record.

Mudeford Suburb of Christchurch
c13 *Modeford*; 1826 *Muddiford*.
The name of the river *Mude* is not found till 1856 (*Mudey*), so the PN is primary '*Muddy ford*'. The river was clearly an obstacle to travel, because the name of the adjacent *Somerford* implies 'ford usable in the summer' (t. Hy II *Sumerford*).

Murrell Green Shrunken village in Odiham
1167 *Morhale*.
OE/ME *Mōrhealh 'marsh nook'. It was at the northern extremity of the former Odiham parish, and lies just west of a pool-forming stream which is a right tributary of the Whitewater.

Naked Man Blasted tree in Rhinefield
So called from a suggestive projecting branch around half-way up.

Nateley Scures and **Up Nateley** Two parishes
1086 *Nataleie*; t. Hy I *Nattelega*; c.1195 *Natelege*.
OE **Natan lēage* (oblique case form of) '(the) wet wood/clearing'.
The word *næt* is not on record, but it would be an exact parallel for
German *nass*, etc. The church of Nateley Scures lies down by the
river Lyde. Up Nateley is, not surprisingly, a little higher. The
wood in question may be the ancestor of the one now bisected by
the M3 motorway. cf. **Netley Marsh**.

The two places are distinguished from the late c13 as 1274
Neteleye Scures (from being held by the de Scures family hailing
originally from *Escures* in Calvados) and 1272 *Upnatelye*.

Neatham
1086 *Neteham*; 1145 *Netham*.
The second type of spelling is commoner, so it is probably OE
*Nēathām 'cattle estate' rather than **(ge)Nēatahām* 'estate of the
royal companions'.

Netherton Hamlet in Faccombe
1434 *Nutherton*; 1438 *Netherton*.
ME 'lower farm or hamlet', i.e. in relation to Faccombe itself; it is
actually at the mouth of the small *cumb* or valley at the head of
which Faccombe stands. The two places were also in the document
of 1438 respectively *Nethurstret* and *Upstrete*.

Netley In Hound
955×958 (c14) (*æt*) *lætanlia*; 1086 *Latelei*; 1239 *Lettelege*.
Ekwall suggests a compound of OE *læte* 'neglected, abandoned' and
lēah 'clearing, wood'. A persistent medieval spelling tradition with
two *t*s suggests rather a first element *lætt* 'lath', thus 'wood where
laths were got' (cf. **Sparsholt**). The former tradition seems earlier.
Forms in *n* do not appear till the c14, possibly as a result of confusion
with **Netley Marsh** about 7 miles away (more if not as the crow
flies); but simple dissimilation of *l...l...* is probable. The original
village site is at *Old Netley*.

Netley Marsh appears as such on maps from 1759.

Netley Marsh
508 (l. c9) *natan leaga*; 1248 *Nateleg'*.

It is now customary to associate the form in the *OE Chronicle* (Ā-and E-versions) with this place, despite the implication that the name went underground for 700 years. Certainly **Natan lēage* cannot have been far from here if *Cerdicesford/Certicesford* in the same annal refers to **Charford**. The story the *Chronicle* gives for the name is pure fabrication, however; the annalist says the name is that of a Welsh king called *Natanleod, Nazaleod* who was killed here with 5000 men by Cerdic and Cynric, 'in consequence of which the district was called *Natanleag/Nazanleog...*'. This is not a W personal name but the name of a wood, 'wet wood', like **Nateley**.

New Brighton District of Emsworth
After the famous *Brighton* (Sx), and so called after the visit of Princess Amelia in 1805 to take the waters. The connection is in the royal association of the Prince Regent with Brighton. There are other *New Brighton*s, e.g. in Chs.

New Forest Forest and (within this) a hundred
1086 *Nova Foresta*; c.1115 *prouincia Iutarum in Noua Foresta, Noua Foresta quae lingua Anglorum Ytene nuncupatur*; 1154 *Noveforest*; 1231 *Nova Foresta Regis*.
Bede, in the *Ecclesiastical History*, puts forward the long-accepted idea that there were Jutes in Hampshire at the time when Angles and Saxons were also active in the conquest. This has been disputed on archaeological grounds, but the tradition remains. Florence of Worcester (d. 1118) continues to retail the story, going so far as to call the New Forest by a derivative of the tribal name, *Ytene* 'Jutes'. (Cf. Ekwall 1953: 132.)
  The forest existed as wasteland before the Conquest. The poor soils rest on Tertiary gravels and sands and can never have supported profitable farming. It was expanded by William I at the expense of more than 20 villages (cf. Muir 1982); hence it was *new* in his time as a legally defined expanded area.

Newnham
t. Hy I *Neoham*; 1167 *Niweham*; 1212 *Niwenham*.
OE **Nīwan hām* (oblique case-form of) '(the) new estate'. The various places called *Newnham* and the like are distributed rather further west than the bulk of the other names in *hām* (e.g. *Nuneham Courtenay* (O)), suggesting that the name functioned more or less as an established lexical expression for a new estate. The manor farm of this Newnham is on a raised patch of Lower Bagshot Sand in the surrounding clay, with easy to work Frilford association soils.

Since the claylands are none too hospitable, there is a clear suggestion in the name that this was a settlement in more marginal land under pressure of population growth in mid Saxon times.

Newtimber Lost DB manor

Lost DB manor of *Neutibrige* in Bosmere hundred, perhaps in Warblington. Probably identical with *Newtimber* in Sx, OE 'new wooden building'.

Newton Valence

1086 *Newentone*.

OE *Nīwan tūne* (oblique case-form of) '(the) new farm'. In 1250 it was held by Wiliam *de Valencia*, hence the manorial element. William's family presumably hailed from *Valence* in Seine-et-Marne (Normandy). That it is a late foundation could be inferred from the fact that the village is on a hill capped with Clay-with-flints; marginal land at the best of times. Of nearby presumably ancient villages, only West Tisted and Medstead are situated on this formation.

Newtown

1218 (*de*) *Novo Burgo* (*de Clere*), *Novus Burgus*; 1252 *Nywebur'*; t. Hy III *nove ville* (*de Sandelford*) (Latin genitive case); 1284 *Nova Villa*; 1316 *Neweton*.

The present name is s.-e., ME 'new town'. It was founded as a commercial venture by the bishop of Winchester in the second decade of the c13, on the lands of his Clere manors; perhaps with a view to imitating, or siphoning off some trade from, Newbury in Brk, the elements in whose name it originally duplicated. The adjacency of places with similar or homophonous descriptive styles, 'the new borough/fort', would have been a sufficient reason for the establishment of a different name for the later and less successful one when the descriptive styles became true names. But in fact Newtown never really got off the ground as a major borough in the c13 and it may have been felt that the ME element *burgh* was simply inappropriate for the place. The qualification *juxta Sandelford* relates to Sandelford, just over the county boundary in Brk.

Norleywood Hamlet in Boldre

Norley is referred to in 1298 *Northlyghesdych*. OE/ME *Norðlēah* 'north wood', i.e. north of South Baddesley.

Norman Court House in West Tytherley

Commemorates the family of *Normand*. The manor was granted to one Roger in 1334.

Norsebury In Micheldever
See **Danebury Hill**.

North Camp Suburb of Farnborough and railway station in Sr
From its position in relation to the later South Camp at Aldershot.
A foundation of 1854.

Northam In Southampton
1086 *Northam*.
Probably OE for 'north hemmed–in land'. The land is the classic
Dodgson *hamm*-1 site hemmed in by the last great bend in the
river Itchen before it reaches Southampton Water.

Northam Lost DB manor in Redbridge hundred
Spelt in the modern way in DB, then lost. Perhaps identical in
linguistic structure, though not in location, with **Northam** in
Southampton.

Northington
903 (c16) (*æt*) *northametone*; 1166×7 *Norhameton'*; 1544 *Northyng-
ton*.
The modern form is a Tudor development. The older name is OE
Norðhǣmatūn 'farm of the north-dwellers'. It is hard to decide
from which place it was thought to be north; perhaps (Old)
Alresford. It is immediately north of Swarraton, a better candidate
if it could be shown conclusively to be an ancient foundation. Late
in the c13 a tradition *Non(e)hampton* arises and is found for 50
years. Since the land belonged to Hyde Abbey in Winchester (from
the c10), the older name may have been altered, by a loose
piece of folk-etymology, to suggest ME *Nunnehampton* 'nuns'
Hampton', but the tradition was scribal only.

Nursling
c.800 *nhutscelle*; 877 (c12) *nuhtscillingæ* [*sic*]; 956 (c12) (*to*) *hnutscil-
lingæ*; 1045 (c11/c12) *hnut scillinga* (*mearc*); 1189 *Nutselling*; 1204
Nutsillinges; c.1230 *Nutschullyng*.
It seems clear that this extraordinary name started as OE *hnutusciell
'nutshell'. We can only guess at the reason. (Ekwall thinks it a
jocular name for a tiny place.) It was modified in later OE by the
addition of the singular -*ing* suffix (Smith, *EPNE*: I, 285–90).
In post-Conquest documents, especially from Winchester, this is
mistaken for the 'tribal' plural -*ingas* suffix or arbitrarily pluralized
as the element *stoc* often is (c.1124 *Nutsellinges*). Evidence for the
loss of the *t* accumulates from 1269 (*Nusselyng*) and the modern
pronunciation is signalled from 1483 (*Nurselynges*).

A comment on **Litchfield Grange** is called for. This appears to be from OE *Hnutuscylf(e)* 'nut(-tree) shelf'. If there were the slightest hint of a *f/v* in the voluminous records for Nursling, I would have no hesitation in taking these to represent the same name-form. The range of ME spellings for the vowel of the second element, *i, y, e, u,* is equally consistent with derivation from OE *scylf(e)*. Nursling is on level, though not elevated, ground. But there is no trace of the required consonant, and the relation between the two names, if any, remains unsolved. The presence of nut-trees in the district is apparently corroborated by the existence of *Nutfield* in Rownhams and *Nutburn* in North Baddesley.

Nurstead Tithing of Buriton
1204 *Nutstede.*
OE *Hnutustede* 'nut-tree place'. The form with *r* is first found in 1586. Similar names in Sf and K have developed the same way, and cf. **Nursling**.

Nutley
1212 *Nutlie*; 1219 *Nutlega*; 1220 *Nutelegha*; 1236 *Nottele.*
Like *Nutley* in several other SCy counties, this is OE *Hnutulēah* 'nut wood', perhaps implying hazel.

O

Oakhanger In Selborne
1086 *Acangre*; 1174 *Achangra*.
OE *★Āchangra* 'sloping wood of oaks'. It later gave its name to
Oakhanger stream, whose original name was applied to **Selborne**.

Oakley, West and **East** Village and hamlet (now a dormitory of
Basingstoke)
and
Oakley, North Scattered settlement in Kingsclere
824 (c12) *acleah*.
OE 'oak wood'. The three hamlets (including North Oakley in
Kingsclere) testify to scattered settlement. The parent village of
West Oakley (now merely *Oakley*) is called 1256 *Chircheacle*, from
the church being there. (There is none in North Oakley even now.)
A further possible mention of the place in AS times is fully
discussed under **Herriard**.

Oakridge In Basing, now district of Basingstoke
S.-e., and on record since the mid c10 (c14) as *acry(c)ge*. The present
estate was built 1952–4.

Oakshott In Froxfield
956 (c12) *ac sceates* (*ford*); 959x963 (c12) *ac sceates* (*geate*).
OE 'oak corner'. Administratively it was at the eastern extremity
of Froxfield parish and therefore a typical *scēat* site. Cf. **Aldershot
Grayshott**, etc.

Odiham
1086 *Odiham*; 1116 *Wudiham*.
The second form, from the Laud MS. of the *OE Chronicle*, gives
the clue that this is OE *★Wudighām* 'wooded estate'. *Hamm* is
unlikely; it is not a classic *hamm* site, and was a royal domain before
1066, strengthening the probability of *hām*.

Old Basing
See **Basing**.

Old Winchester Hill Hillfort in Exton
t. Ed IV (*pastura vocata*) *Oldewyncestre*.
It is not known how or when the association with **Winchester**
took place; it seems to be an early piece of scholarly speculation,
and it may be significant that the mention t. Ed IV is in a document
from Winchester College. The fort itself is mentioned in an AS

period document as (*on*) *eorð burge* (*geat*) '(to the gate of the) earth fort'. An endorsement to this document states that King Eadred added to the grant of land in Exton a mill at the east gate of Winchester. Maybe in this very document there is scope for confusion of the gate of the fort in the text and the gate of the town in the endorsement, giving rise to the idea that the fort was another Winchester.

Oliver's Battery In Basing, Old Alresford and Winchester
All these names testify to the activities of the Parliamentary armies ultimately under Cromwell in the Civil War. They laid siege to Winchester in September and stormed Basing House in October 1645 after another lengthy siege.

The oldest relevant references known to me are 1808 *Cromwell's Battery*, 1866x1869 (1908) *Oliver Cromwell's Battery* (Winchester); 1840 *Oliver's Dell* (Basing) is not the same place as the local Oliver's Battery but commemorates the same events. The Winchester *Battery* seems to have been the best known, and I hazard the guess that the other two duplicate this striking name. References originally involving the surname *Cromwell* have become less respectful as time has passed, possibly in the way that the Devil may have his teeth drawn by being called (*Old*) *Nick*.

Ossemsley House, scattered settlement in Milford-on-Sea
t. Hy I *Osemundeslee*; 1280 *Osmundesle*.
OE/ME 'Ōsmund's wood/clearing'. *Ōsmund* is a man's name, sometimes of Scandinavian origin, though the bearer need not have been a Norseman. Gover and Morris worry about whether this can be the DB manor of *Oselei* and conclude that it cannot. Morris also mentions a form *Osanlea* of 984, which is not certain to be relevant. In fact *Oselei* can be this place if it was called after a regular short-form of Ōsmund's name, *Ōsa*. There are precedents for PNs based on the short-forms of names of people known by longer names; cf. **Bursledon**.

Otterbourne
963x975 (c12) (*to*) *oterburna*(*n*).
OE 'otter stream', a small right tributary of the Itchen.

Outwick In Breamore
1086 *Otoiche*; c13 (*H*)*outwyke*.
OE *⋆Ūtwīc* 'outlying specialized (probably dairy-) farm'.

Overton
909 (c12) *uferantun*, (*to*) *uferatune*; 1086 *Ovretune*.

OE *Uferra(n) tūn(e) 'higher farm (oblique case-form)'. To judge by the modern position of the church and manor, down the river Test, we have to reckon with the sense 'further up the river', as seen from e.g. Laverstoke.

Ovington
963×975 (c12) (æt) ufinctune.
OE 'farm associated with Ufa'.

Ower Manors/hamlets in Copythorne and Fawley
1086 Hore; 1284 Ore; 1327 Oure.
Either OE ofer 'flat-topped ridge' or ōra 'bank, shore, foot of a slope'. Ower in Copythorne overlooks a right tributary of the river Blackwater, from a majestic 44 feet. This is the one that Morris identifies with DB Hore in his Hampshire Domesday. Ower in Fawley, by the shore of Southampton Water, is probably the one meant by Gelling (1984: p.179), who includes this as one of her 'coastal' ōra PNs (cf. **Copnor**).

Owslebury
963×975 (c12) oselbyrig; 1185 Oselbury; 1245 Oselebery; 1272 Oslebergh.
OE *Ōselburh 'blackbird fort'. It is curious that the OE name appears to be a direct compound of the two words, though some c13/c14 forms suggest *Ōselaburh 'blackbirds' fort'. No earthwork is known to me. The village is on top of a hill from which the ground falls away on all sides.

Oxelei DB manor in Rowditch hundred
There is no doubt that the name means 'ox clearing/wood', but it is hard to identify. Possibly Oxleys Copse (1538 Oxlease) in Beaulieu liberty, but that appears to have lǣs 'meadow' as the second element and it is not in Rowditch hundred.

Oxenbourne Tithing of Eastmeon
1200 Oxeburne; 1208 Oxeneburne; 1245 Exeneburne.
OE/ME Oxenaburna 'oxen's stream', a headwater of the river Meon. There are occasional E- spellings representing the older OE genitive plural form exena.

P

Pamber Parish and forest
1166 *Penberga* (village); 1204 *Penberg* (village); 1206 *Penber'*
(forest); 1234 *Pembergh* (forest); 1253 *Penbere* (village); 1306
Pambear (village).
Apparently OE *⋆Pennbeorg* 'hill or barrow with an enclosure or
fold'. Forms from the c13 onwards however suggest the second
element is *bær* 'woodland swinepasture'; the fact of its being a forest
area, with common rights of pannage, may have encouraged this
reinterpretation of the name. *Penn* may be a W hill-name.

Park Farm Beaulieu, DB manor of **Througham**
749 (c12) *Ðruhham*; 1086 *Tru(c)ham*; t. Hy VIII *Througham*.
OE *⋆Þruhhām* 'trough or conduit estate', or perhaps the second
element is *hamm*, in this case land surrounded by former marsh, a
Dodgson *hamm*-2a. The *þruh* would presumably have been for
drainage. (The word could also mean 'coffin'.) *Park Farm* is on the
S fringe of the former estate, which, when emparked, was known
as 1547 *Trougham Parke* or 1606 *Beauley Parke*.
   The DB manor was held by a man named *Colgrin*; *Colgrimes-
more* (displaying the correct form of the name) is found in Beaulieu
in c.1210.

Parsonage Tithing of Kingsclere hundred
1586 *Parsonadge*.
This was a church manor from the AS period (*VCH* IV: 261), and
its name was deliberately opposed to that of 1586 *Lordshipp*, the
tithing representing the royal demesne manor.

Passfield In Bramshott
1639 *Parsfeild*; 1786 *Parcefield*; 1817 *Paswell*.
Not found early. Perhaps for ME *⋆Persilfeld* 'parsley field'.

Paulsgrove In Cosham
c.1300 *Pallesgraffeld*; 1319 *Pale(s)grave*; 1321 *Pallesgrove*.
There are numerous English names where it remains uncertain
whether the original form contains OE *grāf* 'grove', *grōf* 'groove'
in some topographical sense, or *græfe*, *græf* 'diggings'. This is one of
them. If the name is OE, the first element is the man's name *Pælli*.
The present quarry in Portsdown, above Paulsgrove, is modern.

Pauncefoot House, shrunken village in Romsey
1206 *Pancevot*; 1487 (*manor called*) *Paunesfotes* (*Hill*).

Manor of the *de Pauncefot* family, an AN name meaning 'arched belly'.

Pennington and Upper Pennington Suburbs of Lymington
c12 *Penyton*; 1272 *Penington*.

OE/ME *Peni(n)gtūn* 'penny farm', i.e. a farm on which a penny geld was payable. Cf. **Penton Grafton**, **Penton Mewsey**.

Penton Grafton Part-manor, hamlet in Weyhill
1086 *Penitone*; c13 *Penitone Grefteyn*; 1269 *Penytun Gresteyn*.

That part of Penton manor not held by the Meisys, but by the abbey of Grestein in Eure (so in DB; 1167 *Peninton Abbatis*). There is a persistent spelling-tradition with *f* for *s*, e.g. 1316 *Croftyn*, though Gover says that this 'must be a late mistake due to mis-reading of the 17th and early 18th century printed "s".' The prominence as landowners of the Earls of Grafton may have had something to do with the association; or there has been an association with the *Grafton* villages 9 miles NW in W.

Penton Mewsey
1086 *Penitone*; 1255 *Penyton Meysi*; 1272 *Penyngetun*.

OE *Peni(n)gtūn* 'penny farm', i.e. one which had to pay a penny geld. The manor was held in 1212 by Robert de *Meisy* from *Maisy* (Calvados – hence the manorial specifier; the modern aberration is first found 1606 *Pennyngton Mewsey*). Ekwall speculates that this Robert is the one referred to in 1167 *Penintona Roberti*. Distinguished from **Penton Grafton**, next door.

Petersfield
1181 *Peteresfeld*; 1248 *Petresfeud*.

'Peter's open land'. The church dedication is to St Peter. But there are cases of rededication of churches where the saint's name is suggested by the parish name (cf. **Catherington**, *Osmington* (Do)). If appearances are deceptive, perhaps this is OE 'Peohthere's open land'. Since the name is not recorded till the late c12, an open mind on the likely date of origin and interpretation is desirable; on the element *feld* see Gelling (1984: 235–45).

Phoenix Green Hamlet in Hartley Wintney
Thus in 1826. From an inn.

Picket Piece Suburb of Andover
OS 1:50 000. This appears to contain a FN including ME *piked* 'pointed' (cf. Hampshire dialect *peaked* (Cope 1883: 65)), possibly alluding to the tapering piece of land between the two converging roads to Whitchurch. This name and the 1 mile distant *Picket*

Twenty Farm may have influenced each other. This extraordinary name is 1826 *Pickiltrenthay Farm*, possibly corrupt (and euphemistic) for *Piddletrenthide* in Do; but the connection is obscure.

Picket Post Hamlet in Burley
Thus in 1759, but spelt *picked* 1789, 1794 etc. 'Pointed post', cf. **Picket Piece**. Reason unclear, maybe a boundary mark between Ellingham and Burley.

Pignal Enclosure In Denny
1331 *Pigenhull*.
ME 'pigs' hill', with a ME weak plural in *-en*. There is a *Pig Bush* 5 miles away in the same parish, of particular interest for the adjacent *Tantany Wood* (thus 1789), which seems to contain a common dialect word for the weakest pig in the litter, but has in fact been reformed from an obscure earlier 1578 *Tantro meade*.

Pilcot Hamlet in Dogmersfield
1280 *Pylecote*.
OE *Pīlacotu* 'stakes cottages'. Whether this refers to an enclosure type or to the products of the inhabitants is not known.

Pilley Farm and hamlet in Boldre
c.1280 *Pilely*; 1280 *Pililegh*; 1306 *Pillelegh*.
OE *Pīlalēah* 'wood where shafts or piles were got', cf. *Pylewell* (1609 *Pilewells*) in the same parish. Or perhaps the first element is *pyll* 'tidal creek', typical of the WCy but found in minor names as far E as Sx. Pilley and Pylewell are between the Lymington river and a watercourse that may well have been tidal before it was regulated to form a feature in the grounds of Pylewell. This latter possibility could not account for *Pilmore Gate* (1331 *Pillemore*) in Minstead, far inland. There is also an unexplained modern *Pill Heath* in Hurstbourne Tarrant. Pilley was resettled from the cleared DB village of *Pisteslei*. It is unclear whether the names are connected. The DB name may be *Pisestedeslēah* 'clearing/wood of *Pisestede*', this being 'pea place', cf. **Binstead**.

Pitt Manor in Hursley, now in Winchester
S.-e., and on record since the c12. The hamlet is in a dip, so the term may be used in a topographical sense.

Pittleworth Farm in Bossington
1086 *Puteleorde*; 1280 *Puteleworth*; 1341 *Piteleworth*.
Despite sporadic c13 forms with a medial *-s-*, probably OE *Pyttelawyrð* 'hawks' curtilage'; though wildlife names with *wyrð*

are rare, and perhaps a personal name from the word is a preferable solution.

Plain
This word is used in its ordinary sense of 'large tract of open land' both in the New Forest (**Bratley Plain**, *Wilverley Plain, Janesmoor Plain*) and in the Forest of Bere (**Cowplain**).

Plaitford In Melchet Park and Plaitford, originally in Wiltshire
1086 *Pleiteford*; 1234 *Pleitesford*.
Possibly from OE **plēget* 'playing', the name thus being parallel to *Playford* (Sf), 'ford where games took place' (over a right tributary of the Wellow); and more loosely to the several PNs derived from OE *plegstōw* (*Plaistow* (Ess), *Plaxtol* (K)). There are two such PNs in Ha, *The Plestor* in Selborne and *Plastow Green* in Kingsclere.
  Maybe the ford intended was over the stream that formed the old county boundary; a significant place to have games.

Pokesdown Suburb of Bournemouth, now in Do
c.1300 *Pokesdoune*.
ME 'goblin's hill'; unless the ME derivative of OE *pūca* is here a surname. It survives in this capacity as *Pook*. Young (1957: 186) wonders whether the dialect word for 'haycock' (cf. Cope, under *pook, puck*) is involved, but the c13 form with a medial -*s*- speaks against this.

Poland Farm in Odiham
1234 *Palling'*; 1280 *Pollynge, Pullyng'*.
Only two spellings – the earlier 1295 – have final -*s*, so this is probably OE **Pōling* or **Pulling* 'pool place'. Poland is by the river Whitewater.

Polygon, The In Southampton
This district (once well outside the borough boundary) derives its curious name from the development planned and begun in the early 1770s as a self-contained resort for the aristocracy to rival (or outdo) the Long Rooms in Southampton. The frontages of the houses were to be arranged in a regular dodecagon, with the back yards of the properties tapering towards a central hotel intended to be the venue for glittering social occasions. The scheme was beset by financial problems as early as 1773 and was never completed (cf. Patterson 1966: 52–5). Perhaps best known now as the name of the famous hotel which commemorates the scheme, the original hotel having been demolished.

Popham

903 (c16), c.1140 *Popham*.

There is no known element which could explain the first syllable. Ekwall suggested that a short form of OE *popel* 'pebble' (which is continued by Hampshire dialect *popple* (Cope 1883: 69)) may have existed, and Gover noted that since the place is on the Chalk, the reference must be to flints. In fact Popham manor farm is on a patch of Clay-with-flints surrounded by otherwise loamy soil; so Ekwall and Gover may well have been right that it is OE *Pophām* 'pebble estate'.

Popley In Sherborne St John, now district of Basingstoke

Named from *Popley Field Farm* (*Popley Fields House* on the latest OS map, SU 636546), no references to which have been discovered before the mention of *Popley Field* in the Sherborne St John Tithe Award of 1840. Cf. **Popham**. There are field-names in Ha containing *popple/pobble* and the like 'pebble, flint', e.g. 1560 *Poble londe* in Wootton St Lawrence and 1448 *Popehull*, later *Popple Field* (Field 1972) in Curdridge. However, earlier c20 OS maps show our place as *Poplar Field Farm*; and some of the older names may include references to poplars or even to poppies (cf. Smith, *EPNE* II: 70). It is not clear which is the genuine source of the name, but the place does not appear to be on a patch of Clay-with-flints.

Porchester

904 (c12) *porceastra*; 963×975 (c12) *porteceaster*; 1086 *Por(t)cestre*. The frequency of early forms showing *Porte-* is slightly troubling, but there can be little doubt that this is OE *Portceaster* '[Roman] fortification/town at *Port*', where the first element is the anglicized form of the RB/PrW name for Portsmouth Harbour. The Roman fort is still very conspicuous.

Port Way

1298 *Portweye*.

The Roman road (Margary 4b) from Old Sarum to Silchester is ME 'town way', presumably to be understood as the 'way to Salisbury', given the contrasting fortunes of the two Roman towns. In AS charters it is just called *stræt* 'paved road' or *ealdan stræt* '(the) old paved road'.

Portsdown Chalk ridge and hundred

1086 *Portesdone hdr'*; 1167 *Portesdon*; 1175 *Portesdune*.

This contains OE *dūn* 'hill', applied typically to ridges and other hills with a top suitable for a settlement-site, though no English-period settlement on Portsdown is known to me, and there can never have been much water up there to supply a settlement. This element was probably in use very early in English namegiving, say before 800. The hill was so called because it overlooks the *Port*, for which see **Portsmouth**.

Portsea Island

982 (c14) *portesig*; 1218 *Porteseia*.
OE **Portesīeg* 'island at the port (Port)', or elliptically for 'Portsmouth island'. A name of this form is now also applied to the part of dockland from which the Ryde and Gosport ferries depart. *Island* has been added as the element *īeg* has ceased to be understood.

Portsmouth Liberty

501 (c.890, c12) (*æt*) *portesmuðan*; 1114 (*on*) *Portesmuðe*; 1100x35 *Porthesmuda*; c.1125 *Portesmues*.
OE **Portesmūða* 'mouth of *Port*', the anglicized RB/PrW name of Portsmouth Harbour, or possibly 'mouth of the port'. The last-quoted spelling is one of many betraying NF influence.

Portswood Suburb of Southampton

1045 (c12) (*on*) *porteswuda*; 1167 *Porteswuda*.
OE 'wood of the town', i.e. of Southampton.

Posbrook Farms in Titchfield

1202 *Possebroc*.
Possibly OE **Possanbrōc* 'Possa's brook or watermeadow'. The man's name *Possa* is not known for certain to have existed, but may also be found in e.g. *Postwick* (Nf). (*Pusa* and *Passa* are actually found.) The farms lie low beside the smaller channel of Titchfield Haven; though perhaps the sense of *brōc* typical in Sx, 'land beside a stream, watermeadow' is intended.

Poulner District of Ringwood

1300 *Polenore*; 1327 *Polenoure*; 1410 *Pulnore*; 1682 *Powner*.
The second element is *ōra* or *ofer*, both words for 'bank, slope' discussed by Gelling (1984: 173–82). *Ofer* appears to mean 'flat-topped ridge' and *ōra* 'slope, foot of a slope'. The topography of east Ringwood favours the latter. The first element is obscure. If it is not an unknown personal name it may be OE *polleie* 'pennyroyal'. This well-known medicinal mint grows in sandy damp places, and the local soils of the Bursledon association, a sandy loam subject to waterlogging, would provide a good habitat. *Polleie* may only be a book-word, as other vernacular names for the plant, e.g. *dwōstle*, are known; but the form seems to be thoroughly nativized.

Preston Candover
See **Candover**.

Prior's Barton In Winchester
1166 *Berton prioris*.
For OE *beretūn*, see **Abbott's Barton**. This grange farm belonged to the prior of St Swithin's.

Priors Dean
t. Hy II *Dena*; 1198 *Dene*.
OE *denu* 'valley', typically a winding, steep-sided one with a flattish bottom. This suits the site of the manor-house. The manor was held by Southwick Priory, and the modern name is recorded from 1367.

Privett
755 (*æt*) *pryfetes* (*flodan*); 1207 *Prevet*; c.1245 *Pruuet*; 1248 *Privet*.
OE *pryfet* 'privet'. The entry in annal 755 of the *OE Chronicle* means 'at the watercourse of Privett', where Sigebeorht, exiled king of Wessex, was killed by a herdsman. Since there is no stream at Privett, it is not clear what is meant, but Grundy (1922: 54–5) has surmized that *flōde* was a place subject to flash-flooding (cf. **Winslade**).

Prollingworth Lost part-tithing of Titchfield hundred
1241 *Pralingwurth*; c.1350 *Prallyngworth*; 1586 *Prolingworthe*; 1613 *Prowlingworth*.
Obscure. Forms related to the first element seen to be found in *Pralle* (Sx), *Prawle* (D); Ekwall takes the latter to be OE *præwhyll, *prawhyll* 'lookout hill'. The second is OE/ME *wyrð* 'curtilage'. Only a run of three forms in the early c14 (*Prallyngeworth(e)*) suggests that this is a PN with an OE genitive plural first element. We should reckon with the possibility of an OE lexical word **pral-* or the like. Identified by Watts (1984) as a substantial part of the north end of Titchfield hundred, including the modern hamlets of Burridge and Eyers Down in Sarisbury-cum-Swanwick.

Purbrook In Farlington, suburb of Portsmouth
c13 *Pokebroc*; 1248 *Pukebrok*.
OE/ME *Pūcanbrōc 'goblin's brook'. Forms with *r* are found from the c17, e.g. 1675 *Purbeck*. There is room for more work on mythical beings in PNs.

Purewell Suburb of Christchurch
c.1300 *Perewull*; 1327 *Pirewolle*.
OE/ME *Pirigewiell 'pear-tree spring'. Two little streams rise here and flow into Christchurch habour.

Q

Quarley
1167 *Cornelea*; 1269 *Querly*; 1280 *Quereley*.
Possibly OE *Cweornlēah* '(hand)mill wood/clearing'; exact sense unclear, cf. **Curbridge**. It is curious that no ME forms are on record containing both *Qu-* and medial *-n-*. But *corn/curn* is common in ME for *cweorn* and the various forms may be reconciled with such an intermediary. Some spellings suggest the genitive plural *cweorna* or the genitive singular of the related word *cweorne*; but forms with no medial vowel are in the majority.

Quidhampton Hamlet, later village, in Overton
1086 *Quedementun*; 1245 *Quedhamtun*, *Quidhamtun*.
OE 'farm of the inhabitants of *Cwēadhām*', an otherwise unknown PN meaning 'dirt/dung estate'. Or, more directly, 'farm of the inhabitants of the filthy/dung estate'. There are two further *Quidhamptons* in W.

The suspicion that the medial element is *-hǣme-* 'dwellers' rather than *-hām-* is based on the DB form but reinforced by the existence of farms called *Polhampton*, *Northington* and *Southington* in the same parish. Certainly the first (940 (*æt*) *polhǣmatun* 'farm of the dwellers at the pool or at *Pōlhām*', i.e. the pool which is a source of the Test), probably the second (1218 *Norhamet'*) and possibly therefore the third all contain *-hǣme-*. The modern forms of the last two probably stem from the homophony of their medieval and early-modern forms with *Northampton* and **Southampton**. Speakers, or more likely writers in the first instance, have taken action to avoid ambiguity of reference.

R

Rafborough District of Farnborough

An unusual c20 name formed from the initials of the RAF, because of the adjacent aerodrome of the Royal Aircraft Establishment. *Borough* on the analogy of *Farnborough*.

Rake or **The Rake** Partly in Sx

1327 (*ate*) *Rake*.

OE *hrace, hraca*, literally 'throat', topographically probably 'gully, pass'. Rake is in a gap in the hill occupied by **Hill Brow**.

Ramsdean In Langrish

1233 *Ramesdene*; 1248 *Rammesdene*; 1257 *Ramesdune*; 1316 *Rammesdon*.

The spread of medieval forms is ambiguous between *denu* 'valley' and *dūn* 'hill'; some forms may refer to the hamlet and others to Ramsdean down. Analogies with PNs elsewhere suggest that the first element is likely to be OE *hræfn* 'raven' (or a man's name of the same form), especially in the case of the *dūn*. But it could as well be *ramm* 'ram'. The spellings also suit the form of the OE word *hramse* 'ramsons, wild garlic' that typically appears in PNs, as Gover suggests (*see* next entry). No certainty is possible.

Ramsdell Hamlet in Wootton St Lawrence

1170 *Ramesdela*; 1248 *Ramesdelle*.

Very likely OE **Hramsdell* 'dell where wild garlic (OE *hramse*) grew'. There is a tiny valley SW of the place where a stream rises. The element *hramse* often appears in PNs in forms with a vowel between the *m* and *s*. Other formally acceptable possibilities as in previous entry.

Redbridge In Millbrook

c.730 (m. c8) *hreutford*; c.890 (c.1000) *hreodford*; 956 (c10) (*on, of*) *hreod brycge*; 1045 (c11/c12) (*on*) *hreod bricge*; 1086 *Rodbrige*; 1222 *Redbrigge*; 1276 *Rudbrigge*.

OE **Hrēodbrycg* 'reed bridge', probably in the sense 'bridge where reeds grew'. The earlier name was 'reed ford', and it is hard to escape the conclusion that a bridge was built to carry the Dark Age ancestor of the A35 over the river Test sometime close to AD 900. There are still conspicuous reed-beds here.

Redenham Hamlet and park in Fyfield

901 (c14) (*to ðam*) *readen hamme*; 1167 *Redenham*; 1256 *Radenham*.

The AS-period form is good OE 'at the red hemmed-in land', which appears to denote Cunney's Down, N of Redenham Park, which drops away noticeably on three sides. There was a Roman building on the Down. The soils are the red soils of the Carstens association.

Redrice In Upper Clatford
1269 *Rederis*; 1306 *la Rederys*, *la Rederes*.
OE *Rēadan hrīse '(at the) red brushwood-covered land', the precise botanical implications being unknown (dogwood?).

Rhinefield Modern parish carved out of Brockenhurst
1352 *Ryefeld*; 1353 *Riefelde*.
OE/ME *Rȳgefeld 'rye open land'. Gover suggests that the first element may really be the OE adjective *rȳgen* 'rye-grown', but forms in -*n* do not appear till the late c15 (1490 *Rynefeld*). A ME origin for this alternative formation is therefore certain: ME *Rīenfeld.

Later irrelevantly associated with either the *rhines* (drainage ditches) of the Somerset Levels or the European river.

Rhode Farm in Selborne
1086 *Larode*; 1248, 1285 *la Rude*.
OE *rod(u) 'clearing, assart', used as a PN. The forms quoted show the French definite article. The modern spelling is, as so often in PNs and surnames, influenced by that of *Rhodes*; an excess of classical zeal.

Ringwood Town and hundred
955×958 (c14) (*æt*) *runcwuda*; 955 (c14) (*to*) *rimucwuda*; 961 *rimecuda*; 1086 *Rincvede* (manor and hundred).
Ekwall suggests an unrecorded OE *rīmuc, derived from *rīma* 'edge, border'. Ringwood would then be 'border wood', from its position outside the fringe of the New Forest. This is universally accepted. But since it is close to the border with Dorset (2.5 miles away), and since the border parishes have been carved out of Ringwood, an open mind may be called for.

Riplington or **Ripplington** Tithing of East Meon
1195 *Rippledon*; 1207 *Riplinton*; 1209 *Ripplinton*.
OE, apparently *Rippelingtūn 'farm of the elongated thicket', see Smith (*EPNE* II: 84). I assume this since the modern dialect reflex of the word *rippel denotes a thicket. For the formation, cf. Smith (*op. cit.* I: 296 (para. 6(c))).

Roake Farm in Broughton

1325 (*atte*) *Oke*; 1628 *Oke*; c17 *Rocke* (*Downe*).

VCH identifies this with the DB manor of *Mulceltone* (1207 *Michelton*) 'big farm'. The present name means '(at the) oak'; there is a *Roke* farm in Romsey whose name has the same origin. The *R-* has come from misdivision of ME *atter oke*.

Rockbourne

1086 *Rocheborne*; 1155 *Rokeburne*; 1157 *Rocheburna*; 1166 *Rochesburna*.

OE **Hrōcaburna* 'rooks' stream', a right tributary of the Avon. The *-s-* forms, sporadic c.1200, may show the influence of **Rockstead** in the same parish. This was c.1210 *Rokesey*, *Rokesaye*, 1536 *Rocksted*, 1593 *Rocksithe*. This problematic name may be OE **Hrōcesīeg* 'rook's dry ground in marsh', **Hrōcaseað* 'rooks' pit' or less likely **Hrōceshǣð* 'rook's heath'; or elliptically for 'Rockbourne pit/heath'.

Rockford Manor in Ellingham

1086 *Rocheford*; 1167 *Rechesford*, *Rachesfort*; 1286 *Rokeford*.

Too early to be the AN name *Roquefort* 'strong crag'; it was a manor before 1086. It is not obvious what to make of the c12 forms, which suggest confusion with early forms of the *Rochford*s in Ess and Wo; the rest point to OE **Hrōcaford* 'rooks' ford', cf. **Rockbourne** and the DB manor of **Rockstead** in that parish. The ford is over Dockens Water, a left tributary of the Avon.

Rockstead DB manor in Rockbourne

c.1210 *Rokesey*; c13 *Rokesaye*; 1256 *Rockesegh*.

Seems to be OE **Hrōces īeg* 'rook's dry ground in marsh', or 'of *Hrōc*'. This would suit the site of *Marsh Farm*, 1 mile to the W, better. Some Tudor spellings suggest that the second element is either *stede* 'stead, place', *hǣð* 'heath' or *seað* 'pit'. Though only the last is plausible, the first has won through. Cf. **Rockbourne**.

Rollstone DB manor in Fawley

1331 *Rolveston*; 1432 *Rotheleston*.

Probably OE 'Hrōðwulf's farm', but the surviving mentions are late. Morris' edition of DB identifies this with the DB manor of *Roweste*, also in Redbridge hundred, but this name appears to mean 'rough wooded hill' and the name is not therefore to be equated with *Rollstone*. However this need not have been far away; *Row Down* is adjacent to Rollstone.

Romsey

966×975 (c12) *rummæsig*; 971 *rumesig*; c.1000 (c14) (*to*) *rumesige*; 1026 (c12) (*to*) *rumesege*.

OE **Rūmesīeg* 'island of Rūm'. OE *ī(e)g* means 'island' or 'raised ground in marshland'; obviously the latter is meant here, in the Test marshes. It is the commonest element recorded in ancient PNs (cf. Cox 1976: 58). *Rūm* is found as the first element of OE names like *Rūmbeald* (ME *Rumbold*).

Ropley

1172 *Roppele*; 1198 *Ropeleia*; 1245 *Ropele*.

Probaly OE **(H)roppanlēah* 'wood/clearing of Hroppa', a man's name which Ekwall explains as a short-name for **Hrōðbeorht*, the English equivalent of AN *Robert*. The existence of named woods in the parish (e.g. *Charlwood, Monkwood, Lyelands Wood*) may suggest that 'clearing' is the proper translation for *lēah* in the parish name.

Rother River

956 (c12) (*andlang*) *scire*; 959×975 (c12) *scyre*; c.1160 *Schire*.

Originally called **Scīr*, probably OE 'bright', but see further **Sherfield-on-Loddon** on the problems of names apparently containing this element or the homophonous word meaning 'shire' (the Rother briefly constitutes the boundary between Ha and Sx E of Sheet). The present name is a back-formation from that of *Rotherbridge* bridge and hundred in Sx (1086 *Redrebrige*) 'cattle-bridge'.

Rotherfield Park In East Tisted

1015 *hryðerafeld*; 1165 *Ruðeresfeld*; 1167 *Reðeresfeld*.

OE **hryðerafeld* 'open land of cattle'. The tradition with medial *s* is peculiar and unexplained; all spellings between 1165 and 1207 have it, and it may have been a scribal error that was perpetuated in later documents. As to the *park*, there is reference to *the park pale* in 1564.

Rotherwick

c.1100 *Hrytheruuica*; 1193 *Retherwyk*; 1262 *Rutherwik*.

OE **Hriðerwīc, Hryðerwīc* 'cattle farm'.

Rowland's Castle

t. Ed II *Rolokescastel*; 1369 *Roulandes Castell*; 1381 *Roulakescastel*. Whatever this name originally was, it became associated with the hero *Roland* of the twelfth-century French romance. The first part is indeed likely to be a man's name, and, to take it at face value, it may be a Frenchified descendant of a Frankish (continental Germanic) *Hrōdlaik* (or less likely Scandinavian *Hróðlaug*, a woman's name), which would have been introduced after the Norman Conquest. *Castel* 'castle' is also a borrowing from Norman French; the whole thing is a medieval rather than a Dark Age name.

Rowledge Partly in Farnham (Sr)
c.1200 *la Rowedich*; 1759 *Rowlridge*.
OE/ME *Rūgan dīc* '(at the) rough ditch/dyke', probably a boundary mark of the pre-Conquest estate of Farnham (Sr). The modern corruption is seen in the second spelling.

Rowner
948 (c12) (*oþ*) *ruwan oringa* (*gemære*); 1086 *Ru(g)enore*.
OE *Rūgan ōran* '(at the) rough bank'. The form from the AS period, from the bounds of Alverstoke, means 'up to the boundary of the people of Rowner'. Hence also *Fort Rowner*.

Rownhams New parish carved out of Nursling and North Baddesley
1269 (*in bosco de*) *Rowenham*; 1301 *Roghenham*.
From an OE phrase, probably in a dative case form, (*æt þām*) *rūgan hamme* '(at the) rough hemmed-in land' or, more generally, 'enclosure'. The name probably refers to the spur of land formed by the Bracklesham Beds, culminating in *Toot Hill* ('lookout-point hill'), which projects into the lower claylands to the north of the present Rownhams. The motorway service-station here is a well-known viewpoint. The modern form suggests derivation from a surname enshrining the old place-name.

Royden Farm in Brockenhurst
1284 *Reidon*; 1333 *Reydone*; 1573 *Roydon*.
OE *Rǣgandūn* 'doe hill', from *rǣge* 'female roedeer'. The manor is low by the river Boldre, and its lands must be referred to rather than its site.

Rufus Stone or **Rufus's Stone** Near Canterton
Marks the traditional site of the death in 1099 of William II (Rufus) in the New Forest; or rather the site of the tree from which Walter Tyrrell's arrow is supposed to have been deflected into the king. Lord de la Warr placed the stone here in 1745.

Rushington Former hamlet in Eling, district of Totton
1548 *Russhyngton*; 1577 *Risshington alias Rumbridge*.
Not recorded till late. If ancient, perhaps OE *Riscentūn* 'rushy farm', and cf. *Ruskington* (L). *Rum Bridge* is the bridge carrying

the A35 over Bartley Water. It was really a separate place. The stream was earlier forded at the adjacent *Brokenford*.

Rushmoor District
1567 *Rushe more*.
Probably s.-e. from the little valley called now *Rushmoor Bottom*. Chosen as a district name in the 1974 local government reorganization presumably to avoid the competing claims of Farnborough and Aldershot to have the district named after them.

Rye Farms in Odiham
1228 *Rie*; 1294 *la Rie*.
Appears, like *Rye* in Sx, to be ME (*at*) *ther eie* '(at) the island or raised land in a marsh', though precise topographical reasons are far from clear. There is a very small rise in the land just E of Great Rye farm; streams rise to the E and NW of the farms.

S

St Catherine's Hill Hill and fort SE of Winchester
1208 (*sub*) *monte sancte Katerine*.
There was a medieval chapel on the hill dedicated to St Catherine. However, names of this type are always suspicious; does the dedication cloak, and canonize, an earlier PN? *St Ann's Hill* above Allington (W) was earlier *Tan Hill*. Cf. also **Catherington**.
  This name recurs in Hurn, but the earlier records testify to a ford (1316 *Catelineford*).

St Cross 'Hospital' in Winchester
1185 *domus s. crucis* (*extra muros Wintonie*); 1208 *hospitalis Sanctae Crucis*.
The hospital or refuge was dedicted to the Holy Cross. The French name (1395 *Seynt Croys*), or the scribal Latin version seen in the early forms quoted, has clearly been mistranslated to provide a spurious English saint.

St Denys Suburb of Southampton
t. Hy I *Sanctus Dionisius*; 1279 *Seyndenys suburb'*.
From a church dedicated to the patron of Paris.

St Giles's Hill Suburb of Winchester
1208 *mons sanctii Egidii*.
William II granted the right to a fair to be held on the feast-day of St Giles (*Egidius* in Latin), and the fair was held on the hill on the left bank of the Itchen.

St Leonards and St Ives Modern parish carved out of Ringwood
A civil parish uniting a real saint with a fraud. There was a *St Leonard's chapel* in Beaulieu; the saint is often associated with forest districts (cf. *St Leonard's Forest* in Sx). St Ives is 1187 *le Yvez*, 1190 *Yves*, 1212 (*in*) *Yvetis*, and these forms may represent the singular and plural of an OE/ME **īfet(t)* from *īfig* 'ivy', thus 'ivy-grown copse(s)'. The formation may parallel that of **Privett** and that of numerous names in K and Sx which are *-ett* derivatives of words for trees, in the sense 'wood or grove of such and such type of tree'.

St Mary Bourne
1185 *Borne*; 1188 *Burna*.
OE *burna* 'stream', i.e. the **Bourne Rivulet**, whose name perpetuates the ancient one. The place was a chapelry of Hurstbourne Priors, and the presumable early dedication is recorded in 1476

Maryborne, 1483 *Borne S(an)c(t)e Marie*. The present church is dedicated to St Peter and the date of the rededication is unknown.

Sandford Farm in Kingsclere
c.1240 *Santforde*; 1248 *Sanford*.
ME 'sand ford', over a right tributary of the Enborne; s.-e. since the stream flows over the exposed Bagshot Sands. This was one of the manors of **Knowl** mentioned in DB.

Sandleheath Hamlet/estate in Fordingbridge
1536 *Sandelheath*; 1590 *Sandhill Heathe*.
The second form gives the game away; named from the 'manor' of *Sandle* (1210 *Sandehill'*), s.-e., presumably originally located on the outcrop of Bagshot Sands here. The present place is actually on the London Clay.

Sanhest Lost DB manor in Boldre hundred
Probably OE *Sandhyrst* 'sandy wooded hill'. Gover says it may be near the present *Sandy Down* (1331 *Sandidon*).

Sarisbury
Before 1538 this is recorded only in a document of the reign of Edward I (as *Sarebury*). It is obscure, and the suggestion that it duplicated the name of *Salisbury* does not seem likely. A Tudor antiquary may have taken it that way and thereby made the suggestion true.

Sarson Farm in Amport
This is an unusual name in several respects. It is first found as 1203 *Anne* (cf. **Abbot's Ann**), said in this Curia Regis roll to be held by Richard *le Salvage* (the surname is 'savage'; 1242 *Anna Savage*). The name stabilizes in the late c13 as (e.g. 1269) *Sauvageton* 'Savage's farm', like **Monxton** a very late formation with ME *tūn* 'farm' (cf. Smith, *EPNE* II: 193, 198). The modern name is an extreme attrition of this (1597 *Sarston*).

Satchell Farm in Hamble
1251 *Shotteshale*; 1548 *Shotshall*; 1586 *Shaltshall*; 1766 *Shotshall alias Satchell*.
OE/ME *Sceotteshealh* 'nook of land of Sceot(t)', a person with a name meaning 'the Scot' or, if the name is very ancient, 'the Irishman'; cf. **Shoddesden**. The sequence *sh...s...* [ʃ...s ...] gave speakers problems, as the record reveals; they ultimately switched round.

144

Sclive Unidentified DB manor in Boldre hundred

Uninterpreted. The second part seems to be OE *clif* 'cliff'. Earlier identifications with **Highcliffe** in Christchurch and *Muscliff* in Holdenhurst both place *Sclive* in the wrong hundred. If it was near the Bishop of Winchester's other land in the DB Boldre hundred, we would need to look to *Inchmery House*, just west of Lepe in Exbury, the only place where there is a modern sea-cliff, however low. This name is not found before 1609 *Inchmary*.

Searchfield Farm in Charford

1270 *Estchardeford Secchevill'*; 1346 *Secchevylle*.

A manorial name commemorating the *de Secheville* family, who have not, however, been recorded in connection with Charford. The forms with *r* date from the c17, and the reformation to *field* from the c16.

Segenworth Farms in Titchfield

982 (c14) (*to*) *suggincgwyrðe*; 1242 *Sugginwrth*; 1280 *Soggynwrth*; 1325 *Suckyngeworth*; 1329 *Suggyngeworth*.

OE *Suggingwyrð* 'Sugga's curtilage'. The *-e-* forms are in evidence from the e. c16 (1530 *Segengworth*). The man's name apparently consists of the OE word for 'hedge sparrow'. But there is no parallel in the entire English place-name record which would license the interpretation of this name as 'hedge sparrow(s') curtilage'.

Selborne

903 (c16) *seleborne*; 1086 *Selesburna*; 1201 *Seleburne*.

Clearly named from what is now called *Oakhanger Stream*; disregarding the form in DB it appears to have been OE *seala burna* 'stream of sallows'.

Setley Hamlet in Brockenhurst

Occurs as *Setle* in 1331. Appears to mean 'planted wood', though this would have needed enclosing against roaming animals and enclosure of the royal forest for any purpose was illegal till 1483. (That does not mean it never happened.) Possibly therefore includes *sett* 'stunted', as Gover suggests for *Set Thorns Inclosure* (Rhinefield); though the chances of that including *set* 'planted' are significantly higher in view of the date of the first record, 1595. The 1483 Act provided for coppicewood to be surrounded with a thorn hedge until it had matured.

Shalden

1046 (c12/c16) (*be*) *scealdedeninga* (*gemære*); 1167 *Scaldedene*; 1282 *Shalden*.

OE *Scealde denu '(the) shallow valley'. The earliest form means 'by the boundary of the people of Shalden'. The name has obviously migrated. Shalden is on top of a ridge surrounded by rather steep, narrow valleys. Maybe the one to the east, where *Shalden Park Wood* is situated, is intended; the valley to the west was probably **Thedden**, another case where a present-day *denu* name is situated high.

Shamblehurst Farm in Botley, later in Hedge End
1174 *Scamelherst*; 1212 *Samelhurst*.
OE *Sceamolhyrst*, in one of two senses: literally 'bench wood' (where suitable wood was got) or figuratively 'wood on a bench' (shelf of level ground). *Hyrst* usually means 'wooded hill', which does not go well with the second possibility. It could, obscurely, imply 'wood where benches/tables were set up'.

Shave Wood in Minstead
An ancient wood, predating the **Inclosures**, in the New Forest management category 'Ancient and Ornamental'. Contains a common, but unexplained, form of OE *sceaga*, ME *schawe* 'wood', 'strip of woodland on field border'. Also in *Shaves Green* (1540 *Shaves greene* (Ellingham)) and *Shave Hat* near Bratley in Broomy Walk/Minstead.

Shawford Hamlet, now village, in Compton
1208 *Scaldeforda*; 1233 *Scaudeford*.
OE *Scealdan forde* '(at the) shallow ford', over the Itchen.

Shedfield Modern parish carved out of Droxford
956 (c12) (*to*) *scida felda*; 1256 *Schidefeld*.
OE *scīd* meant 'split wood, billet', 'shingle' or 'board', and Kökeritz (1940: 179–80) suggests that Shide (Wt) has a name embodying this word in the sense 'footbridge'. The present name means 'open land associated with more than one *scīd*', and the precise interpretation is unclear. A Roman road (Margary 420) crosses four minor streams close to Shedfield (within the parish). Maybe fording them was assisted by boards at some stage in their existence. A slight possibility is OE *scydd* 'shed, temporary building', and hence 'open land of the sheds'.

Sheet Modern parish carved out of Petersfield
c.1210 *Syeta*; 1236 *Shete*; 1281 *Schyte*; 1316 *Schute*.
OE *scīete* 'corner, nook', a derivative of *scēat* well evidenced in place-names. Sheet is in the angle between two headwaters of the river western Rother, and Sheet Common constituted the north-

eastern corner of Petersfield parish, surrounded by woodland into the c20.

Sherborne St John

1086 *Sireburne*; 1167 *Shireburne Johannis*; 1245 *Shirburne*.
Probably OE *Scīra burna '(the) bright stream'. The forms suggest this; on the other hand the proximity of *Shirlen's Copse* in Newnham (1365 *Shirlond*) and *Shear Down Farm* in Hannington (1334 *Scirdoune*) leaves a nagging suspicion that the word *scīr* 'shire' might be involved in some way because of the proximity of the county boundary with Berkshire. See the discussion under **Sherfield-on-Loddon**.
   The manor was held by Robert *de Sancto Johanne* in 1242, and the form of 1167 suggests earlier ownership by the same family. Distinguished from **Monk Sherborne**.

Sherfield English

c11 (c14) *scirefelde*; 1086 *Sirefelle*; 1256 *Shirefeud*.
Probably OE *Scīra feld '(the) bright open land', cf. **Sherfield-on-Loddon**. However the whole problem of names of this type is reviewed there. The manor was held by Richard *le Engleys* 'the Englishman' in 1325. It is uncertain whether any contrast with **Frenchmoor** is intended. The manorial specifier is mainly to distinguish it from Sherfield-on-Loddon.

Sherfield-on-Loddon or Sherfield upon Loddon

1167 *Sirefelda*; 1212 *Scirefeld*.
OE **Scīr(a) feld* '(the) bright open land', possibly meaning 'sparsely wooded'. If the name once denoted a larger area than the modern parish, we should reckon with *scīr* 'shire' as the first element, as we are not far from the Berkshire border. But the bulk of the spellings do suggest the inflected adjective 'bright'. See below. Distinguished by central administration as *on Loddon* and the like from the mid c16, in contrast to **Sherfield English**. For the same reason, in earlier times (e.g. 1280), occasionally distinguished as *Warblynton* from the family of Thomas de *Warblinton*, which must have originated in **Warblington**.
   There are several names in the county containing OE *scīr* as the first element, but whether in the sense 'bright' or 'shires' should be discussed. Those attested in early times are all (except perhaps **Shirley**) consistent with an origin in *scīra*, *scīre* or *scīran*, definite inflected forms of the adjective. But all except one are close to border territory, and also consistent with an origin in *scīra* 'of the shires'. **Sherfield-on-Loddon** church is just over 3 miles from

Berkshire, **Sherfield English** is less than a mile from a salient of Wiltshire. **Monk Sherborne** and **Sherborne St John** would have been less than 5 miles from Berkshire before the transfer of Mortimer West End to Hampshire. Other local PNs are *Shirlen's Copse* (1365 *Shirlond*) in Newnham and *Shear Down Farm* (1334 *Scirdoune*) in Hannington, neither more than 6 miles from Berkshire. It would be reasonable to speculate that the northern edge of Hampshire was added relatively late to the county, before which time it was a bulwark or no man's land between the two counties or the administrative areas that were their ancestors. **Shirley** in Millbrook is not near a boundary, but it might be OE *Scīrlēah* 'shire wood/clearing', with *scīr* in the singular (see its entry below). The DB hundred of *Shirley* comes to within 3 miles of the Dorset boundary and is adjacent to **Ringwood** hundred (cf. this name). **Shirrell Heath** may also contain *scīr* 'shire', but in exactly what sense is uncertain.

This difficult problem is even more complex, because consideration of the **Clere** names seems to lead us in the opposite direction and to take *scīr* to mean 'bright' after all.

Shipton Bellinger

1086 *Sceptone, Sceptune*; 1167 *Shipeton*; 1270 *Shupton*; 1291 *Schipton*.
OE *Scēaptūn* 'sheep farm', a frequent name-type. *Bellinger* is from the name of the lord in 1296, Ingelram *Berenger*, the modern form showing dissimilation of *r* to *l*. It is not known from which other *Shipton(s)* it is distinguished (possibly *Shipton Holms* (New Forest)).

Shirley In Millbrook, suburb of Southampton

1086 *Sirelei*; 1227 *Schirleg'*; 1253 *Sherley*.
There are two possibilities: either OE 'bright wood/clearing', in a compound form with an uninflected adjective; or 'shire wood/clearing', but there is no evidence that a shiremoot ever met here. If such evidence ever turns up, it will probably show that the name dates from the period when Southampton was the capital of the county and gave it its name. Cf. **Sherfield-on-Loddon**, where *Shirley hundred* is also discussed. If the second interpretation is right, there may be an implied contrast between **Portswood** 'wood of the town' and Shirley 'wood of the shire'.

Shirrell Heath In Shedfield

826 (c12) (oð ðæt) *scirhiltæ*; 939 (c12) (of) *scyrhylte*.
The name is not found again till embodied in the complex form *Sherrill heath* (1695). OE 'bright wooded land', the second element

being *hylte*, a derivative of OE *holt* 'managed wood, grove'; or 'shire wood', in some uncertain sense. Cf. **Sherfield-on-Loddon**.

Shoddesden Farms in Kimpton
1086 *Sotesdene*; 1265 *Schottesdene*; 1269 *Shottesden*.
Probably OE 'valley of Sceot(t)', used as a personal name rather than meaning 'the Scot/Irishman', cf. **Satchell**. Or was the ancestry of *Agemund* who held the manor before 1066 that of an Irish Viking? His name is Scandinavian in origin. The modern forms emerge in the c16 (1579 *Shaddesden*, 1699 *Shodsdeane*). Gover thought that the DB manor of *Soresdene* was in fact Shoddesden; it is otherwise unidentified, and there have long been two significant farms here. They may have turned up in DB as *Sotesdene* and *Soresdene*, a mistaken distinction. *VCH* (IV, 342) equates *Soresdene* with **Sarson**, and there is indeed a family connection between the DB lord of *Soresdene*, Waleran venator 'the hunter', and the later lords of Sarson. Certainty is not possible; both places are in Andover hundred as the DB *Soresdene* is. *Soresdene* is, however, not an ancestor of the name of *Sarson*.

Sholing In Itchen
1251 *Sholling*; 1255 *Schollinge*.
The name is first recorded rather late, and it is not fully clear whether it is an *-ingas* folk-name or a singular *-ing* name. If the former, the name may be OE **Sceolingas* 'people associated with a person called *Sceolh*' (a nickname either meaning 'crooked' or 'squint-eyed'); if the latter, an interpretation 'sloping place' is possible. The village lay on land between two streams, gently shelving SW to the place where they join. But the universal medieval spelling with *-ll-* speaks against both possibilities.

Silchester
c2 *Kaléoua*; c4 *Calleva*; c6 *Caleba*; 1086 *Silcestre*; c.1200 *Selechæstre*; 1227 *Cilcestre*; 1236 *Cilecestre*; 1294 *Cylchestre*; 1322 *Sylchestre*; 1349 *Chilchester*.
The ancient name of this Roman city was Brit. **Callēuā*, PrW **Callīw*. This was a derivative of the word giving rise to W *celli* 'grove' (less likely its direct ancestor). From this point, two theories have been propounded. Either the ancient name persists, with OE *ceaster* 'Roman town/station' added to it; or it is an entirely English name with an unrecorded derivative of the word *sealh* 'sallow tree' as the first element. Gover inclines to the first view, Ekwall to the second. Henry Bradley suggested to Grundy (1927) that the first element was OE *sȳl* 'pillar'. But in that case we would expect some

u spellings in ME. The entire problem is reviewed in Coates (1988a). The 'sallow' theory is improbable on ecological grounds (compounding the philological difficulties (1) that Ekwall invents derivatives of *sealh* rather liberally, and (2) that the balance of early spellings favours a one-syllable first element). The 'survival' theory runs into difficulties because the expected forms in initial *C-* do not appear till the c13, before which we find uniformly *S-*. Coates slightly favours the 'survival' theory, but the matter should be left open still.

Sinah Common In Hayling Island
Appears 1440 *Seynor*. Maybe a descendant of OE **Sæganōra* 'bank at the marsh', i.e. the marshes of Langstone Harbour. The word **sæge* is not on record but has continental Germanic counterparts.

Skidmore DMV in Romsey
1227×1245 *Scudemore*, 1412 *Skydmore*.
Takes its name from a family the present form of whose surname is often also *Scudamore*. This is of uncertain origin, but could be accounted for formally as AN *escu de more* 'shield of a moor'. Reaney in his *Dictionary of English Surnames* takes the surname to derive from a SW place-name (presumably this one, had he known of it), but that cannot be right, as PNs beginning with *Sk-* are not expected in the SCy – they are usually of Scandinavian origin. Moreover there is a further Norman 'surname' manor in Romsey, **Pauncefoot**.

Slacham Lost DB manor in Fordingbridge hundred
OE **Slāhhām* 'sloe estate'. Has been identified with **Sloden Inclosure** in Fordingbridge (SU 207132), though the formation of the names is not identical.

Slackstead Two hamlets in Farley Chamberlayne
903 (c16) *slastede*; 1269 *Slacstede*; 1350 *Slaghstede*.
OE **Slāhstede* 'sloe-place/site'. The [k]-sound for earlier [x] (OE *h*) is paralleled in e.g. **Heckfield** and in *Hick'stead* (Sx). For *stede*, see Sandred (1963). The chalk downs are good blackthorn country. Distinguished now as *Upper* and *Lower S.*

Sleaford Hamlet in Headley
1245 *Sleyford*; 1336 *Slayford*.
OE **Slegeford* 'killing ford', the reason for which is unknown. Not from the *Slea* stream, whose name is a modern back-formation from the PN.

Sloden Inclosure In Ashley Walk parish
Recorded 1243 *Sloudon*. OE **Slōhdūn* 'bog hill'. Above, and edged

by, *Latchmore Brook*, whose name means 'leech pool' or 'boggy pool' (1391 *Lechemere*); more likely the latter, to judge by Sumner's topographical description (1972: 34).

Slufter's Inclosure In Minstead
No early spellings discovered. I guess that it derives from an earlier PN amounting to 'bog', ultimately from OE *slōhtre*, for which there are parallels in continental Germanic languages. A stream flows through the plantation. Possibly, though a little less likely, from the ancestor of 'sloe-tree'.

Smannell In Andover
t. Ed III *Smethenhulle*; 1432 *Smethull*; 1652 *Smanhill*.
OE *Smēðenhyll* '(at the) smooth hill' is rather more likely than *Smiððanhyll* 'smithy hill'. The reference is to the gentle rise above Finkley farm.

Snoddington Manor in Shipton Bellinger
1086 *Snodintone*; 1269 *Snodintun*.
OE *Snoddingtūn* 'Snodd's farm'.

Soberton
1086 *Sudbertune*; c12 *Subertune*; 1280 *Suthberton*.
OE *Sūðberetūn* 'south grange farm', i.e. south from **Meonstoke/Corhampton** (cf. the names of these). It became a grange of Beaulieu Abbey in 1205.

Soldridge In Medstead
1233, 1245 *Solrigge*.
OE *Solhrycg* 'wallowing pond ridge', i.e. one of the small elevations W and E of the present village. The general characteristics of the land here could be deduced from the existence of *Dry Hill* N of the hamlet, dryness requiring special mention.

Solent, The Arm of the sea
c.730 (m.c8), c.890 (c.1000) *soluente*; 948 (c12) (*utt on*) *solentan*; 1395 *le Soland*.
Of uncertain meaning, but a name of an ancient type. Remarkably similar names are found about 2000 years ago in Sicily, on the coast of Africa, and in the Adriatic (this last being an island). It appears to be Indo-European in form, but cannot be positively attributed to any known IE language. It is discussed at great length in Coates (1988a).

The name originally denoted the whole channel including **Spithead**, for the form of 948 appears in the bounds of Alverstoke, adjacent to the spit from which Spithead takes its name.

Solent Breezes Estate in Hook

A s.-e. 1960s fancy name for a caravan site which appears as a permanent feature on the current OS 1:50 000 map despite its largely seasonal occupation.

Somerford Suburb of Christchurch
See **Mudeford**.

Sopley

1086 *Sopelie*; t. Hy I *Soppeleia*; 1152 *Soppeley*.
OE **Soppanlēah* 'Soppa's wood/clearing'. This man's name has been inferred from other PNs. It is legitimate to wonder if an OE **soppa* 'milksop' existed; only *sopp* is recorded, but there are continental Germanic parallels for a **soppa*. If so, this is 'sop wood' in a topographical sense; the village centre is by a marsh in the Avon valley.

South Ham, West Ham Districts of Basingstoke

These names clearly include *hamm* 'hemmed-in land', but it is hard to determine in what sense. They may represent the *Hyghehamme* 'high *hamm*' recorded in c.1250. They are higher in the dry upper valley of the Loddon than the centre of Basingstoke is.

South Hay Shrunken village in Binstead

There is a *Hay Place* in the same village from which it lies S. That is 1362 *Heyes* 'enclosures' (placed by Gover under Alton).

South View District of Basingstoke

S.-e.; it is on the south flank of the hill commemorated by the name **Oakridge**.

Southampton

842 (l. c9) *hamwig* (a continental spelling); c.973–1015 *hamwic* (coins); 825 (c12) *homtun*; 837 (e. c12) (*æt*) *hamtune*; 900 (e. c11) *hamtun*; 924–39 *amtun* (coins); c.973–c.1025 *aamtun* (coins); 962 (m. c12) *æt suthamtunam*; 980 (m. c11) *suðhamtun*.
This name has been extensively discussed by Rumble (1980), and his account should be consulted by interested readers. There are many mentions of the c11 and before showing that the generally used name of the place was *Hamtun*, representing an earlier **Hammtūn*, OE 'hemmed-in land town', referring to its situation between the Itchen and Test estuaries. The site was much more obviously a Dodgson-2a *hamm*-site before the reclamation of land in the Test estuary for the New Docks. The alternative name-tradition was *Hamwīc*, 'hemmed-in land trading-place', often cited by archaeologists and historians in the once-off c8 Rhineland

German form *Hamwih*, a custom which should be discarded. There is little reason to suppose that the two names represent separate places; rather they are likely to be names for the town in its topographical or administrative (*tūn*) and mercantile (*wīc*) aspects. The town is distinguished as *South*ampton as early as the *OE Chronicle* (*Suðhamtun*, s.a. 980 (m. c11), C-text), and it has been surmised that this was an invention at a place for which North- and Southampton were equally important. Abingdon (O), on a major through-route from Southampton to the Midlands, where the C-test of the *OE Chronicle* was written, seems the likely candidate. This is where the bulk of the examples of this name-form stem from or derive from at second hand. This name-form does not begin to become general, however, till the high Middle Ages, and plain *Hampton* is found as late as 1465/6; it is this form which appears in the name of the county. The abbreviation *Hants* represents the AN version of OE *Hamtūnscīr*, for which *Hantescire* in DB can stand as a model.

The modern suburb *Hampton Park* contains, of course, a fancy revival of the older simple PN.

Southbourne Suburb of Bournemouth, now in Do
A purely modern name, curious as the place is not south of any bourne. *VCH* (V: 134) says it was formerly *West Shore*, i.e. from the perspective of Christchurch.

Southbrook Tithing of Micheldever
t. Hy III *Suthbrok*; 1586 *Southbroke*.
ME 'south of the brook', i.e. Micheldever stream; opposite is *Northbrook* (1256 *Northbrok*).

Southsea
1545 *le South Castell of Portesmouth*; 1579 *Southsea ca.*; c.1600 *Southsea Castle*.
Although the name seems transparent, there is no obvious reason why a place on land should be called *south sea*. The name is at first that of the Tudor castle, and we must suppose it is so named from being beside Spithead rather than Langstone or Portsmouth Harbours, unless the *-sea* has been abstracted from other local names like **Portsea**, **Hilsea**, *Horsea* and treated as an element.

Southwick
c.1140, 1212 *Sudwic*; t. John *Suwyca*; 1291 *Suthwyk*.
OE/ME *Sūðwīc* 'south specialized farm'. *Wīc* often means 'dairy farm' in particular. It is not clear from what perspective it is south. Perhaps from the fact that it is just south of the Roman road from

Chichester to Bitterne – one of the farms opposite could have been a 'north wick'; or from **Wanstead Farm**, less than 2 miles ENE. No significant connection with Hambledon, the parish immediately N, is known.

Sparsholt

901 (c11) (æt) *sweoresholte* (error confusing *p* with the runic letter *wen* (*w*)); 1047×1053 (c12) (æt) *spæresholte*; 1167 *Speresholt*.

OE *Spearresholt* 'managed wood producing spears, spars, rafters', a useful appurtenance close to a large town and military centre like Winchester. This name has influenced that of *Spursholt* in Romsey, which was 1227 *Perscete* (OE *pirigescēat* 'pear-tree nook'), via form 1601 *Spurshott*.

Spithead Arm of the sea

First mentioned by name in 1629. It denotes primarily the spit of **Haslar**, at the heel of which is **Gilkicker Point**; its underwater extension is *Spit Sand*, on which *Spit Sand Fort* stands.

Spursholt House in Romsey

See **Sparsholt**.

Stakes In Farlington, suburb of Portsmouth

Originally *Frendstaple*.

t. Hy I *Frundstapla*; t. Hy II *Frendestapele*; c.1200 *Freondestaple*; 1441 (*maner' called*) *Stake*.

Apparently OE *Frēondesstapol* 'friend's post', or perhaps 'Friend's', i.e. a personal name. Possibly the same element in the plural (*frēonda*). The precise meaning is unclear. Ekwall gives a more complicated – and less satisfactory – origin in the personal name *Frēomund*, reduced rather drastically. The modern name is from the family of *Stake* holding the manor in 1248. They apparently gave their name to the place rather than taking it from it.

Stamshaw or Stampsey In Portsmouth

1236 *Stamnesho*; 1292 *Stampneshou*.

There are odd transformations later, e.g. 1294 *Scampnesho*, 1333 *Stamelleshou*, c.1600 *Stampsey*. OE 'heel of land, promontory (*hōh*), marked with a (stem- or stern-) post'. The first element appears to be an OE *stamn*, not attested, but related to the *stemn* that gives us *stem*(*-post*), and paralleled by German *Stamm*; possibly a borrowing from the equivalent word in Low German, *stamn*, in pre-Hanseatic trading contacts.

Stanbridge Two manors and DMV in Romsey

'Stone bridge' (1236 *Stanbridge*) spanning the Test. Cf. **Awbridge**.

The two manors in the c14 were distinguished as *Earls* (*Comitis*) and *Ranville*; the former was held of the Earl Marshal (initially by Simon de Montfort) and the latter by the *de Raunvile* (*Ranville*) family, hailing from *Ranville* (Calvados, Normandy).

Standon Hamlet in Hursley
1167, 1171, 1249 *Standen(e)*.
OE *★Stāndenu* 'stony valley', i.e. the one followed by the modern A31.

Stanpit DB manor in Christchurch
1086 *Stanpeta*; c.1170 *Stanputta*.
OE *★Stānpytt* 'stonepit, quarry'. The outcrop here is of brickearth/valley gravel.

Stanswood DB manor in Fawley
1086 *Staneude*; 1283 *Staneswode*.
Gover suggests 'wood belonging to **Stone**' in the same parish. This seems probable.

Stapely Farm and tithing in Odiham
1184 *Stapeleg'*; 1201 *Stapeleya*; 1206 *Stapelleg'*.
OE *★Stapollēah* 'post wood', i.e. presumably where timber suitable for posts could be got, rather than one marked with a post.

Steep
c12 *Stepe*; c.1200 *Stupe*; c.1230 *la Stiepe*.
Clearly OE *stīepe* 'steep place', from *stēap* 'steep'. There is quite a steep drop from the downland to the Weald here.

Steventon
1086 *Stivetune*; 1167 *Stiuintona*; 1200 *Stiventon*.
A possible *-ingtūn* derivative of an unrecorded OE man's name *★Stifa* 'stiff', as Gover speculates. However, the name recurs at *Steventon* (Brk), *Stevington* (Bd, Ess), *Steeton* (YWR x2) and *Stewton* (L). Much more likely therefore OE *★Styf(ic)ing-tūn* 'farm at the place of grubbed-up trees' (see *★styfic* in Smith (*EPNE* II: 166)).

Stockbridge
1221 *Stocbrugge*; 1227 *Stocbrigge*.
OE/ME *★Stoccbrycg* 'log bridge', i.e. presumably that is how it was constructed. The absence of Stockbridge from DB may be accounted for by the presence of the *Sumburne* held by William of Eu in Somborne hundred, for Stockbridge was known as *White Somborne* in the early Middle Ages (Hill 1975). Hill's identification

of this place with the *Brige* (Brit. 'hill(s)') of the Ravenna Cosmography need not be accepted (cf. Rivet and Smith 1979).

Stoke Hamlet in St Mary Bourne
900 (c11) (*æt*) *stoce* (*be hysseburnan*); 1208 *Stokes*.
OE *stoc* 'dependent farm, grange farm', held at various times by the monks of Abingdon (O) and St Swithin's. Also called 1255 *Crockerestok* 'potters' Stoke' (or possibly with *Crockere* as a surname) to distinguish it from **Alverstoke**, **Stoke Charity**, etc.

Stoke Charity
1086 *Stoches*; 1256 *Eledestoke*; 1276 *Elledestok*; c.1270 *Stokecharite*; 1276 *Eldestok(e)*; 1364 *Oldestoke*; t. Jas I *Old Stoke Charitie*.
Originally just *Stoc* 'dependent farm, grange farm', i.e. of Micheldever, held by Hyde Abbey. Ekwall suggested, in a letter to Gover, that the earliest qualifier of the name represents OE *ǽlede* 'burnt'. This was later taken as *eald* 'old', developing regularly in one tradition into the *Old Stoke* of modern times (still on the OS map as a house name, SU 485377). The manor was held in 1276 by Henry de *la Charite*, hence the other tradition. The two traditions merge in an early Stuart document.

Stoke Park Modern parish carved out of Bishopstoke
1291 (*in*) *parco de Stok*.
The medieval *park* was an enclosed hunting-ground within a major manor. The manor here was the Bishop of Winchester's. See **Bishopstoke**.

Stone In Fawley
c.730 (m. c8) (*ad*) *Lapidem*; c.890 (c.1000) (*æt*) *stane*; 1086 *Stanes*.
The place mentioned by Bede is now usually placed here; though in earlier writings one of the **Stonehams** was preferred, presumably only because they were more significant and better-known places. Stone is right for his story, since the Isle of Wight is involved, and Stone is at the Solent end of a local Roman road (Margary 423). It is quite probable that a Roman-period artefact is commemorated in the name. *Stansore Point* nearby may be an early derivative from this name ('bank/shore of Stone').

Stoneham North and South
932 (c13/c14) (*æt*) *stanham* (North); 1086 *Stoneham* (North); 1086 *Stanham* (South).
Both names have the same origin. They were distinguished in medieval times as *Abbot's* and *Bishop's* Stoneham, being held by

Hyde Abbey and the see of Winchester respectively. The place-name is OE *Stānhām* 'stone estate', either from stone-built buildings or from the character of the land.

Stoney Cross Crossroads in Minstead
A reference to the metalling of the Roman roads (Margary 422 and 424) which intersect here is possible, but the place is in any case on a patch of plateau gravel.

Stour River
944 (c15) (*on*) *sture*; 968 (c14) *stour*; t. Hy I (*ripam de*) *Stour*.
There are several *Stours* in England, e.g. also in K and Ess/Sf. Ekwall relates it to the *Stura* in Italy and gives it an Indo-European background allowing it to mean 'strong, powerful river'; though citing words meaning 'pole' does not make the theory convincing. There are philological difficulties in connecting it instead with an unattested OE relative, **stōr*, of the ON word *stórr* 'big', which would otherwise be seductive because the name seems only to attach to relatively major rivers. Instead, Smith (*EPNE* II) derives it from an OE relative of Low German *stūr* 'unfriendly', Norwegian *stūr* 'gloomy'.

Stratfield Saye and **Stratfield Turgis** Two parishes
1053×1066 (c13/c14) *stratfeld*; 1086 *Stradfelde, Stradfelle*.
OE **Strǣtfeld* 'open land by the paved road', i.e. the Roman road (Margary 4a) from Silchester to London, also known as *The Devil's Highway*. One manor was held by John de Stutevill' in 1244 (cf. c13 *Stratfelde Stuteville*) and later by Richard de Say (cf. 1263 *Stratfeldsay*). The other, smaller one was held by the Turgys family from the late c13 (cf. early c13, 1287 *Petit Stratfeld, Stratfeud Turgis*). Both specifiers are Norman surnames; the first comes from the PN *Sai* in Orne (Normandy); the second is a Frenchified form of the Scandinavian given name *Þórgils*.
Stratfield Saye house is the seat of the Dukes of Wellington, hence the adjacent *Wellington Monument* and *W. Country Park*.

Stratton, East
903 (c16) *strattone*; 1167 *Strattona*.
OE **Strǣttūn* 'paved road farm'. The road is the Roman road from London to Winchester (Margary 42a). The place is *East* Stratton from 1316 (*Est Strattone*) in contradistinction to *West Stratton* a mile away in Micheldever (recorded as so named from 1250). It is not known whether they were ever a single farm.

Street In Christchurch, tithing of Christchurch hundred
1248 *Strete, Strate*; 1429 *la Strete*.
Clearly 'street', but in a medieval sense e.g. 'highway'; there is no known Roman road hereabouts.

Stroud In Langrish
1327 (*atte*) *Strode*.
OE *strōd* 'marsh covered with brushwood'. Stroud overlooks a headwater of the Rother.

Stubbington Submember of the new parish of Crofton
1086 *Stubitone*; 1202 *Stubinton*.
OE *Stubbingtūn* 'farm at the *stubbing*' or land characterized by stumps, cleared land.

Sudberie Lost DB manor in Bermondspit hundred
The PN is not found after DB, but appears to have a name meaning 'south fort/manor', OE *Sūðbyrig* (dative case). It is possible that this is the later *Preston House* in Preston Candover, which is 1167 *Candiura Stephani*, 1328 *Stevenbur'* ME 'Stephen's manor', a name-type common in the Home Counties (cf. **Bransbury**). This would have to be the 'south manor' from being in the detached part of Bermondspit hundred, south of the block of villages from Dummer to Herriard which constituted its DB heartland. Otherwise, account should be taken of the earthwork SW of Ellisfield below which is *Berrydown* farm; or possibly *Moundsmere Manor* in Preston Candover.

Sunwood Manor in Buriton
1194 *Sunnewurda, Soneworde*; 1207 *Sunewurth*.
OE *Sunnanwyrð* 'Sunna's curtilage'. The form in -*wood* is found from 1759.

Sutton Scotney Hamlet, now village, in Wonston
1086 *Sudtune*; 1235 *Suttun'*.
OE/ME *Sūðtūn* 'south farm', in relation to *Norton* in the same parish rather than to the village of Wonston itself, which is to the east of here. *Scotney* from Walter de *Scotney* who held the manor in 1235; his family hailed from *Étocquigny* in Seine-Maritime, Normandy (cf. *Scotney Castle* in Lamberhurst (K)).

Swampton DB manor in Kingsclere hundred, tithing of St Mary Bourne
1086 *Suantune*; 1248 *Swanton*; 1269 and thenceforward *Swamptun*.
To judge by the earliest forms, on the face of it, OE 'swan farm'. There is no trace of the medial -*e*- which would make 'swains'

farm' likely. The forms in -*mp*- are, however, inexplicable starting from *Swantūn*. Most likely therefore *Swammtūn* 'mushroom/toadstool farm'; this element has not been recorded in PNs before.

Swanmore
1205 *Suanemere*; 1207 *Swanemere*.
OE *Swanamere* 'swans' pool'. The spelling -*more* would have been substituted late when the original second element had come to be pronounced with the obscure vowel [ə].

Swanthorpe House in Crondall
1233 *Swanethorp*; 1248 *Swandrop*; 1541 *Swantroppe*; 1586 *Swandrope*.
OE *Swānaþrop* 'herdsmen's secondary settlement', with the implication that the site is a permanent village replacing an earlier seasonal herdsmen's settlement.

Swanwick Submember of Sarisbury parish
1185, 1210 *Suanewic(h)*; 1236 *Swanewik*.
OE *Swānawīc* 'herdsmen's specialized farm', possibly a dairy farm.

Swarraton
903 (c16) *Swerwetone*; 1135x1154 *Serueton*; 1207 *Sherueton*; 1242, 1250 *S(w)arweton*.
Ekwall suggests that the first element is a reduced form of *Swærwæd* 'heavy ford' (i.e. over the right-bank tributary of the Itchen entering below Alresford). Grundy, following Bradley, suggests the first element is a pre-OE stream name. The latter cannot be right; PrW *sw-/su̯- is non-existent (Jackson 1953: 525–6). Perhaps it is OE *Swearðwatūn* 'pelt farm', i.e. farm supplying dressed or undressed animal skins, if OE *sweard, swearð* 'pelt' is for Gmc *swardu-, swardw-* as Germanic and Baltic cognates seem to suggest. For a trace of the *u/w* in the second syllable to be preserved, the name would have to be of high antiquity. The 'oldest' spelling is preserved only in a c16 copy of a spurious document, but it looks a fair ancestor for the modern name.

Sway Modern parish carved out of Boldre
1086 *Sueia*; 1227 *Sweia*; 1248 *Sweye*.
Possibly OE *swæð* 'track', surviving in a Normanized form, which would not be surprising close to a centre of the royal court's activity like the New Forest. Ekwall suggests a river-name (for *Avon Water*; this name is entirely modern) deriving from OE *swēge* 'sounding', but this seems a bit weak. Although the phonology is tricky, OE *Sūhege* 'sow enclosure' might fill the bill.

Swaythling In North Stoneham

909 (?c11/c12) (*be*) *swæðelinge*; 932 (c13/c14) (*to*) *swæðelingeforda*, (*of*) *swæðelingforda*; 1045 (c12) (*on*) *swæðeling wylle*.

Despite five separate mentions in AS times, and despite the remarkable similarity of these, the name remains difficult. Swaythling seems to have been the name of the stream now called *Monk's Brook* which falls into the Itchen here; the form of 1045, apparently 'the stream (called) Swaythling', may support this view. It may be a singular -*ing* name based on OE *swaðul* 'smoke, (??) mist', and if so therefore *Swæðeling '*place of mist*'. *It would be interesting to know more about the microclimate of the area.* OE *sweðel* 'wrappings, swaddling-bands' might be considered, in use as a topographical term, but the stream is not especially winding and nothing else would seem to justify such a name.

Sydmonton Modern parish carved out of Kingsclere

1086, 1200 *Sidemanestone*; 1169 *Sidemanton'*.

Certainly OE *Sīdemannestūn 'Sīdemann's farm'. A man of this name was *Sydeman minister* who signed the Ecchinswell charter of 931 (c12). Grundy speculates (1927: 260) that it was he who gave his name to this village. Romsey Abbey held the manor, and presumably the advowson, of Sydmonton in 1086; Sydeman the priest may have held it of an earlier abbot. In 1586 we find the interesting corruption *Sidemountaine*; this was a time when speculative etymology was a popular pastime among the learned (and semi-learned).

T

Tadley
909 (c12) (æt) tad(d)anleage; 1205 Taddele.
Mention of toads (OE tādige or a possible short-form *tadda)
suggests that lēah here be interpreted as 'meadow, pasture' rather
than 'wood/clearing'. The matter is more open if the first element
is the same word used as a man's name (cf. Tadlow (Bk)). If the
first form is good OE, the personal-name interpretation may be
better, because it is a genitive singular form.

Talbot Village Suburb of Bournemouth, formerly in Do, now returned
Named in the mid c19 after the local landowners Mary Anne and
Georgina Charlotte Talbot.

Tangley
1174 Tangelea; 1212 Tangelie.
OE *Tang(a)lēah 'wood/clearing at the projecting point(s) of land'
(see under tang in Smith (EPNE II)). Tangley church stands on a
small promontory between two small dry valleys, and there are
slightly larger promontories on either side of this one. The first
element may therefore be in the plural, as all the medieval spellings
indicate.

Tatchbury Fort in Copythorne
903 (c14) tachburi; 1086 Taceberie; 1227 Tachebir'.
The second element is byrig, the dative case of OE burh 'fort'; there
is an ancient fortification here. The first is quite unclear. It may be
a man's name *Taccea, derived from *tacca 'teg, young sheep' or
the known personal name Tacca, Tæcca. There are two medieval
spellings with Th-, dating from 1272, 1475, which might suggest
the first element is OE þæc 'roof, thatch'; the PN could then be
'thatched manor'. If so, all the other spellings and modern form
would have to be put down to AN influence.

Temple Farm In Selborne
1240 (manerium) de Templariorum de Sudinton; 1256 Suthinton.
The manor was ME *Sūth in tūn 'south in (the) village'. It was
granted to the Knights Templar in 1240 and the feudal name has
supplanted the older one. The complex Temple Soddington alias
Temple Sothington is found as late as 1617.

Test River

877 (c12) (*on*) *terstan*; 901 (c11) (*on*) *terstan*; 1045 *tærstan stream*; 1234 *Terste*; 1425 *Test*.

A problematic name. The string of OE spellings (only a sample is given) leaves no doubt what the name was in AS times, *Terste/-a*, and there begins the problem. No English etymology can be offered. Equally, no PrW name should contain *-st-*, since this combination was simplified to *-s-* during the Brit. period or earlier. The PrW form must have had a vowel between the *-s-* and *-t-*. But if so it would probably have been stressed and therefore not lost. Leaving aside this point, a form pronounced in PrW *Tristǫn* (if one could have existed) could have given OE *Terste* by the processes described in detail by Jackson (1953: 524–5). Such a name resembles superficially the common RB *Trisantona* seen in e.g. *Trent*, *Tarrant*. But its relation to this name is problematic.

Testwood In Eling, suburb of Southampton

1174×1199, 1207 *Terstewode*; 1362 *Testwode*.

OE/ME 'wood (*wudu*) by the Test'; see **Test**. The DB manor of *Lesteorde*, *Lestred* has been held to be Testwood, but nothing can be made of the forms as they stand.

Thedden Grange-farm in Alton

1168 *Tedena*; 1203 *Þuddene*; 1207 *Theddene*; c.1270 *Thutdene*.

OE ★*Þēotdenu* 'valley with a water conduit'. The name has migrated to the farm from the broad valley below (cf. **Shalden**). It is not hard to imagine that there was a villa in it in Roman times supplied with piped water from Alton's spring(s). The mouth of the valley is at Will Hall (see **Alton**). But this is pure speculation.

Throop Hamlet in Holdenhurst, now suburb of Bournemouth, in Do

c12 *la Throup*; 1201 *Latrop*; 1540 *Throppe*.

OE *þrop* 'secondary settlement', i.e. of Holdenhurst.

Thruxton

1167 *Turkilleston*; 1244 *Turkeleston*; 1269 *Trokeleston*; 1325 *Thrukeleston*; 1442 *Throkeston*; 1670 *Thruxon*.

The first element is a man's name of Scandinavian origin. Since there is a suspicion (*VCH* IV: 387) that this is one of the old *Anne* manors registered in DB, the name may be post-DB in origin (cf. **Monxton**, **Sarson**), and the name will then be a fully anglicized version of the Scandinavian, *Thorkill* No tenant of this name is known, however. The attrition of the name can be followed in the series of forms cited. It had clearly reached the modern pronunciation, or nearly so, by the mid c15.

Tichborne

c.909 (c12) *ticceburna*; 938 (c12) (*be*) *ticceburnan*; 1235 *Ticheburne*. OE 'kid stream', containing the nominative singular or genitive plural of an unattested relative (*ticce*) of the word *ticcen* 'kid'. (Cf. **Titchfield**, **Tisted**.) It may be *Ticcea*, a masculine by-name based on the word in question. The stream is the upper course of what is now counted as part of the river Itchen.

Tidbury Ring
See **Tidworth**.

Tidgrove DB manor in Kingsclere
1086, 1176 *Titegrave*.
OE *Titangrāf* 'Tita's grove' or managed wood.

Tidworth, South or Tedworth

979×1015 (c14) (*æt*) *tudanwyrðe*; 1086 *Tedorde, Todeorde*; 1203 *Tudewrth*.
OE *Tudanwyrð* 'Tuda's curtilage'; on the form *wyrð* see **Ashmansworth**. If the first citation for 1086 is correct, it shows an early hint of the later development of the name with the front vowels *i, e* which is not otherwise found till the c14/c15 (1362 *South Tedeworth*). Distinguished from *North Tidworth* just across the county boundary in W. The same man's name (which may be connected with Brit. names in *Touto-*) appears to feature in *Tidbury Ring* in Bullington, 18 miles ESE of here (1019 (*of, to*) *tudan byrig*), though not in *Tidcombe* (W, 7 miles NE, 1197 *Titecumba*), which contains the personal name found in **Tidgrove**.

Timsbury Parish, later in Michelmersh
1086 *Timbreberie*; 1252 *Timberbury*.
OE *Timberburh* or *(ge)Timbreburh*; the meaning is thus uncertain as between 'fort' and 'manor-house' and 'built of timber' or 'marked with a timber building'. Only archaeological findings can elucidate this. Its low-lying site is clearly not that of a typical prehistoric hillfort.

The forms in -*s* which eventually prevail (strangely, in view of how transparent the form of the name was) are found from 1236 (*Timbresbury*). This suggests that the PN was taken as including a personal name of a possessor or tenant, leading me to think that 'manor' is the likelier interpretation. But this is not certain.

Tiptoe In Hordle
From a surname of French origin recorded since the c13 in this area
(c13 *Typetot*)

Tisted, **East** and **West** Two parishes
932 (c12) *ticces stede* (West T.); 941 (c12) (*æt*) *ticcestede* (West T.)
1086 *Tistede* (West T.).
OE *Ticces stede 'kid's place' or 'place of a man called *Ticce* 'kid''
The expected word for 'kid' is *ticcen*, but clearly an *n*- less form
existed (cf. **Tichborne**, **Titchfield**). The places are distinguished a
1234x1236 *Westistude* and 1263 *Est Tystede*, and so to the present day

Titchfield
982 (c14) (*on*) *ticcefelda*, (*to*) *ticcanfelde*; 1086 *Ticefelle*; 118.
Tichesfeld; 1218 *Tychefeld*.
OE 'open land associated with *Ticcea', a man's name derived from
the OE *ticcen* 'kid'. Otherwise, if an alternation of forms found i
an early c10 boundary clause for Ampfield is to be taken seriously
ticcenesfelda/ticcefeldes, the present name may actually be **Ticce(n)
feld* 'kids' open land', a two-stem nominal compound involving
the noun *ticcen* or *ticce. (Cf. **Tichborne**, **Tisted**.) But in an
important note, Finberg (1964a: 58) observes that the place in whose
bounds *ticcanfelde* occurs is stated to be in the Isle of Wight. If we
remove this form from the list above, the spread of spellings become
consistent. probably therefore Ticcefeld 'kid open land'.

Totford Farm and hamlet in Northington
1167 *Totefort*; 1201 *Toteford*.
OE *Tottanford 'Totta's ford', over the stream flowing from th
Candovers to the Itchen.

Totton In Eling, suburb of Southampton
1086 *Totintone*; 1174x1199 *Totyngton*.
OE **Tot(t)ingtūn* 'farm of Tot(t)a'. It is usual to identify the D
manor of *Dodintune* in Redbridge hundred with this place too
though not on the linguistic evidence. There was an actual *Dod*
who held the extinguished manor of *Bedecote* in the New Fores
before 1066. On some late maps (1817) a form with an unrounde
vowel *Tatton* is found (cf. **Breamore**).

Toyd Farm In Martin, former submember of separate parish, onc
in Do
c13 *Tohyde*; 1255 *Twyd*; 1518 *Twohide*.
OE *Twāhīda 'two hides'; cf. **Fyfield**. Obviously related to th
geld which it was liable to pay, but nothing is known of its histor
in the c11/c12.

Tuckton Suburb of Bournemouth, now in Do

1248 *Tuketon*; c.1300 *Tocketon*.

Probably OE *Tuccantūn* 'Tucca's farm'. Cf. **Tufton**. A late form of Tuckton shows the same development, 1727 *Tuffen alias Tuckton*. Gave its name to *Tucktonia*, the famous model village.

Tufton

1086 *Tochiton*; 1189×1199 *Tokinton, Tokintun*; 1256 *Tuketon*.

OE either *Tuccantūn* or *Tuccingtūn* 'Tucca's farm' (cf. **Tuckton**). The development to *f* presupposes a change of [k] to [x], but no such thing shows up in the record. The *f* is seen first in 1580 *Tufton*. It is of great interest that the Dark Age trackway from Winchester to Whitchurch, Litchfield and the Kennet Valley was 901 (c14) (*on*) *tuccinge weg*, c.1250 *Tokingweie*, apparently containing the same personal name. It passes within half a mile of Tufton village.

Tunworth

1086 *Tuneworde*; 1193 *Tunnewrthe*; 1244 *Toneworth*.

OE *Tunnanwyrð* 'Tunna's curtilage'. There is a similar name in Mx.

Twinley Manor In Whitchurch

1615 *Twynlie*.

Gover suggests 'double wood'. Although the form is late, however, it almost certainly represents OE (*æt*) *twǣm hlǣwum* 'at (the) two barrows', from the two long barrows immediately adjacent.

Twyford

963×975 (c12) *tuifyrde*; 1086 *Tuiforde*; 1189 *Twiferd*.

OE *twīfyrd* 'double ford'. The Itchen today runs here in two and then three main channels. One is crossed by the ford referred to in **Shawford**; this appears to be the ford downstream from Twyford over the eastern channel. It is not known how the river has changed its bed in 1,000 years, if at all. There are *Twyfords* elsewhere, e.g. Brk, Bk, all by double fords.

Tytherley, West and **East** Two parishes/manors

1086 *Tiderlei* (both), *Tederlege* (either), *Tederlec/-leg* (either); 1218 *Tuderle*; 1252 *Tuderlegh*.

OE *Tīedreleah* 'fragile wood', as perhaps of a newly established plantation. Distinguished as 1212 *Westuterlie*, 1291 *Estuderlegh*. After DB most simplex forms may refer to East T., as the tradition acknowledging West T. by separate name seems to be early. East T. may thus be the parent settlement.

U

Up Nateley
See **Nateley Scures**.

Upham
c.1170 *Upham*.
OE 'upper estate' or 'upper hemmed-in land'. The village stands on a rise with noticeable descents on all sides, whilst a typical *hamm-2b* site falls on three sides. This makes the former more likely, therefore OE *Upphām.

Upton Grey
t. Hy I *Huppeton*; 1202 *Upton*.
OE/ME *Upptūn 'higher farm'. This name is a problem, for the whole of the eastern end of Bermondspit hundred is on a relatively level plateau varying between about 100 and 125 metres above sea level. If anything, the site of Upton Grey is fractionally lower than the surrounding area. It may be 'up' from the point of view of Hoddington manor in the same parish, but one has to go slightly down before one goes up! Perhaps we should take into account the mysterious phrase *upicenes hlywan,* in the bounds of the Hoddington charter of 1046, said by Grundy (1927: 279) to refer to a barrow, but I cannot make anything of it. (It is not by the river Itchen. *Hlywe* means 'shelter'.)

The manor was acquired by John de Grey in c.1260, the family name deriving from *Graye* in Normandy.

Utefel Lost DB manor in Rowditch hundred
Vtefel in DB; apparently OE *Ūtefeld 'more distant open land'.

V

Vernham Dean or Vernham's Dean

1210 *Ferneham*; 1232 *Fernham*; 1410 *Farnhamsdene*.

The original settlement name may be OE **Fearnhām* 'bracken estate', but the *Farnham* in Sr is certainly *Fearnhamm* 'bracken hemmed-in place', i.e. 'nook, corner, enclosed area', typically land surrounded on three sides by some natural obstacle. The use of *hām* in PNs died out early, so *hamm* is more likely if this is not an ancient place.

The modern name means 'valley of Vernham', though the genitive form of the PN in the new name is unusual in a creation of c. the c15 (1410 *Farnhamsdene*). However there is variation on this point; the OS one-inch county index (1974) gives an 's in the parish name but none in the village name. The place is in the broad valley above the source of the Bourne Rivulet at Upton, a typical *denu* 'wide flattish-bottomed valley'. It is distinguished from *Vernham Street* (1324 *la Strete*) on the hill to the east. The *V-* is not recorded till the reign of Elizabeth I, but it is a truly ancient Wessex dialect feature dating back to at least late OE (cf. e.g. Fisiak 1984). The fact that only *F-* shows up in early records is a tribute to centralized administration.

The history of this PN is, however, more complicated, for during the AS period it was known at one time as *Æscmere*, or formed part of this (cf. Grundy 1927: 281–3). cf. **Ashmansworth**.

Vyne, The Manor in Sherborne St John

1531 *The Vyne*.

S.-e. It has been said that this is the earliest English name coined specifically to designate a house. The estate was previously called *Sherborne Cowdray* (1272 *Syrburne Coudray*) from the family of Fulk *de Coudray* who held it in 1251. There are numerous places in Normandy called *Coudraie* 'hazel coppice', and Gover's speculation that it may have to do with *Cowdray* in Midhurst (Sx) may be unnecessary. But he asserts that the family of Peter de Coudray who gave their name to *Cowdray Copse* in Herriard actually did come from Cowdray in Sx.

W

Wadwick Hamlet in St Mary Bourne
1306 *Wad(d)ewyke*; 1636 *Wadewick*.
OE *Wadanwīc* 'Wada's specialized farm', probably a dairy-farm.

Walhampton Manor in Boldre
1086 *Wolnetune*; c12 *Wolhampton*; 1262 *Welhamton*.
Possibly *hāmtūn* 'estate' by a *weall* 'wall' or *walu* 'ridge, baulk, weal'. What the first element refers to is unclear. Later confused with **Wallington** (thus 1669; 1327 *Walynton*).

Walkford Farm, hamlet and **Glen** in Milton, now Christchurch East
1280 etc. *Walkeford(e)*.
Ekwall suggests an old stream-name *Wealce* 'the rolling one'. Gover considers this too and mentions OE *Wealeca*, a male personal name, as an alternative for the first element. Possibly a ME form 'ford that needs to be crossed at a walk' (i.e. (1) not on horseback or (2) not at the trot; ctrst **Arford**) is a simpler solution. Just possibly also 'ford where fulling took place', because an early meaning of *walk* was 'to full cloth'.

Wallington In Fareham
1233 *Waletune*; 1307 *Waleton*.
Although recorded only late, apparently OE *Wēalatūn* 'serfs'/Britons' farm'. For the implications of this see Cameron (1980). Such names are often associated with important RB estates, in this instance Porchester.

Wallop, **Nether** and **Over** Two parishes/manors
1086 *Wallope*; 1130 *Wallop*; 1201 *Walhop*; 1204 *Welleope*; 1217 *Welhop*; 1221 *Wellop*; 1227 *Wallehop*; 1242 *Wollop*; 1291 *Wolhope*.
This is a most difficult name. It appears to contain OE *hop* 'constricted valley' (cf. Gelling 1984: 112), and if so it is the only PN south of the Thames to contain the word in this sense. Gelling wonders if a colony of Midlanders was responsible. In some desperation Ekwall postulated a form of *wiellhop* 'stream valley' that must date from before the time of *i-* umlaut, i.e. probably before c.550, viz. an established compound *weallhop* where the [j] triggering *i-* umlaut had been lost. Gelling (*loc. cit.*) also notes that *weall* would not be expected in Hampshire. Rather perhaps it is a name of pre-English origin. There was a correspondence in *Antiquity*

in the 1930s, culminating in an article by Jackson (1939), associating Wallop with *guoloppvm, id est cat guoloph* in the *Welsh Annals* (caput 66). If the name is indeed Welsh, the PrW form behind these c8 renderings must be **Wolopp*, and what that might mean is anybody's guess. The form *guoloph* seems to show a Welsh spelling of a date later than that at which *Wallop* became an English name, if *ph* is for [f]. But this solution does not account for spellings in *e*.

The two Wallops are distinguished from the late c13 as 1271 *Netherwellop* and 1280 *Overwellop* from their respective positions along the Wallop Brook. *Middle Wallop* of course lies between them. The powerful landholding Wallop family, hailing from here, is commemorated in e.g. **Farleigh Wallop** and *Wallopswood Farm* in Soberton.

Waltham, Bishop's Parish and chase
904 (c12) *waltham*; 909 (?c11/c12) (*to*) *wealthæminga* (*mearce*); 963×75 (c12) (*æt*) *wealtham*.

OE *wealdhām* 'woodland estate', in a technical sense (cf. Huggins 1975). Places bearing this name appear to be establishments operative very early in AS times, and were royal woodland domains. This place is occasionally *Suthwaltham* in the Middle Ages (ctrst **Waltham, North** and variously also *Waltham Episcopi* or *Bisshoppeswaltham* and the like. The document of 904 records the grant of the estate by King Eadweard ('the Elder') to the see of Winchester. The form of 909 means 'to the boundary of the inhabitants of Waltham'. The earlier name for the chase was 1301 *Hordareswode*, 1307 *Hordereswode*, which looks suspiciously as though it contains OE *hordere* 'treasurer' (i.e. of the bishopric?). The term *chase* was originally applied to non-royal hunting grounds, as opposed to the royal *forest*.

Waltham, North
909 (c12) *wealtham*; 1167 *Waltham*; 1208 *Norwaltham*; 1291 *Waltham parva*.

North, *Parva* to distinguish it from *Bishop's Waltham*. For full discussion see **Waltham, Bishop's**. It may be of significance that before the Conquest the king held land in the adjacent manors of Dummer, Oakley and Steventon. On Saxton's map of 1611 it unaccountably appears as *Coldwaltham*, perhaps confused with the place of that name in Sx.

Wanstead Farm and shrunken village in Southwick
1201×1212 *Wenstede*; 1212×1217 *Wanstuda*.

OE **Wennstede/Wennstyde* 'bleb or wen place', like *Wanstead*

(Ess). The farm is right on top of a smooth hill.

Warblington

1086 *Warblitetone*; c.1170 *Warbligetona*; 1186 *Werblinton*; c13 *Warblin(g)ton(e)*.

There are several formal possibilities for this, all involving the OE woman's name *Wǣrblīð*, as Ekwall surmised in *DEPN*. It may be ⋆*Wǣrblīðantūn* 'Wǣrblīð's farm', ⋆*Wǣrblīðingtūn*, the same in essence, or ⋆*Wǣrblīðingatūn* 'farm of those associated with Wǣrblīð'. Possibly there was variation involving more than one of these forms. Further variants on the name(s) seem to have been current in the Middle Ages and later: cf. *Warbelton* (c.1230) and *Warlington* (1542). These may be an error and a spelling analogue for the nearby *Farlington* respectively.

Warborne Hamlet in Boldre

c12 *Wereburne*; t. John *Wereborne*.

Probably OE ⋆*Weraburna* 'stream with weirs or fish-traps', though no stream is visible on the OS 1:50000 map.

Warnborough, North, Warnborough Green Village/hamlet in Odiham, and Warnborough, South Parish

973×974(c12)(*æt*) *weargeburnan*(?South); 1046(c16)(*on*) *weargeburninga* (*gemære*) (?South); 1276 *Northwargheburne*; 1291 *Suthwargheborgh alias Suthwargheburn*.

OE ⋆*Weargaburna* 'felons' stream', where malefactors were drowned. (Cf. Kristensson (1981), Arngart (1983), Sandred (1984) for discussion of a similar, though not historically identical, name in Nf, once thought to have a common origin with *Warnborough*.) Puzzlingly, there is not a trace of a stream now at South Warnborough (below *Wells Hill*), to which the earliest forms appear to refer. North W. is on the river Whitewater. Grundy (1927: 286–7) confidently identifies the OE forms with South W.; however there is no boundary clause to the relevant charter and considerable uncertainty about the course of the bounds written in 1046. We must reckon with the original Warnborough being N., or that N. and S. once form some kind of unit which the OE name denoted.

In the c13 both PNs are rationalized as containing ME *burgh*, and the *n* migrates to the first syllable to compensate. Occasional forms are found with *gh* or *n* in both elements (1291 *Suthwargheborgh*, 1235 *Warnburn'*).

A reason to pause before accepting this rather dramatic etymology wholesale is that no origin is known for the common dialect word *werg* 'willow', which makes good sense with *burna*.

Warnford

1053 (*æt*) *wearnæforda*; 1086 *Warneford*.

If Ekwall was right about the existence of a hypothetical OE ★*wrǣna* 'stallion' (from *wrǣne* 'randy'), then this is 'stallion's ford', or the ford of a person so named. But more likely it is 'ford of Wǣrna', where this name is a short-form of an OE man's name like *Wǣrnōð*. The ford is across the river Meon.

Warsash Submember of Hook parish

1272 *Weresasse*; t. Ed I *Weresasche*.

OE ★*Wǣresæsc* 'ash-tree of a man called *Wǣr*'. OE boundary clauses are known to contain references to trees associated with individual people; perhaps on the boundary of their estates. Alternatively it might be 'ash of/by the fish-weir or fish-trap'; on which objects cf. Watts (1985).

Waterlooville Modern parish

Takes its name from *The Heroes of Waterloo* inn on the road from Portsmouth to Guildford (modern A3). *Ville* names enjoyed a brief vogue in the early to mid part of the c19, cf. *Cliftonville* in Hove (Sx) and Margate (K), *Rosherville* in Gravesend (K) and *Frithville* (L, Holland). The use of a fashionable French element in this particular name seems rather spiteful. The place was earlier 1759 *Whateland End*, 1817 *Waitland End*, attested too late for certainty about its origin.

Watership Down Part of chalk scarp in Sydmonton

1432 (*atte*) *Watershipe*.

OE *wæterscipe* 'conduit, artificial watercourse'. The Down takes its name from the farm of the same name, on the other side of the natural depression containing the village of Sydmonton. There is evidence of ponding on the E edge of the park.

Weeke Suburb of Winchester

1248 *Wike*; c.1270 *Wyke*.

OE *wīc* 'specialized farm', often a dairy-farm. (Cf. Ekwall 1964 on this very common PN element.)

Well Hamlet in Long Sutton

1237 (*la*) *Welle*.

OE/ME *wiell*(*e*) 'spring'. There is a pond here.

Wellow Stream and parish/manor, later two parishes, later reunited

672 (m. c12) (*on*) *welewe* (stream); 873×888 (c11) (*æt*) *welewe* (manor); 1086 *Weleue* (manor).

This seems to be an old name for the river **Blackwater**, and may be the *Velox* recorded in the c6 *Ravenna Cosmography* (Coates 1981: 69). The name recurs in that of the *Wellow* in So. It may represent a Brit. *ꝑelꝑo-; this would be the source of W *gwelw*, an adjective now translated 'pale blue' but originally meaning 'colour of milk as it begins to ferment'. Ekwall on the other hand derives it from a root meaning 'turn', and conjectures that the Wellow is the 'turning' river. But there cannot be many streams in the SCy that have no bends. If the *Ravenna* form belongs here, the British name is rendered into Latin as if meaning *velox* 'swift'.

DB implies there is one manor. There are two medieval parishes, distinguished as 1310 *Estwelewe* and 1461 *Westwelwe*.

Wellsworth In Idsworth
1222 *Waleswrthe*; 1236 *Welleswrth*; and occasional forms without *s*.
OE *Wealeswyrð 'Wealh's curtilage', or possibly 'Welshman's curtilage' (cf. Cameron 1980: 46). There are Roman remains nearby.

West End Modern parish carved out of South Stoneham
1607 *Westend*.
Since this place is not the west end of any parish, nor west from any nearby place of any significance, its name may be from OE *wæstenne* 'waste, wilderness'. It is a mile or so from *Wildern*, formerly in Botley and now in Hedge End, whose name is certainly from ME *wilderne* 'wilderness'. West End stands on a patch of Plateau Gravel. Both places stand on or adjacent to the damp and potentially thickly wooded soils of the Wickham 3 and 4 associations, and the waste referred to may have been virgin woodland.

West Ham see **South Ham**.

West Meon
932 (c12) (*æt*) *meone*.
See river **Meon** and **East Meon**.

Westbury
1086 *Wesberie*.
The 'west manor' in Eastmeon (Eastmeon hundred), though assessed as part of Meonstoke hundred in DB.

Weston In Itchen
c11 (*to*) *westtune*; 1245 *Westone*.
OE 'west farm', SW in relation to Sholing in Itchen. But it may be named from the viewpoint of Old Netley, whose *West Wood* is adjacent.

Weston Tithing of Buriton
c12 *Westeton*; 1278 *Westington*.
OE, either ⋆(*be*) *westan tūne* '(place) west of the farm/village', or
⋆*west in tūne* 'west in the village'. The situation could be characterized by either expression; most later spellings suggest the second.

Weston Colley In Micheldever
Found from 1280 as *Weston(e)* 'west farm', i.e. seen from Micheldever. *Colley* is a late addition which does not appear to commemorate
a family; it seems to be a PN which could have a number of different
sources, and which may or may not have been applied as a surname.
If it was a local PN, it may be linked with the *Blackcrate Cottages*,
Black Wood in the same parish; such names may be indications of
charcoal burning (cf. Hoskins 1967) and the PN may contain ME
col '(char)coal'. But this is uncertain.

Weston Corbet and **Weston Patrick** Two parishes
1086 *Westone* (Patrick); 1203 *Weston* (Corbet).
OE 'west farm'. The Westons are west of South Warnborough, but
it may be better to think of them in relation to Hoddington, like
them in Bermondspit hundred, from which they are south-west, or
Upton Grey, which lies between the Westons and Hoddington.
The feudal elements come from the family of *Corbet* 'crookback',
who held one manor in 1203, and from *Paterik* de Chaworces, who
held the other in 1257. These are both distinguished from **Weston
Colley** in Micheldever.

Westover Liberty, now in Do
c13 *Westour'*; 1263 *Westur'*; c13 *Westouer(strond)*; 1313 *Weste-
stures*; 1319 *Westovere*.
Gover says 'it is clear that the original was OE (*be*) *westan Stūre*,
"(place) west of the Stour".' It is true that this expression describes
its location; it comprised all Hampshire west of the Stour, viz.
Holdenhurst and part of Christchurch. On the other hand the forms
do not tell such a straightforward story. There is a strong suggestion,
going right through to modern times, that the name was ⋆*Westofer*
'west promontory'. Warren Hill (which ends in **Hengistbury
Head**), an arm of land enclosing Christchurch harbour, is a fine
ofer site as described by Gelling (1984), though no village is known
there. However, it is south of Christchurch borough, not west. On
balance, then, Gover is right, but the name has clearly been *understood* as 'west promontory', or perhaps as 'west, over (the harbour)',
at various times in its history. Just up the river Stour is *Iford* in
Holdenhurst, which is 1272 *Uvre*, c13 *Evere*, i.e. OE *yfer*, which

Gelling (1984: 178–9) claims to be identical in meaning with *oter*.

Wey River

672×674 (c13) (*endlonge*) *waie, waie(muþe)*; 956 (c.1225) (*on*) *wegan*; 1190×1193 *Waie*.

A pre-English river-name duplicated in the *Wye* and the Do *Wey*. Celtic origin is not provable; rather from some language spoken in England before British. Ekwall (1928) derives it from the Indo-European root **u̯egh*- 'move', and postulates the only philologically convincing way of linking the phonology of *Wey* with that of *Wye*.

Weyhill

c13 *Leweo*; c.1270 *la Wou*; 1318 *Weo*; 1379 *la Wee*.

Despite there being no AS-period records, this name shows every sign of deriving from OE *wēoh* 'idol', commonly taken to mean '(heathen) shrine, temple' in PNs. The place may have had a colourful religious history; a Christian Roman hoard was found here. Continental Gmc relatives of OE *wēoh* may have a Christian meaning. It is not now regarded as certain that names of this type actually refer to material signs of AS paganism.

We find 1399 *Wee alias Ramrugge*. *Ramridge House* is on the side of a spur to the NW of the present village, which occupies the spur used by the Andover to Devizes road (A303). *Hill* is not added to the simplex name till 1571.

Wherwell Village and priory

955 (c14) *hwerwyl*; 959 (c14) *werewelle*; 1052 (c12/c11) (*to*) *hwerwillom, hwærwellan*.

OE **Hwerwiell(as)*, literally 'cauldron spring(s) or stream(s)', hence 'bubbling stream(s)'. The church and priory are on an island formed by the multiple channels of the merging rivers Test and Dever. The eddies in the Test are well known.

Whitchurch

909 (c12) *hwitan cyrice*; 1001 (*æt*) *hwitciricean*.

OE '(the) white church'. The most likely interpretation is that the church was whitewashed. But Bede noted that *Whithorn* in Wigtownshire was called c.730 (*æt*) *hwitan ærne* or *candida casa* 'white building' merely because it was stone-built.

Whitehill In Selborne

No early forms are known, but since it is on the chalk the name is probably s.-e. An early name for it may be c.1270 *le Whitestigele* 'white bostal or steep hill-path'.

Whitenap Suburb of Romsey
1280 *W(h)ytenharpe.*
OE/ME '(at the) white harp'. OE *hearpe* is found in several PNs, all offering difficulties of interpretation, and as a final element is usually taken to mean '(salt-)sieve'. Whitenap is some way from the main branch of the river Test, even if this were tidal in the Middle Ages and thus could sustain salterns. The river is not now tidal above the marshes north of Totton.

Whitewater Stream, left tributary of the Blackwater
Deliberately named in contrast to the **Blackwater** with which it merges at the boundary with Brk? There is no obvious reason for the name. Part of its upper reach may in 973 be called *weargburna*; this is treated under **Warnborough**.

Whitsbury Formerly in Wiltshire
1132x1135 *Wiccheberia*; 1168 *Wicheberia.*
Ekwall suggests this contains OE *wice* 'wych-elm', presumably yielding a PN *Wiceburh* 'fort of the wych-elm(s)'; there is no convincing trace of the genitive plural. The *burh* is obviously the hillfort now called *Whitsbury Camp* or *Castle Ditches.*

Whitway Hamlet in Burghclere
1245 *Wytewey*; 1280 *Whyteweye.*
OE/ME 'white way', presumably from the track just south of here up on to the chalkland of the Downs, now the A34 and no longer white.

Wickham
826 (c12) (*oð*) *wichæma* (*mearce*); 925x941 (c14) (*æt*) *wicham*; 1086 *Wicheham*; 1167 *Wicham.*
It is now generally accepted that OE *wīchām* is an established compound denoting 'small Roman town or villa complex', containing a borrowed form of the Latin word *vīcus* 'street, quarter, district' (cf. Gelling 1988: 67–74). What is not clear is whether it denotes a physical entity (e.g. stone buildings) or a legal or tenurial one as well (i.e. a sign of persistent Roman administrative activity). Roman settlement, including a cemetery, is known within a radius of 5 miles of Wickham, and it is on the Roman road from Chichester to Bitterne. Perhaps the RB *Clausentum* (see **Bitterne**).

Widley Extinguished parish in Cosham, submember of Southwick parish
1242 *Wydelig'*; 1256 *Wydelegh.*
OE/ME *Wīdan lēage* '(at the) broad clearing/wood'.

Wield

1086 *Walde*; 1167 *Walda Episcopi*; 1256 *Welde*.

OE *weald* 'forest', i.e. a large tract of ancient unfelled woodland, later 'wooded downland' (cf. Everitt 1977). There is still a fair amount of woodland in the surrounding area. The modern long vowel is in evidence from the c15 (1428 *Weelde*). The manor was held by the Bishop of Winchester in the c12, hence the form of 1167. *Upper* and *Lower Wield* are 1369 *West-* and *Estwelde*.

Wigley In Copythorne

1189 *Wigelega*; 1256 *Wygele*.

OE *★Wicganlēah/Wicgenalēah* 'beetle wood/clearing'.

Wigston Lost manor in Beaulieu

1086 *Wigarestun*; 1578 *Wygeston*.

Despite the five centuries between the records, the equation is reasonable; the DB manor was in Boldre hundred. OE 'Wīggār's or Wihtgār's farm'.

Wildern In Hedge End

See **West End**.

Wildhern Hamlet in Andover

1635 *Wildherne*.

Either ME *wilde herne/hurne* 'wild corner' or *wilderne* 'wasteland, wilderness', cf. **Wildern** in Hedge End.

Will Hall House in Alton

See **Alton**.

Wilverley Post Boundary mark of Rhinefield and Burley

Recalls *Wilverley Wood* and *Lodge*, recorded in various guises since the c17. *Wilverley Inclosure* is on a patch of the Barton Sands amid an area of Plateau Gravel, and was clearly intended to support better quality (broadleaved) timber (cf. **Inclosure**). The origin of the primary PN is a matter of speculation.

Wimpson In Millbrook, suburb of Southampton

1236 *Wnemanneston*; 1269 *Wynemanestun*.

OE 'Wineman(n)'s farm'. The very reduced form is foreshadowed in 1580 *Wymston*.

Winchester

c2 *Ouénta*; c4 *Uenta Belgarum*; c.730 (*a civitate*) *Uenta quae a gente Saxonum Uintan cæstir appellatur*; 731 (c10/c11) *wintan-*, *wentancestre*; 855 (c10) *wintanceastre*; 961 (c12) *wenta*.

There is no difficulty about this name as an English name. It represents the RB name, *Venta*, inflected and compounded with OE *ceaster* 'Roman fort, station, town'. The RB form appears in the *Antonine Itinerary*: *Uenta Belgarum* was the chief place of the Belgae, the immigrant bearers (aristocrats) of the Iron Age C culture to parts of S Britain.

Venta is a greater problem. It was also the name of Caister-by-Norwich and Caerwent (*Venta Icinorum*, *Venta Silurum*), and appears, for instance, in the name of the fort *Glannaventa*, identified with Ravenglass (Cu). The element in question is not British, and may predate the P-Celtic languages in Britain. It has Indo-European parallels like *vênd* 'place' in Albanian. All we can safely say is that *Venta* is a name coined in some Indo-European language, probably meaning '(chief) place (of a tribe)'. This is discussed in greater detail by Coates (1984a).

The form of the PN current in medieval documents is the latinized form *Wintonia* or *civitas Wintonia/Wintonie*.

Winchfield

1229 *Winchelefeld*; 1249 *Winchefeld*; c13 *Wyncheffeud*; 1299 *Wynchesfeld*.

OE 'open land by a nook' (*wincel*), the loss of *l* adjacent to *ch* being usual. The court farm is by a small indentation in the 250ft. contour line.

Windenaie DB manor in Whitchurch or really **Woodhay (East)**

1086 *Windenaie*.

Morris associates this difficult DB name with a boundary mark (*on*) *whitan leasheal* '(at) the nook of Whitewood' in Whitchurch; he does not spell out his reasons, simply citing earlier authorities, and concedes that its spelling, bar the first *n*, could easily represent **Woodhay (East)**, and that is what Gover takes it to be. Both Whitchurch and East Woodhay are in the appropriate hundred, Evingar.

Winklebury District of Basingstoke

c.1290 *Wiltenischebury*; 1407 *Wyltenysshbury*; 1443 *Wynnyshbury, le Wynlysbery*; 1578 *Wincknersbury*.

This remarkable name has undergone many irregular transformations. Gover notes that, in a Romsey context, one Walter *le Wyltenysshe* is mentioned in an Assize Roll of 1289. This makes it very likely that we have to do with a surname meaning 'hailing from Wilton (W)', though its form is without any perfect parallel that I know of (the nearest being *Kentish*, *Devenish*; these two county-derived names suggest that '*Wiltonish*' is elliptical for

'*Wiltonshire-ish*', so to speak). Given this, the present name must be 'manor associated with the *le Wyltenysshe* family'. In this case *burh* could be 'fort' rather than 'manor', in view of the earthwork within which the school now stands, though the adjacent (now lost) *Bury Farm* supports either interpretation. But the association of a ME surname with *bury* from *burh* 'fort' would be remarkable indeed.

The modern name has clearly been influence by the name of the hillfort *Winklebury* in Berwick St John (W), though this is 45 miles away.

Winkton In Christchurch
1235 *Wyneketon*; 1236 *Wineketon*; 1280 *Wynketon*.
OE *Winecantūn* 'Wineca's farm', the man's name being a pet-form of a name in *Wine-* 'friend'. Morris in his edition of the Ha *Domesday* identifies this place with *Weringetone*, which is quite out of tune with all the other spellings. He also has to juggle with the hundred boundary; *Weringetone* was in Shirley whilst Christchurch and Winkton were in Egeiete.

Winnall Suburb of Winchester
1204 *Wilehale*; c.1270 *Wynehale*; 1272 *Wilenhale*.
The first spelling is typical of the earlier records, so the place is probably OE *Wilighealh* 'willow nook'. (The West-Saxon dialect form *welig*, recorded in the Isle of Wight and Brk, does not seem to be responsible for this name.) Winnall stands on the left bank of the river Itchen where willows are likely enough. The later forms either arise by dissimilation of *l* to *n* or testify that the name is really *Wiligenhealh*, with an adjectival form as the first element.

Winslade
1086 *Winesflot*; c.1270 *Wynnesfloud*; 1270x1280 *Winesflode*.
OE *flōde* means 'gutter, intermittent spring' (cf. Smith, *EPNE* I: 178, Gelling 1984: 22); and cf. **Privett**. It is not clear what can have been referred to; there is no stream here now. The name means 'watercourse of Wine', a common OE man's name. The sequence of two fricatives [sf] gave difficulties, and in the c13 we find 1236 *Wyneflod*, and by 1399 the ancestor of the modern name *Winslode*. The later development is as if the name contains OE *lād* 'lode, watercourse, drainage ditch', or rather *gelād* 'difficult passage' (Gelling 1984: 73–6); forms in *a* are found from Tudor times.

Winsor Manor and village in Copythorne
1167 *Windesore*; 1222 *Windlesore*; 1272 *Windlesovere*.
This belongs to a class of names (including *Windsor* (Brk)) which

Ekwall was thought to have solved once and for all as OE *Windelsōra* 'windlass bank', i.e. a bank equipped with a device for hauling boats out of the water. The trouble with Ekwall's theory is illustrated by the Ha place. Winsor is between what are no more than two trickles, left tributaries of the Bartley Stream. No boat can ever have got within miles of here. Gelling (1984: 181–2) hesitantly suggests instead that the etymology is correct but that it refers to the means of pulling vehicles up steep or muddy slopes, but this is least convincing for Winsor. The late c13 apparent substitution of the descendant of OE *ofer* 'flat-topped ridge' for *ōra* 'bank, shore' is not unusual.

Wintershill In Durley
1272 *Wintershull.*
OE/ME 'hill of *Winter*', a personal name seen also in *Winterslow* (W), unless this name is late enough to contain the common ME surname.

Winton Suburb of Bournemouth, now in Do
Part of the estate of Mary Anne and Georgina Charlotte Talbot (cf. **Talbot Village**), whose relative the Earl of Eglinton was created Earl of *Winton* in addition in 1859 (Young 1957: 193–4).

Wolverton
1086 *Ulvretune*; 1167 *Wulfertona.*
OE *Wulfheretūn* 'Wulfhere's farm'. The absence of medial -*s* is curious, but with parallels elsewhere (e.g. **Awbridge** and *Edgarley* (So) but mainly in the NCy and Midlands). Some forms suggest the synonymous OE *Wulfheringtūn* (1248 *Wlfrincton*), but they are all of the c13. The spellings do not strongly suggest the female name *Wulfrūn* instead.

Wonston, South Parish and estate
901 (e. c11) (*on*) *wynsiges tune*; 1086 *Wenesistune*; c.1124 *Wonsin-tone*; 1171 *Wonsyngtone.*
Early called OE *Wynnsigestūn* 'farm of Wynnsige', a man's name, with medieval evidence of a shift to the (?nearly) synonymous *Wynnsigingtūn*.

Wood Green Village, extraparochial area
Tucked into the NW extremity of the New Forest, it is known by this name from the mid c17. The wood is *Godshill Enclosure*, which separates the village from the rest of the New Forest; that is named from *Godshill* in Ashley Walk. *Green* is a common SCy name for a secondary settlement.

179

Woodbury Tithing of Romsey

1303 *Wobbury*; 1311 *Wopbury*; 1330 *Wopabury*; 1586 *Wobury*.
First element obscure; second OE *burh* 'fort, manor' or its ME
derivative. Gover points to the word/name *wopbincg* in some AS-
period charter-bounds of East Meon.

Woodcot or **Woodcott**

1086 *Odecote*; 1167 *Wudecota*.
OE **Wuducotu* 'wood cottages', a familiar and frequent name.
There was a further Woodcott in Kingsclere (1242 *Wodecote*,
possibly 1023 (*on*) *wudacotan*), whose origin is the same. Cf.
Woodmancott.

Woodfidley Wood in Denny

c.1250 *Wolphydelegh*; 1331 (*boscus de*) *Wolfydeleye*; 1338 *Wulfede-
le*; 1665 *Woodfidly*.
Possibly OE **Wulfhilde lēah* 'Wulfhild's wood', containing an OE
female personal name. A Wulfhild was associated with Hyde Abbey
in the early-mid c11. The loss of an *l* between two others is not
surprising. The modern name contains an analogical reformation
after the word *wood*.

Woodgarston Farm in Wootton St Lawrence

945 (c14) *wealagærstun*; 1256 *Wodgarston*.
The earliest record, if reliable, shows that the name was originally
OE 'serfs' paddock'. More specifically, names derived from OE
wealh may often be taken as early names denoting enslaved, or at
least subjugated, Britons (cf. Cameron 1980). In this connection, it
is significant that Roman buildings are recorded in this parish. The
later PN is 'wood paddock'; either a renaming has taken place, or
the original name has been analogically altered to suit the parish
name. Rumble (1983) identifies the AS-period name rather with
Gaston's Wood in Chineham.

Woodhay, East

1144 *Wydenhaya*; 1171 *Wydehaye*; t. Ric I *Wodeheya*.
Possibly OE **Wuduhege* or **Wudugehæg* 'wood enclosure (using
artificial fences)' (cf. Coates 1988a). If so, the first element may be
in its earlier form *widu*. It is more likely that it was originally *wīd*
'broad', and that the name means 'broad enclosure'. *East W*. (1350
Estwydehay) by contrast with West Woodhay over the boundary
in Brk. This may be the DB manor of **Windenaie**, which has been
alternatively identified with *Whitnal* in Whitchurch.

Woodmancott or Woodmancote

903 (c16) *woedemancote*; 1086 *Udemanecote.*

OE * *Wudumannacotu* 'woodmen's cottages/hovels', a name paralleled in Sx, for instance, and maybe having the same import as *Woodcote* (e.g. in Bramdean). Still adjacent to woodland. T e parish may have been carved out of the Candover estate(s); it can scarcely be an ancient parish/manor with such a name, suggesting a temporary or permanent residence for those performing a special task for the manor, even though it was one by the time of DB.

Woolbury Ring Earthwork in Little Somborne

947 (c14) (*beniþan*) *welnabyrig*; 1553 *Wolebury*; 1593 *Wulbury Hill*; 1817 *Worlbury Hill.*

Not clear. Possibly OE 'fort of riches', with reference to treasure as often with barrows, but I have not otherwise come across *wela* 'wealth' in the plural, nor is *wela* the normal word for loot in this sense. If it contains *wiellena* 'of the springs/streams', there is a near-parallel in *Welbury* (YNR). However Woolbury Ring is nearly 2 miles from the nearest flowing water, the river Test, and the valley which it dominates is dry. The OE form is compatible with the genitive plural of a tribal name in *-e*, but no appropriate one is known.

Woolmer Forest

970 (l. c13) *wulfamere* (pool); 1236 *Wulvemar'* (forest).

Takes its name from the pool referred to in 970, 'wolves' pool'. The pool is near Longmoor Camp. The forest is referred to in a Close Roll in 1236.

Woolmer Post New Forest boundary mark

Contains an ancient PN * *Wulf(a)mere* 'wolf pond', cf. **Woolmer Forest**. The pond is referred to as c.1280 *Wolmereslak*, and the valley below was clearly *Wulf(a)denu* (cf. 1296 *Wolvedenesheved*, the 'head' of it).

Wools Lost tithing of Romsey

Originally *Wells*, s.-e., 1236 *Welles*. Forms with *o/u* are found from the early c16, as in the case of *Wool* (Do).

Woolston

1086 *Olvestune*; 1236 *Wlveston*; 1280 *Wolveston.*

OE * *Wulfestūn* 'Wulf's farm'. In 1284 a form *Wolverichestone* appears apparently referring to this place, and this clearly means 'Wulfrīc's farm'. The two names could conceivably have referred to the same man, but the true significance of the alternating forms is not known. A Wulfrīc was the grantee of seven hides of land at Millbrook, 4 miles away, by king Ēadwīg in 956 (document 636 in Sawyer's catalogue). But the name was a common one and not too much should be read into this fact.

Woolton Hill In East Woodhay
Apparently the same as the *Woulthorne* recorded in 1604. *Woolton House* is close to a spring which runs to the Enborne; perhaps therefore OE *Wiellþorn* 'spring (haw)thorn', but the records are too late for certainty.

Wootton New Forest manor
See **Wootton St Lawrence**.

Wootton St Lawrence
990 (c12) (æt) wu:datune; 1086 *Odetone*.
OE 'wood farm', possibly 'farm by a wood'. The two main settlements in the parish are distinguished as 1308 *Up* or 1318 *Overe* and 1312 *Nuther* (i.e. 'nether'). The church of St Lawrence is in the latter place. Distinguished from the *Wootton* in the New Forest, a DB manor, whose name has the same origin, as does that on the Isle of Wight.

World's End In Hambledon
Known as such since 1759. A common (esp. c18/c19) name for the back of beyond. It is close to the southern boundary of its parish.

Worldham, East and West Originally two parishes; now one
1086, 1176 *Werildeham*; 1212 *Worildham*; 1204 *Werldham*.
One manor is recorded in DB, but the two places are distinguished in the c13. Very likely OE *Wǣrhildehām* 'estate of Wǣrhild', an unrecorded but perfectly regular woman's name. Ekwall's ingenious, but almost hilarious, alternative involves an OE *werhielde* 'wood-grouse (i.e. capercaillie) slope', but this once thickly forested country is not capercaillie habitat and surely can never have been.

Records from the c13 suggest that an alternative name-form arose: 1280 *Wordeleham*, still on record in 1789 *Ward-le-ham*.

Worthy Three (originally four) parishes
825 (c12) (æt) worþige, worðige (Martyr Worthy); 854 (c12) (to), æt worðige (?Headbourne Worthy); 904 (?c16) (to) worthigsætena (mearc) (Headbourne Worthy); 904 (?c16) (andlang) worthihæma (mearc) (Headbourne Worthy); 955x958 (c14) (æt þan twan) worþigum (?King's and Martyr Worthy); 1001 worðig (?Headbourne Worthy); 1026 (c12) wurthige (Abbot's Worthy in King's Worthy); 1086 *Ordie* (all).

These four adjacent villages, *Headbourne*, *King's* (including *Abbot(t)'s*) and *Martyr Worthy*, stand in a block on the right bank of the Itchen. They may have formed a single estate at some early period; they are all undifferentiatedly called *Ordie* in DB, though the AS document of 955×958 refers to 'the two Worthys', so there must have been at least two recognisably distinct manors/settlements both called *Worðig* by the mid-c10. Much of the area was donated by King Ēadgār to Brihthelm bishop of Winchester in 961 as if part of an area called *Eastune* (see **Easton**, and below). The identifications in the form-list above are those of Gover, supported, in the cases which both authors mention, by Grundy, whose topographical work is valuable even though his philology should be viewed with caution.

The collective name derives from OE *worðig* 'curtilage', though it is not clear why a word for a small enclosed unit should form the name for such a large one. Nor is it clear why this name should occur so much further east than all the other instances of the element in major names (except in one c12 spelling only of **Blendworth**). It is a characteristically south-western element, the furthest instance east otherwise being in *Hamworthy* in Dorset. Maybe there is something in Grundy's speculation (1926: 127) that the name is really *Worð-īg* 'curtilage island'; there are several sizeable islands in the multiply dividing river Itchen hereabouts. But much more information would be required before one could pursue this idea with confidence. It might be better to treat the SW distribution as a matter of time rather than geography. If the element *worðig* was current as (especially) Devon was being anglicized, perhaps this was the period at which the Worthys were being established. They would then be an interpolation into a landscape already full of English names. It seems that the area must have been a (largely) royal estate of the highest importance.

Abbot's Worthy (1248 *Abboteswrth'*) was held by Hyde Abbey from AD 909, though prior to that date, and in the grant document, it was called *Easton Worthy* ((*with*) *easton worðige*) from being across the river Itchen from **Easton**. Abbot's Worthy may have been, or have included, the five hides granted in 1026 (c12) by Canute to bishop Lufinc of Winchester, which therefore would have been detached from the royal domain of King's Worthy. Because the topographical interpretation of the several AS charters of this area is difficult, and the size of the manors therefore hard to determine, it is not clear whether these last two statements about the holding of the land contradict one another.

The inhabitants of Headbourne Worthy were referred to in the charter of AD 909 (?c11/c12) in the phrase (*be*) *hide burninga* (*gemære*) 'by the boundary of those of Headbourne', and the stream entering the Itchen here was 854 (c12) (*into*) *hydiburnan*, apparently 'stream of the hides'. (The hide was a land-area unit of c.100–120 acres, considered capable of supporting one family and household. Cf. **Hyde Abbey**.) The precise import of this name is unknown. Headbourne Worthy is also known from the c13 as *Count's Worthy* (1291 *Wordy Comitis*) or *Worthy Mortimer* (1303 *Wordy Mortimer*) from being held (in 1212) by Roger Mortimer, the bearer of a family name probably reflecting activity in the Crusades, 'Dead Sea'.

King's Worthy was held by the king before and at the time of DB (and see the comment on Abbot's Worthy above).

Martyr Worthy (1243 *Wordi Lamartre*) was held in 1201 by Henry la Martre, whose surname is of French origin, 'the marten'.

Worting
960 *Wyrtingas*; 1086 *Wortinges*; 1195 *Wertinges*.
The form of 960 appears, in the light of the medieval developments, to be a good OE form, but what it might mean is uncertain. Names of this form are standardly *-ingas* derivatives of personal names, and are usually, on that basis, called 'folk-names'. No personal name of the right shape is known, however. We might guess that a nickname ★*Wyrta* based on *wyrt* 'herb, vegetable' existed. Ekwall points out that a name *Worta* may exist in a c10 boundary clause; but such a name could not be the base of the present PN because *-ingas* names cannot be conclusively proved ever to show *i*- umlaut (cf. Coates 1984b). Maybe it is rather a name exhibiting the plural form of a singular ★*wyrting* 'herb garden'.

The *-s* forms persist into the early c14, though clear forms without it appear already in the c13.

Wyke Three farms in St Mary Bourne
OE *wīc* 'dependent farm, dairy farm' (1236 *Wikes* possibly represents an early plural, but there are unexplained 'plural' forms of elements like this in early ME). We find 1280 *Wyke Prioris* (i.e. of the prior of St Swithin, Winchester, who held Hurstbourne Priors), and 1313 *Wyke Daundely*, commemorating a lord of the manor with the surname *d'Andelys*, from a PN in Normandy.

Wymering Extinguished parish in Cosham
1086, 1184 *Wimeringes*; 1167 *Wimeringa*; 1260 *Wimering*.
A folk-name ★*Wīgmæringas* 'people associated with *Wīgmær*', used as a place-name, as in *Hastings* (Sx).

Y

Yateley
1236 *Yattelegh, Yatelegh.*
This seems to be OE/ME 'wood at the gates', with an analogical genitive plural **genata* for OE *gata*. The reference may be metaphorical, to the 'gates' of Berkshire, over the river Blackwater. Alternatively **Gēatanlēah* 'Gēata's wood/clearing'.

Yavington Manor in Avington
900 (c12) *ebincgtune*; 1086 *Ebintune*; 1280 *Yabyngton*.
OE 'Eabba's farm'. The modern form with *v* is on the analogy of the parish name.

SELECT BIBLIOGRAPHY

Historical, geographical and other background works

BARING, F.H. (1917) 'The Aclea[h]. I. Of the battle in 851. II. Of the synods in 782 etc.', *Papers and Proceedings of the Hampshire Field Club*, 8, pp. 95–9.

BIDDLE, M. (1976) 'Hampshire and the origins of Wessex', in SIEVEKING, G. de G., *et al.*, eds, *Problems in Economic and Social Archaeology*, Duckworth, London, pp. 323–42.

COPLEY, G.J. (1954) *The Conquest of Wessex in the Sixth Century*, Phoenix House, London. (Uses the now outdated chronology of place-name types.)

COPLEY, G.J. (1986) *Archaeology and Place-names in the Fifth and Sixth Centuries*, BAR (British series) 147, Oxford.

EVERITT, A. (1977) 'River and wold: reflections on the historical origin of regions and pays', *Journal of Historical Geography*, 3 (1), pp. 1–19.

EVISON, V.I. ed. (1984) *Angles, Saxons and Jutes*, Clarendon, Oxford.

FINBERG, H.P.R. (1964a) *The Early Charters of Wessex*, Leicester University Press, Leicester.

FINN, R.W. (1962) 'Hampshire', in DARBY, H. C. and CAMPBELL, E.M.J., eds, *The Domesday Geography of South-East England*, Cambridge University Press, Cambridge, pp. 287–363.

GRIGSON, G. (1959) *The Englishman's Flora*, Hart-Davis, London.

HILLS, C. (1979) 'The archaeology of Anglo-Saxon England in the pagan period', *Anglo-Saxon England*, 9, pp. 297–329, esp. pp. 313–15.

HOCKEY, S.F., ed. (1974) *The Beaulieu Cartulary*, Southampton University Press, Southampton.

HOSKINS, W.G. (1967) *Fieldwork in Local History*, Faber and Faber, London.

JARVIS, M.G., *et al.* (1984) *Soils and Their Use in South East England*, Lawes Agricultural Trust, Harpenden (Soil Survey of England and Wales, Bulletin 15).

KENNEDY, A.G. (1985) 'Disputes about "bocland": the forum for their adjudication', *Anglo-Saxon England*, 14, pp. 175–95.

MUIR, R. (1982) *The Lost Villages of Britain*, Michael Joseph; London.

MUNBY. J., ed. (1982) *Domesday Book: Text and Translation, Vol. IV: Hampshire*, Phillimore, Chichester.

PAGE, W., gen. ed. (1900–12) *Victoria History of the Counties of England. Hampshire*, Constable, London (reprinted Dawson, London, 1973), especially volumes III–V. (Volume editors: I & II: H.A. Doubleday and W. Page; III & IV: G.H. Gotley and W.J. Hardy; V: W. Page.)

PATTERSON, A.T. (1966) *A History of Southampton 1700–1914, vol. I,* Southampton University Press, Southampton.

RACKHAM, O. (1976) *Trees and Woodland in the British Landscape,* Dent, London.

RACKHAM, O. (1980). *Ancient Woodland: Its History, Vegetation and Uses in England,* Arnold, London.

SAWYER, P.H. (1968) *Anglo-Saxon Charters: An Annotated List and Bibliography,* Offices of the Royal Historical Society, London.

SIMS-WILLIAMS, P.P. (1983) 'The settlement of England in Bede and the *Chronicle*', *Anglo-Saxon England,* 12, pp. 1–41, esp. pp. 24–5.

STAGG, D. J., ed. (1979) *A Calendar of New Forest Documents: 1244–1334,* Hampshire County Council, Winchester (Hampshire Records Series, vol. 3).

STAGG, D.J., ed. (1983) *A Calendar of New Forest Documents: The Fifteenth Century to the Seventeenth Century,* Hampshire County Council, Winchester (Hampshire Records Series, vol. 5).

STENTON, F.M. (1970) *Anglo-Saxon England* (3rd edition), Oxford University Press, Oxford.

SUMNER, H. (1972) *The New Forest* (new 3rd edition by M. Ridley), Dolphin Press, Christchurch.

TAVENER, L. E., (1957) *The Common Lands of Hampshire,* Hampshire County Council, Winchester.

TAVENER, L.E. (1969) 'The geological structure of the New Forest', in EDILN, H.L., ed., *New Forest. Forestry Commission Guide* (4th edition), HMSO, London, pp. 22–5.

YOUNG, D.W. (1969) 'The history of the forest woodlands', in EDLIN, H.L. (as previous entry), pp. 33–41.

Authoritative general works on place-names and their linguistic background

CAMERON, K. (1988) *English Place-Names* (4th edition), Batsford, London.

EKWALL, E. (1960) *The Concise Oxford Dictionary of English Place-Names* (4th edition), Oxford University Press, Oxford.

FIELD, J. (1972) *English Field-Names,* David and Charles, Newton Abbot.

GELLING, M. (1976) [Section on habitative elements in her] Introduction to *The Place-Names of Berkshire,* vol. III, Cambridge University Press, (EPNS vol. 51), pp. 822–33. (The only relatively complete – but still provisional – discussion of habitative elements as a group.)

GELLING, M. (1984) *Place-Names in the Landscape,* Dent, London.

GELLING, M. (1988) *Signposts to the Past* (2nd edition), Phillimore, Chichester.

JACKSON, K.H. (1953) *Language and History in Early Britain,* Edinburgh University Press, Edinburgh.

NICOLAISEN, W.F.H., GELLING, M. and RICHARDS, M. (1970) *The Names of Towns and Cities in Britain,* Batsford, London. (Revised reprint 1986. Covers the names of larger places only.)

RIVET, A.L.F. and SMITH, C.C. (1979) *The Place-Names of Roman Britain*, Batsford, London.

SMITH, A.H. (1956) *English Place-Name Elements* I/II, Cambridge University Press, Cambridge (English Place-Name Society vols. 25 and 26).

Specialist literature on place-names and their linguistic background

ARNGART, O. (1983) 'The place-names Weybourne and Wooburn', *Journal of the English Place-Name Society*, pp. 5–8.

BARING, F.H. (1909) 'Crundels', *English Historical Review*, 24, pp. 300–3.

BRADLEY, H. (1928) 'English place-names', in *Collected Papers*, Oxford University Press, Oxford, pp. 80–109 (previously in *Essays and Studies by Members of the English Association*, 1910, pp. 7–41).

CAMERON, K. (1968) 'Eccles in English place-names', in BARLEY, M.W. and HANSON, R.P.C., eds, *Christianity in Britain, 300–700*, Leicester University Press, Leicester, pp. 87–92. (Also in Cameron (1975), pp. 1–7.)

CAMERON, K., ed. (1975) *Place-name Evidence for the Anglo-Saxon and Scandinavian Settlements*, EPNS, Nottingham.

CAMERON, K. (1980) 'The meaning and significance of OE *walh* in English place-names', *Journal of the English Place-Name Society*, 12, pp. 1–53 (with appendices by various writers).

COATES, R. (1981) 'Rivet and Smith, *The Place-Names of Roman Britain*', review in *Journal of the English Place-Name Society*, 13, pp. 59–71.

COATES, R. (1984a) 'Remarks on "pre-British" in England; with special reference to **ɥentā*, **ciltā* and "**cunāco-*"', *Journal of the English Place-Name Society*, 16, pp. 1–24.

COATES, R. (1984b) 'On an early date for Old English *i*-mutation', in CRÉPIN, A., ed., *Linguistic and Stylistic Studies in Medieval English*, Association des Médiévistes anglicistes de l'Enseignement supérieur, Paris, publication 10, pp. 25–38.

COATES, R. (1986) 'Mendip', *Nomina*, 10, pp. 5–9.

COATES, R. (1988a) *Toponymic Topics*, Younsmere Press, Brighton. (Contains papers on The Solent, Silchester, and the element *hæg*.)

COATES, R. (1988b) 'Middle English *badde* and related puzzles', *NOWELE*, 8, pp. 91–104.

COLE, A. (1982) 'Topography, hydrology and place-names in the chalklands of southern England: *cumb* and *denu*', *Nomina*, 6, pp. 73–87.

COLE, A. (1985) 'Topography, hydrology and place-names in the chalklands of southern England: **funta*, *æwiell*, and *æwielm*', *Nomina*, 9, pp. 3–19.

COLE, A. (1987) 'The distribution and usage of the OE place-name *Cealc*.' *Journal of the English Place-Name Society*, 19, pp. 45–55.

COX, B. (1973) 'The significance of the distribution of English place-names in *hām* in the Midlands and East Anglia', *Journal of the English Place-Name Society*, 5, pp. 15–73.

COX, B. (1976) 'The place-names of the earliest English records', *Journal of the English Place-Name Society*, 8, pp. 12–66.

DIETZ, K. (1985) 'Ae. *bēocere* 'Imker', me. *bīke* 'Bienennest' und die Ortsnamen auf *Bick-*', *Anglia*, 103, pp. 1–25.

DODGSON, J. McN. (1966) 'The significance of the distribution of the English place-name in *-ingas*, *-inga-* in south-east England', *Medieval Archaeology*, 10, pp. 1–29. (Also in Cameron (1975), pp. 27–54.)

DODGSON, J. McN. (1967a) 'The *-ing-* in English place-names like Birmingham and Altrincham', *Beiträge zur Namenforschung* (new series), 2, pp. 221–45.

DODGSON, J. McN. (1967b) 'Various forms of Old English *-ing* in English place-names', *Beiträge zur Namenforschung* (new series), 2, pp. 325–96.

DODGSON, J. McN. (1968) 'Various Engish place-name formations containing Old English *-ing*', *Beiträge zur Namenforschung* (new series), 3, pp. 141–89.

DODGSON, J. McN. (1973) 'Place-names from *hām*, distinguished from *hamm* names, in relation to the settlement of Kent, Surrey and Sussex', *Anglo-Saxon England*, 2, pp. 1–50.

EKWALL, E. (1928) *English River-Names*, Oxford University Press, Oxford.

EKWALL, E. (1953) 'Tribal names in English place-names', *Namn och Bygd*, 41, pp. 129–77.

EKWALL, E. (1964) *Old English wīc in place-names* (*Nomina Germanica*, 13), Lundequist, Uppsala.

FINBERG, H.P.R. (1964b) '*Charltons* and *Carltons*', in his *Lucerna*, Macmillan, London, pp. 144–60.

FISIAK, J. (1984) 'The voicing of initial fricatives in Middle English', *Studia Anglica Posnaniensia*, 17, pp. 3–16 (and seven maps).

GARDINER, M. and COATES, R. (1987) 'Ellingsdean: a Viking battlefield identified', *Sussex Archaeological Collections*, 125, pp. 251–2.

GELLING, M. (1974) 'Some notes on Warwickshire place-names', *Transactions of the Birmingham and Warwickshire Archaeological Society*, 85, pp. 59–79. (Mainly about the elements *lēah* and *tūn* and their distribution.)

GOVER, J.E.B. *et al.* (1942) *The Place-Names of Middlesex*, Cambridge University Press, Cambridge (English Place-Name Society, vol. 18).

HUGGINS, R.M. (1975) 'The significance of the place-name *Wealdhām*', *Medieval Archaeology*, 19, pp. 198–201.

JOHANSSON, C. (1975) *Old English Place-Names and Field-Names Containing 'lēah'*, Stockholm Studies in English 32, Stockholm.

KRISTENSSON, G. (1981) 'The place-name *Weybourne* in Norfolk', *Sydsvenska Ortnamnssällskapets Årsskrift*, pp. 76–80.

PADEL, O.J. (1985) *Cornish Place-Names Elements*, English Place-Name Society, Nottingham, vols. 56/57.

RUMBLE, A.R. (1987) 'OE *Bōc-land* as an Anglo-Saxon estate name', *Leeds Studies in English*, 18, pp. 219–29.

SANDRED, K.-I. (1963) *English Place-Names in -stead*, Acta Universitatis Uppsaliensis, Uppsala.

SANDRED, K.-I. (1984) 'A river-name, a linguistic change and the importance of non-linguistic evidence', in *Florilegium Nordicum* (Sigurd Fries Festschrift), Umeå, pp. 240–7.

WAKELIN, M.F. (1969) *'Crew, cree* and *crow*: Celtic words in English dialect', *Anglia*, 87, pp. 273–81.

WATTS, V.E. (1983) 'Medieval fisheries in the Wear, Tyne and Tweed: the place-name evidence', *Nomina*, 7, pp. 35–45.

ZACHRISSON, R.E. (1924) 'The French element', in MAWER, A.H. and STENTON, F.M., *Introduction to the Survey* [of English Place-Names], Cambridge University Press, Cambridge (English Place-Name Society, vol. I (i)).

Specialist material on Hampshire place-names

COATES, R. (1988c) *A Bibliography of Place-Names in Hampshire and the Isle of Wight: with a section on Hampshire dialect*, Younsmere Press, Brighton.

COPE, W.H. (1983) *A Glossary of Hampshire Words and Phrases*, Trübner, London, for the English Dialect Society (vol. 40) (reprinted Kraus, Vaduz, 1965). (Includes dialect words in place-names.)

GOVER, J.E.B. (1961, MS. only) *The Place-Names of Hampshire*. (Unpublished. There are copies in the Hampshire Record Office at Winchester, in Southampton and Nottingham University Libraries, in the Ordnance Survey library at Southampton, in private hands, and in the keeping of the EPNS.)

GRUNDY, G.B. (1920–5) 'On place-names in general and the Hampshire place-names in particular', *Papers and Proceedings of the Hampshire Field Club*, 9, pp. 221–261.

GRUNDY, G.B. (1921–8) 'The Saxon land charters of Hampshire, with notes on place- and field-names', *Archaeological Journal*, 78, pp. 55–173; 81, pp. 31–126; 83, pp. 91–253; 84, pp. 160–340; 85, pp. 188–96 (index). (To be used with caution; the philology is not reliable. Grundy's bound, autographed offprints are in Senate House Library, University of London.)

GRUNDY, G.B. (1922) 'The meanings of certain forms in the Anglo-Saxon charters', *Essays and Studies*, 8, pp. 37–69.

HILL, R. (1975) 'The manor of Stockbridge', *Papers and Proceedings of the Hampshire Field Club*, 32, pp. 93–101.

JACKSON, K.H. (1939) 'Wallop', *Antiquity*, 13 pp. 105–6.

KÖKERITZ, H. (1940) *The Place-Names of the Isle of Wight* (*Nomina Germanica*, 9), Appelberg, Uppsala.

LLOYD, A.T. (1964) 'The place-names of Hampshire', in MONKHOUSE, F.J., ed., *A Survey of Southampton and its Region*, Southampton University Press, Southampton/British Association for the Advancement of Science, London, pp. 177–88.

RUMBLE, A.R. (1980) 'HAMTVN alias HAMWIC (Saxon Southampton):

the place-name traditions and their significance', in HOLDSWORTH, P., ed., *Excavations at Melbourne St., Southampton, 1971–6*, Southampton Archaeological Research Committee Report 1; CBA Research Report 33, pp. 7–20.

RUMBLE, A.R. (1983) 'The historical and onomastic evidence', in MILLETT, M. and JAMES, S., eds, 'Excavations at Cowdery's Down, Basingstoke, Hampshire, 1978–81', *Archaeological Journal*, 140, pp. 263–71.

WATTS, D.G. (1984) 'Prallingworth – a lost locality identified', *Papers and Proceedings of the Hampshire Field Club*, 40, pp. 134–6.

YOUNG, D.S. (1957) *The Story of Bournemouth*, Robert Hale, London.

INDEX